X

Writing for your Life #4

Writing for your Life #4

edited by

Jonathan Bing

PUSHCART

ISBN 1-888889-12-8 (hb)
ISBN 1-888889-17-9 (pb)

For information address
Pushcart Press
PO Box 380
Wainscott, NY 11975

Distributed by W. W. Norton & Co.

CONTENTS

INTRODUCTION

Not long after I became the Interviews editor at *Publishers Weekly*, I paid a visit to the Manhattan offices of the *Paris Review* to speak to George Plimpton, the man who has, perhaps more than any other living writer, established the author interview as a staple of American journalism. In the course of casually discussing his method of writing his latest book, a biography of Truman Capote narrated in the voices of Capote's many friends, critics and nemeses, Plimpton unfurled a scroll of taped-together manuscript pages the length of the room. What lay on the floor between us, he explained, was one of hundreds of transcripts of interviews he had conducted, then carefully condensed and reshuffled into a narrative that traced the skyrocketing arc of Capote's career.

That scroll of raw, unedited transcript—Plimpton called it a python—has struck me ever since as a potent symbol of the peculiar challenges faced by the author of a *PW* Interview. Distilling the repetitions and longueurs of natural conversation (few writers, after all, speak in perfect paragraphs) into a pithy portrait of an artist and his or her oeuvre is a feat that can at times seem as daunting as that of charming a deadly snake.

But the difficulty of transmitting the raw material of lived experience into a seamless narrative is precisely what's made the *PW* Interview one of the most popular features of the magazine. Few other interviews offer so thorough a study of the writing life, from the writer's creative ferment and purpose, to the vagaries of the publishing world, the challenges of breaking into print for the first time, or of sustaining a career in a precariously shifting marketplace. Rarely does one find so detailed a portrait of writers struggling with deadlines and storylines, bristling with ideas and opinions.

Sandwiched between book reviews and news stories, the interview occupies a singular space in a magazine. It attempts to block out the noise and hype of the industry and to serve as a reminder of the creative process that makes it all possible.

Chief among the considerations that have guided my choices of what to include in this anthology from recent *PW* Interviews are that the authors be good talkers, have a unique perspective on the business of being published, and that their work, taken together, reflect the diversity of the book world. Here you'll find newcomers with edgy ideas, like Rick Moody and Edwidge Danticat; novelists in midstream taking risks with new material, like Mary Gordon and James Salter; titans of popular fiction, like Sue Grafton and Nora Roberts; leading practitioners of the memoir, like James Alan Mcpherson and Maria Flook; and high-caliber reporters, critics and editors with trenchant opinions about the culture business. The profiles of Brian Moore and Alfred Kazin were among the last interviews granted by these distinguished writers. The interviews with Frederick Barthelme and Tom Wolfe are glimpses of the authors in surroundings that cast their writing personae in sharp relief, a riverboat casino and a splashy publicity tour, respectively.

Like any magazine feature, the Interview reflects the work of many hands. *PW*'s librarian Gary Ink, has time and again provided background for the Interview and assembled the bibliography for this volume. The most valuable resource, however, has been the constant guidance of Sybil Steinberg, the chief Forecasts editor at *PW* and for many years before me, the Interviews editor, who has not only helped maintain the finely balanced lineup of writers who comprise the Interviews section week after week, and cast a merciless eye on the prose of every contributor, but has helped shape my own literary tastes in the process.

JONATHAN BING
Interviews Editor
Publishers Weekly

Writing
for your
Life
#4

BERYL BAINBRIDGE

Aᴜᴛʜᴏʀꜱ ɪɴ ᴘᴇʀꜱᴏɴ often seem utterly different from what their work might lead one to expect; and with Beryl Bainbridge this is the case in spades. Those familiar with her exactingly written, poetic and often harrowing accounts of people caught up in famous historical moments would never envisage the warmly chatty person who comes to the door of her small row house not far from Regent's Park in London.

Not that things are entirely staid and bourgeois in Bainbridge land. The first thing a visitor encounters inside the front door is a life-size plaster statue of St. Patrick with his staff broken (by an overeager grandchild, of which Bainbridge has several) and an enormous stuffed buffalo whose horns are so wide one has to turn sideways to make it through the narrow hallway and into the bright little living room, where a fire burns in the hearth on a mild October morning.

After seeing many pictures of her in which she seems to be hamming it up for the camera as Edith Sitwell used to do, with strange hats or peculiarly gloomy expressions, Bainbridge in person is—well, fun. She has a cheerfully self-deprecating manner, lively eyes and a fund of gossip, and even in her mid-60s, she still cuts a handsome figure.

At the moment she seems to be very much the flavor of the month. At the time of *PW*'s visit, her latest novel, *Master Georgie*, published stateside by Carroll & Graf, was the favorite for the highly prestigious Booker Prize—for which she had been shortlisted no less than four times previously. (In the voting, two weeks later, she lost narrowly to Ian McEwan.) Bainbridge has been the subject of a number of recent newspaper and magazine interviews; socially, too, her life has become somewhat of a whirl. The very week of the interview there was a big, dressy party for the centenary of her long-time publisher, Duckworth, a reading by the Booker shortlist authors, a reception for the Booker's 30th anniversary, a show of paintings by her former husband and a TV shoot.

"It's feast or famine, isn't it?" she declares with a sly gleam in her eye. She is talking from the viewpoint of what one enthusiastic reviewer of her work called "an older, tougher Britain," one in which she grew up. She was born in Liverpool in 1934, Depression days, "and you can imagine the conditions we lived in." Indeed: unheated homes but for pungent and smoky coal fires, baths once a week in water heated on the stove. It tends to build a certain stoicism in the face of today's often imagined hardships, says Bainbridge. "I think the biggest change for most people in my lifetime, more than the Pill or the fact that now nearly everyone has a car and a TV, is reliable hot water, and being warm."

Hers was no rapid plunge into the writer's life. Bainbridge left school at 16 to go on the stage, playing small ingenue roles and touring the country, as repertory theater groups did in the 1950s and 60s. In one role she remembers having to shave her head to appear as a boy—perhaps one reason her hair today remains long and luxuriant, with a fringe that recalls the early-60s beat look. Then came marriage, to artist Austin Davis, and two children to bring up, then a liaison with writer Alan Sharpe and another child, before she could start to think about writing, which she began simply as a way to help make ends meet.

Her first novel, *A Weekend with Claude*, was published in 1967 under the Hutchinson imprint, New Authors Ltd., which brought out only first novels. A year later, Hutchinson published *Another Part of the Wood*. "I got 25 pounds for the first one, and I imagined people would stop me in the street." She laughs, and chokes a little on the latest cigarette; she has been chain-smoking, lighting them from the fire. "When the next book was turned down and nothing else happened I got a bit uneasy and stopped writing for a time."

Then one day she got a phone call from Anna Haycraft, wife of Colin Haycraft, the publisher of the venerable firm of Duckworth. "Your stuff is pretty awful," she remembers Haycraft saying, "but there's something there. What else have you got?" What she had was *Harriet Said*, which became the first of her titles with the house that remains her primary publisher to this day. Anna's advice to her as a writer was succinct: "Write about what you know, get yourself a good plot and cut out all the adjectives." Colin too had his own notions:

"He didn't really like fiction, and he made me think about every sentence; he was incredibly strict about using the right word. I had to keep looking things up in the dictionary."

Under this stern regime she produced a novel a year for the next six years, including *The Dressmaker, Sweet William* (both later made into movies), *The Bottle Factory Outing, A Quiet Life, Injury Time* and *Young Adolf* (which fantasized a visit to Liverpool by the Nazi dictator as a teenager). All this time, she said, she was getting no advances, and earning only very small royalties, and life continued to be the sort of struggle where she often had to borrow to get through the week.

With the U.S. publication of *Harriet Said* in 1973, George Braziller became her regular American publisher, and Bainbridge and Braziller became close friends. (The walls of her house, which are crowded with family pictures and odd mementos, bear several pictures of them together, with her children, in happy visits to New York and elsewhere.)

Then, around the time of *The Birthday Boys*, her first real breakthrough success, they had a rather painful falling out. Bainbridge, who still calls Braziller "a lovely man," said she gave him a copy of the manuscript when he came to London, "then when he got back to New York he sent a letter saying, 'It's not my kind of thing,' almost as if he had never known me." That was nearly five years ago, and they haven't been in touch since, though she regrets it, and wishes she could pluck up the courage to call or write to find out what went wrong.

Braziller is equally fond of Bainbridge, and blames the coolness on Haycraft (who died five years ago) and on the agency Braziller admits he introduced Bainbridge to, after years of being unagented—the John Johnson agency, where Andrew Hewson represents her. "Colin was very possessive of Beryl, and wanted $40,000 for 'Young Hitler,' which isn't the sort of money I could afford, but I paid it to keep her," he told *PW*. "Then at the time of *Birthday Boys*, I heard it was being offered around by her agents' American representatives, as if I didn't exist. Then they asked for the American rights to all her earlier books. I knew she needed the money, so I let them have them." But, he said, he didn't want a continuing breach between them, and was determined to write Bainbridge and seek a reconciliation.

In the event, it was Kent Carroll of Carroll & Graf who snapped up *The Birthday Boys*, and who has been doing very well by—and out of—her ever since. She is deeply loyal, and despite many offers from bigger publishers on both sides of the Atlantic, would not think of leaving her current stalwarts. "I want to stay with the people who wanted me in the first place. Anyway, I prefer smaller publishers; you feel more at home there."

That her real recognition as a writer came only after a long string of quirky novels based on a strongly comic sense of character still surprises her, as does the moment of change. "It's strange how fate works, very peculiar," she says. "Colin Haycraft had just died, and my son needed a big lump sum to buy a house, which I couldn't afford. Then Robin Baird-Smith, the new president at Duckworth, came around and asked me what I wanted that would persuade me to stay. Just like that, I said 'A three-book contract,' though I'd never had one before. Off the top of my head I said I'd write about the *Titanic*, the Crimea and Dr. Johnson." She wanted to go back into history, she says. "I felt I'd used up my childhood in all the other books."

The Birthday Boys, her dazzlingly brilliant fictional account of Captain Scott's ill-fated Antarctic expedition, gave her the idea of writing about the great ship. "Scott died in March 1912, and the next month the *Titanic* sank. It was all somehow related, and I felt I was really getting to know the period."

After stellar reviews on both sides of the Atlantic, *The Birthday Boys* became a big seller in paperback, and the book on the *Titanic* disaster that followed, *Every Man for Himself,* sold strongly from the start. "The film didn't hurt, of course," grins Bainbridge. "I think a lot of people thought my book was a novelization." *Master Georgie,* which takes three odd Liverpudlians on a journey into the hell of the Crimean War but is also about early photography, undying love, deceit, illusion, courage and the benefits of a classical education, was chosen as (never mind the lost Booker) one of *PW*'s Best Books of the Year.

It has been often pointed out how brilliantly the famous Charge of the Light Brigade, which is what most people remember from the Crimean War, takes place very distantly offstage in Bainbridge's novel, in the same way that the sinking of the *Titanic* is incidental to a number of human dramas in that novel. "There's no point in writing about what everybody knows, and I don't want to have any hindsight. I pretend I'm there, at the time, like the people I'm writing about, and I can't let them know what they wouldn't know."

She does prodigious research—her tables are piled with books on Dr. Johnson and his period, ready for her next foray. "I could never have tackled subjects like this with my old publisher," she confides. "He'd have questioned everything. But everything you want is there. You just have to read up on it."

Her writing methods are drastic, a form of total immersion not many writers could sustain, and which perhaps helps account for the starkness and grip of the resulting vision. "I'm not one of those people that can just write a few hours a day and have a normal social life the rest of the time." She shuts off the phone, draws the curtains, and for five months—roughly the time it takes her to write a new book—she plunges without interruption into her fictional world. She writes until she can write no more, stays in her nightgown, sleeps on her couch, sends out for takeout food, and if inspiration fails, takes a tumbler of Scotch. "I have to be careful, though, because I find one drink tends to lead to another." Also, "I spend half my time calculating how big the pages are, how many words on each, so I'll know when I've done enough." That's one way of ensuring her books' remarkable brevity and concentration. Another: "I throw away 12 pages for every one I finish. I cut like mad, all the time."

Her new book is due in March, and already, with an October lost to the social and publicity whirl, she feels she's fallen behind, since she can't start without a title, and so far hasn't come up with one she likes. *An Afternoon at Mrs. Thrale's* is one she has toyed with, "but would enough people know who she is?" (She was Dr. Johnson's landlady, and Bainbridge has unearthed some material that hints that she sometimes had to lock him in his room when the mad fit was on him. "Did she whip him?" she asks, with mock-prurient glee.)

Despite the flagrantly outrageous decor of her house, where towels ostensibly from the *Titanic* hang in the bathroom alongside Crucifixion carvings, Bainbridge likes to portray herself as a grandmotherly figure whose main concern is for the future of her children and grandchildren. "I want to get together all my documents and papers for them against the time I die." Success, she finds, though very slow in coming, "is very nice, even late in life. I never had expectations, you see. I think struggle is probably good for the soul, as long as you don't go under."

She remains unperturbed by the oddball reputation that seems to cling to her. "People say I'm eccentric, but I don't see how you can be eccentric and still write hundreds of words a day, and pay the bills, and own a house, and baby-sit for six grandchildren every week."

JOHN F. BAKER
November 9, 1998

ANDREA BARRETT

Rochester, N.Y., home to corporate headquarters for Eastman Kodak and for Xerox, styles itself "The World's Image Centre." It is a city much concerned with capturing the past and, indeed, a city that finds the past palpable in the present. Along the expressways that divide the town, Kodak billboards beam the golden-yellow hue indelibly associated with that firm's brands. Heneath their patina of rust-belt obsolescence, aging factories are reminders of an industrial heyday, while well-preserved residential boulevards march towards the city limits, evoking a statelier era.

In her own way, Rochester resident Andrea Barrett has become a leading light of the image industry. She doesn't ply the trade of a scientist or an engineer; rather, she crafts powerfully vivid works of fiction, most recently *The Voyage of the Narwhal,* an epic of 19th-century polar exploration (Norton). In 1996, Barrett surprised the publishing world by winning the National Book Award for fiction, in a decision that startled many industry insiders. Since then, the powerful volume that garnered the prize, the story collection *Ship Fever,* has won additional acclaim. Yet Barrett herself remains something of an enigma. To understand Barrett, it helps to understand that if she seemed to come from nowhere to take home NBA laurels, she actually came from a place long devoted to the science of making memory tangible.

Memories both personal and historical saturate Barrett's shady, barn-red three-story home, which lies not far from The George Eastman House, Rochester's noted museum of photography and cinema. Photographs of China and the Arctic recall Barrett's travels. A 1911 *Encyclopedia Britannica* set—the edition most treasured by historians—fills several bookshelves, while the coffee table offers a volume titled *Voices of the Spirit World,* which contains communications from the great beyond transcribed by a spiritualist medium and published in Rochester in 1855. The collection's most striking figure is its curator, Barrett herself: a lanky woman whose animated face peers out from under a crown of long tresses. Barrett's own voice is tremulous; her long sentences emerge in the torrent characteristic of a shy person determined to be voluble.

Barrett has often sought to seclude herself with her work, and, when she has emerged, she has often eschewed the role of author. "Until recently," she confides, "hardly anybody here knew I was a writer—they knew me as my dogs' mother, walking around the neighborhood." She is still adjusting to the attention brought by the success of *Ship Fever.* "The phone plagues me," she sighs. "I really can't make something new unless I feel that at least for a while it's completely secret," she says. "I can't work on it. I can't think about it. I don't sell books before they're done, and I don't show them to my agent or my editor."

Yet Barrett is poised to become a more public figure in the wake of *The Narwhal*'s publication. Her new novel resembles many of the stories in *Ship Fever* in its 19th-century setting and in its choice of a scientist as its protagonist. But by unfurling a larger canvas with *The Narwhal,* Barrett extends into new territory her uncanny ability to make stories of science past illuminate today's world. *The Narwhal* imagines the travails of botanist Erasmus Darwin Wells, who signs on to a polar expedition led by his sister's dashing but dangerously immature suitor. The novel's drama eventually encompasses not only how they search for a previous, lost team of explorers, but also how they navigate the sea of publicity when they return to their native Philadelphia.

Barrett, too, has felt the allure of extreme climes. A year ago last June, with the support of a Guggenheim Foundation grant, she traveled to the northern coast of Baffin Island, where she gathered much "visceral detail" for the book. Still, Barrett expresses some bafflement at the prospect that *The Narwhal* might bring her a still larger public. "I thought I was writing a deeply obscure book," she avers, "about some mid-19th-century Arctic explorers and naturalists," about "material that ought not to be of interest to anyone but me." But people have likened *The Narwhal,* she says, to the adventure tales that have swept into the mainstream recently, from John Krakauer's *Into Thin Air* to fellow Norton author Sebastian Junger's *The Perfect Storm* and, of course, the ultimate iceberg saga, *Titanic.*

"The idea of this as an adventure story is very funny to me," Barrett says with a giddy laugh. "What I was after was much more ruminative.

In fact, although the research I was drawing from is full of adventure, I think this book is much less full of adventure. Its people are painters and writers, they're thinking and mulling, they're seeing, they're looking. They're not going out and slashing polar bears to death."

Barrett shares the scientific bent and love of the outdoors characteristic of her protagonists. Born in Boston, she grew up largely on Cape Cod, where her childhood days on the beach instilled a deep feeling for the ocean and a passionate interest in natural history. By age 19, she had graduated from Union College in Schenectady, N.Y., with a degree in biology. On a first foray into graduate school—at the University of Massachusetts in Amherst—Barrett studied zoology, a discipline in which she remains enmeshed: on this day, her writing desk bears a textbook open to pages illustrating various jellyfish. " 'The Littoral Zone,' " a *Ship Fever* story, "is going in a Norton Anthology," Barrett explains, "and the editors asked me to write footnotes."

Barrett would later return to U. Mass to study medieval and Reformation theological history. It was during this second sojourn in graduate school that she became conscious of her true vocation. "Writing papers about the Inquisition or the early days of the Franciscan order, I was going through exactly the same process I use now to make my fiction," she recalls. "I'd go to the library and pull out everything, fill my room and become obsessed with the shape and the texture of the paper, and the way the words look, trying to make it all dramatic. At some point I realized: 'hey, this isn't history, and I'm not a scholar.' "

Subsequently, Barrett moved to Rochester, where her husband was doing an M.D./Ph.D. program. The couple lived a bleak, monastic existence, residing in a "crumbling graduate student housing tower." Barrett took secretarial jobs in science and medical labs, where, she recalls, "if it was slow, I could put paper in the typewriter and pretend I was typing notes—and I just started writing this novel." Barrett characterizes her first effort—never published—as "unspeakably horrible. I'd go to the library and get other novels and read those, and books about how books are put together, and criticism, and then I'd write. It was an awful experience and the book was awful. And I spent forever doing it." This lonely apprenticeship stretched from the end of 1977 until Barrett's first visit to Breadloaf, in 1984.

Barrett first went to Breadloaf "as what they call a contributor, the lowest rank of what used to be an infinite hierarchy—which is to say that I paid cash money. I'd written one or two little stories, and I brought them up for the workshop. But of course I had the novel in my purse, as does everyone who goes to a writer's conference."

Barrett's first big break arose from a workshop with Nicholas Delbanco and Thomas Gavin. Delbanco, says Barrett, "did two incredibly generous things." First, "he offered to read my novel, and then he read it up there. Now that I teach [in the M.F.A. program at North Carolina's Warren Wilson College], I realize how improbable and impossible that is." Then, she continues, Delbanco "sat me down and said that I could probably be a writer if I wanted to be, that I had a voice, but that I had learned to write on this novel and could never save it, and that I should throw it out and move on. Which I also now realize is an incredibly difficult thing to say to a writer—and it was exactly what I needed. It was the best thing anybody ever did for me. I cried for a day, and then I threw it out, and then I wrote *Lucid Stars*."

Through subsequent trips to Breadloaf, Barrett met Wendy Weil, who became her agent. Editor Jane Rosenman, then at Delacorte, bought Barrett's intergenerational saga, which traces how a family of strong women learn to rely on each other for help in life's crises. Barrett cherished Rosenman's nurturing support, and the editor and press so esteemed *Lucid Stars* that they chose it to launch its Delta imprint for paperback originals. *Secret Harmonies,* more tightly focused on a musically gifted woman's mixed experience of marriage, followed as a Delacorte hardcover.

Barrett finds her diverse work "strangely of a piece, in the sense that I've always relied quite heavily on research to provide both the plot of my novels and the stuff that is the background of the characters' lives."

But one real transition, to Barrett's mind, came with *The Middle Kingdom,* a novel about an American who visits China with her biologist husband, published by Pocket after Rosenman moved to that press in 1990. (Like *Secret Harmonies* and *The Forms of Water*—a novel that chronicles the twilight journey of an elderly ex-monk—it was reprinted as a Washington Square paperback.) Where her first two novels were "some uneasy fusion of research, perception of contemporary life and fragments taken from my own life or the lives of people I knew," *The Middle Kingdom,* Barrett says, "really bears no relation to my own life, and yet I was able to use the spine of my trip there in 1986 as a way to access through research a whole other set of lives. That was a kind of revelation."

The cerebral ambitions of *The Middle Kingdom* and, especially, of her subsequent novel, *The Forms of Water*, found Barrett departing from the mainstream at Pocket. The *Ship Fever* collection marked a still more radical departure. Funded by a NEA grant, and nearing despair over her novel's perceived lack of commercial viability, Barrett set out to experiment with the short story form. Intense research into the history of natural science and medicine bore fruit in a stunning series of vignettes of past and present scientists—among them Linnaeus and Mendel—culminating in the title novella, in which a young Canadian doctor becomes so consumed by his work saving sick Irish immigrants that he himself falls victim to their affliction.

Yet when Barrett submitted *Ship Fever* to Pocket, the outcome was a parting of the ways between author and publisher. Rosenman now says that she "felt that Andrea's luminous writing would be better served by a hardcover publisher more exclusively devoted to literary fare." Cast out of the world of conglomerate publishing, Barrett landed at Norton, where *Ship Fever* prospered under the solicitous wing of Carol Houck Smith. Barrett lauds Smith as an "amazing person. I don't think that *Ship Fever* was an easy book for her to buy, and then she was so solidly behind it; she fought for it like an archangel."

The attention to *Ship Fever* has opened up diverse new audiences for Barrett, and she is slowly learning to recognize signs of the public's appreciation. She tells, for example, of a visit this past spring to a Washington, D.C., high school, where "a gifted teacher" invited her to meet a class that had read her stories. "They were such amazing students, so engaged and articulate," she says. What's more, as Barrett discovered to her delight, the students had an unexpected tribute up their sleeves. The whole class wore long white lab coats—donned, it turned out, not for some preceding home economics class, as Barrett at first surmised, but rather as a humorous tribute to her and her scientific protagonists. Barrett will continue to win accolades. But she will long remember how these young readers so fittingly styled themselves her fellow workers in the endeavor to bring together the imaginative worlds of science and literature.

SAMUEL BAKER
August 10, 1998

11

FREDERICK BARTHELME

ARRIVING ON HIS ritual Thursday night expedition to Biloxi's Casino Magic, Frederick Barthelme is greeted warmly at the house bank and credit union, where they're only too pleased to cash his personal check. It's a surprisingly large check for a "decidedly midlist" author (as Barthelme flippantly but somewhat regretfully calls himself), whose latest novel, *Bob the Gambler,* is about the ruinous toll gambling exacts on a Mississippi man and his family.

Barthelme's hero, Ray Kaiser, gets so hooked on blackjack and roulette that this novel (his seventh but the first from Houghton Mifflin) seems to carry an implicit warning: Gambling can be hazardous to your psychological, physical and financial health. When talking about his book, Barthelme is blunt about gambling's seductive powers. "There's absolutely no question that it's an addiction, as powerful a drug as anything I've ever seen. Worse than cigarettes, cocaine, heroin."

Strong sentiments, but Barthelme hasn't let them deter him from Biloxi's casinos. He's as habitual as Ray Kaiser, if not nearly so impulsive and demonic. That's apparent when he takes a low-roller from *PW* on one of his pilgrimages a few weeks before the publication of *Bob the Gambler.* Also along for the ride is his younger brother, Steve, another of the four writing Barthelmes—a "Flying Wallenda" brotherhood (according to Frederick) that includes the late Donald, whose whimsical, collagist *New Yorker* stories made him the highest flier, and Peter, a mystery novelist.

With a fistful of "play" money, Barthelme sets off for the Casino Magic's blackjack tables. In his gray polo shirt, jeans and mesh slippers, the amiable, 54-year-old author is as casually retro as most of the other players. "Six one and a shade" (in his own words), he moves with a bulky, happy-go-lucky grace, looking a bit like Hemingway with his neatly trimmed, silvery beard. (For *PW* readers, he proposes: "Why don't you just say I look like a large Montgomery Clift?")

Momentarily distracted en route to the blackjack game, Barthelme surrenders four $100 bills to a no-armed bandit—a high-tech slot machine that uses push buttons, rather than a lever, to part gamblers more efficiently from their money. Losing $400 is "like nothing," he says. "You can get down $1000 and come back real easy."

Barthelme gets down real easy—and fast—at blackjack, even though he's playing at a table with his lucky dealer, John. It was John, the novelist says, who recently urged him to try number eight at a nearby roulette wheel. With odds of 35 to one, Barthelme bet $50 and won $1750. "I managed to lose it later, so it really didn't matter. But it was really quite amazing."

When *PW* suggests that it's about as amazing as Rick's ability to pick the winning roulette numbers in *Casablanca*, Barthelme (who's also known as Rick) insists that it's naive and melodramatic to suspect a rigged wheel in such a "highly policed" casino. Instead, he attributes John's called shot to intuition, coincidence, quantum mechanics, morphic resonance "with a little bit of salt," and his experience as a croupier. "These things simply happen and we don't have any ready way to understand or explain them," he says.

In the four years since "floating" casinos (camouflaged barges) docked on Mississippi's Gulf Coast, Barthelme has regularly commuted the 70 miles from Hattiesburg, where he directs the creative writing program at the University of Southern Mississippi and edits the *Mississippi Review*. "Yes," he says. "I have been keeping score— and no, I'm not ahead."

"When I started gambling," Barthelme adds, "I wasn't clear about how tightly it can grip you. There's a point you reach when you're losing where you just don't care any more about the money. It's like, I've lost so much already that it seems silly to worry about spending another thousand to get it back."

Whatever his losses, they're surely not as crunching as those of Ray Kaiser, the narrator of Barthelme's novel, whose stepdaughter jokingly calls him Bob (sometimes Bub) the Gambler. An "architect, husband, an ordinary guy, a middle-class Ford-Explorer–driving guy with wife, child, dog, house . . . a few blocks off the beach," as he describes himself, Ray overnight becomes "the guy in the newspaper who loses everything at the casino."

Shuffling credit cards from the rapidly depleting deck of plastic in his wallet, Ray drops $43,000 "and change" during a feverish, agonizing, sleepless stretch of 36 hours at the Paradise casino. "The way I played," he admits, "was a kind of probable suicide."

Though she's not nearly as suicidal, it's Ray's wife, Jewel, who initially persuades him to join her at the Paradise, as a way of relieving the daily dullness, the boredom with the cineplexes and the shopping malls, the "beach crap." Starting off as small-fry winners at the one-dollar slots, they soon discover they are, in Jewel's words, "natural-born losers," whose ultimate losses include their house, cars, TVs, stereos, furniture.

Yet Barthelme says he's not being ironic or facetious at the end of the book, when they convince one another that they're spiritually better off for losing. "For them, it's a positive experience," he says, "because it takes an anesthetized couple, in the sense that we're all anesthetized, and it wakes them up."

Despite the negative effects of the Biloxi casinos on Barthelme's bank account, they've only expanded and enriched his literary territory. Beginning with his debut collection of short stories, *Moon Deluxe* (S&S) in 1983, most of his books—including a second story collection, *Chroma* (S&S, 1987), and such novels as *Two Against One* (S&S, 1988) and *The Brothers* (Viking, 1993)—have been situated on or near Mississippi's Gulf Coast, which has become as much Barthelme's "postage stamp of native soil" as Faulkner's Yoknapatawpha County or Nelson Algren's Division Street.

The coastal highway from Gulfport to Biloxi is recognizably Barthelme country. After passing through stretches of white beach and aristocratic Southern homes, the road turns into an "outlet mall version of Las Vegas" (as the novelist calls it in the opening pages of *Bob the Gambler*) marked by hundreds of temples to tackiness.

However shabby and transient, it's a landscape that not only agrees with but also largely defines Barthelme's seriocomic characters, many of whom are physical and spiritual vagrants. Divorced and involved in loose relationships, they move from one generic condo to the next, haunting the shopping centers and strip malls, talking and eating and drinking aimlessly, obsessed with their cars, their stereos, all their material goods, indulging their ravenous appetites for junk food and what the writer calls "slop/scuzz/scum/slime/trash/junk" culture.

Like so many of his characters, Barthelme lives in—or occasionally occupies—an impersonal condo, in a Hattiesburg development. His bedroom office seems inordinately neat for a writer's working quarters, while the rest of the house is austerely, minimally furnished, with a few museum posters and a Bauhaus book on a coffee table. "I work here and that's all that happens," says Barthelme, a bachelor, who indicates that he does most of his living at the home of a woman friend.

If Barthelme's characters seem excessively verbose, especially in his later fiction, that may be due in part to his practice of dictating his books into a tape recorder, lately while driving between Biloxi and Hattiesburg. Because brand names figure so conspicuously in Barthelme's fiction, and his characters talk in such a discursive, colloquial style, the author has become a brand name himself, according to critics: a K-Mart realist (or is it a Wal-Mart minimalist?), along with Raymond Carver, Ann Beattie and their many imitators.

Barthelme says he can't complain about his treatment by critics, especially not the *Vogue* review of *The Brothers* by Bret Easton Ellis, who called him "one of the most distinctive prose stylists since Hemingway." Even so, he adds with caustic laughter, "I would rather have sold some books."

In common with a lot of his contemporaries, Barthelme has been a migratory writer, moving from Simon & Schuster to Weidenfeld & Nicholson to Viking. For *Bob the Gambler,* he defected from Viking to Houghton Mifflin, along with his editor, Dawn Seferian, whose editorial eye, he says, is "really quite extraordinary. She made liberal suggestions on this book, every one of which was on target."

Accounting for a family that's produced so many writers, Barthelme says it was "built into the system," social as well as genetic. Born in Houston, Barthelme and his siblings (three brothers and a sister, Joan, whom he calls "the fastest gun") were raised in a "quite serious but playfully intellectual, very verbal" atmosphere. His mother was a teacher, his father an architect, and they put a high value on wit, charm and fast repartee—"pot shots disguised as jokes." Frederick studied architecture at the University of Houston but dropped out in 1967 and set off for New York, hoping to find a career as an artist.

His brother Donald, 12 years older, was living there at the time, amazing readers with his fabulist stories, and Frederick was soon experimenting with fiction himself, as an offshoot of his conceptual art.

When he started publishing stories in William Shawn's *New Yorker* during the early 1980s, Barthelme acquired both a valued editor, Veronica Geng, and an agent, Andrew Wylie. "He wrote me two or three letters," Barthelme says of Wylie. "I liked the sound of them, so I called him up and we got along splendidly. He was my ideal version of an agent, rough and tumble and quick—the kind of guy who might be able to get a reasonable amount of money for a literary work in a market that didn't prize it."

Instead of resenting the fraternal competition, Donald, who had been publishing in the *New Yorker* for a decade, encouraged his literary efforts, Barthelme says, reading his manuscripts and offering editorial suggestions—among them one piece of advice he has steadfastly and perversely ignored. "He kept telling me, 'Take the weather out, take the weather out.' That's why my goal in life is to write a book that consists of nothing but weather."

Needing to free himself of Donald's influence, Barthelme headed for Johns Hopkins University in 1976, where he studied with John Barth, learning about narrative and plot strategies, qualities that were notably, and deliberately, absent from his brother's work.

During his nearly two decades in Mississippi, Barthelme has found the state both enlightened ("Nothing like the myth of Mississippi") and congenial for a number of reasons, not the least of which is the culture of the Gulf coast, which Barthelme treats with off-handed affection, confessing that he's "completely enthralled" by the decay and the tackiness of his "dinky coast town," as he refers to Biloxi in *Bob the Gambler.*

The casinos, which he expects will make Biloxi America's third ranking gambling theme park, after Vegas and Atlantic City, have only added another layer of ticky-tack ugliness, both to his delight and dismay: "It's grotesque by definition, and wonderfully so, from my view. But it's not nearly as much fun as I thought it was going to be. I wish I could make as much writing as I lose at the casino."

With *PW* watching, Barthelme offers a live demonstration of his bad luck at the Casino Magic blackjack table. As John the Dealer claims another pile of his $25 chips, Barthelme jokes: "You're trying to hurt me. If I keep losing with such authority, I'm going to get up and find a table where I can win."

Barthelme doesn't call it a night until 11 the next morning. *PW* makes an earlier exit, but not before Barthelme persuades us to feed three dollar bills into a slot machine, just to know the thrill of winning or losing. The $3 stake quickly grows to $14.50, a decent payoff. But Barthelme insists on going for the $25,000 jackpot, and in a few minutes it's all gone. "Now," the author says, smiling wickedly, "you've had the complete gambling experience."

JOHN BLADES
October 6, 1997

JOHN BAYLEY & IRIS MURDOCH

In a detached house on a leafy suburban street in North Oxford lives a remarkable pair who between them have helped shape the literary landscape of contemporary England: John Bayley, former Oxford professor of English, for over 30 years a noted critic, and a recently fledged novelist; and his wife of 40 years, the eminent novelist and philosopher Iris Murdoch. And they live, as Bayley says in his new and heartbreaking book about their life together, "like naughty children."

For Iris has suffered for over four years now from advancing Alzheimer's disease, and though Bayley cares for her devotedly, and alone (he determinedly refrains from seeking any kind of live-in help), the house and garden are in an advanced state of neglect. "We've never been much for housekeeping," Bayley says cheerfully, in what has to be the understatement of the year. On a street of well-kept homes smiling in the mellow fall sunshine, the Bayley establishment, with its unkempt front garden and dark, encroaching trees strikes a note of somber heedlessness.

Indoors, the *PW* visitor is ushered to a sagging chair that has to be hastily cleared of a tottering pile of books and magazines, one of three seats ranged before a dead TV set whose screen peers from among the clutter. A crowded window ledge offers a sort of snapshot of the chaos that overspreads the house: It contains a video of Fred Astaire's *Shall We Dance?*, some half-eaten slices of salami, a few broken crackers, a bowl half-full of crusted oatmeal, a couple of coffee cups with dried, milky sediment, a scattering of paper towels, a CD of a Wienawski violin concerto, and a small potted plant that looks to be in its last throes. A row of similarly afflicted plants, victims of Iris's obsessive over-watering, lines a shelf.

The house's inhabitants are in not much better trim than the house. Bayley, an energetic wisp of a man of 74 whose eyes explode with eagerness behind his glasses, but whose razor seems to have missed several patches of stubble, is in ancient carpet slippers and a well-worn pullover: his 80-year-old wife, gray hair unruly over her wide brow, is in a grubby housedress. Their unkempt appearance, however, fades almost instantly from consciousness under the on-slaught of Bayley's stammering rush of witty, sometimes bitchy, words, his utter openness—and the solicitous affection with which he treats Iris. For that celebrated pug face (as he likes to describe it), with the firm chin, the thoughtful eyes and the hint of perpetual in-ner amusement, is now an anxious mask in which the eyes dart from side to side in search of reassurance, and sometimes close as if in mo-mentary sleep or resignation.

It is chilling to associate this shadowy creature with the writer of more than 30 novels, beginning with 1954's *Under the Net,* which in their very personal blend of fantasy (Murdoch was a very early magic realist), myth, keen psychological insights, humorously inside knowl-edge of English bohemian life and lightly worn philosophical under-pinnings, made her *the* woman writer for the first postwar English generation. Nearly all her books are still in print in Penguin editions, and came out in the U.S. as Viking hardcovers.

Bayley talks of his wife with enormous pride, still apparently as be-dazzled by her achievements as he was when, as a young graduate student, he first sought to woo the already renowned philosophy pro-fessor. "For 30 years she wrote a book a year, regular as clockwork," he says. "Didn't you, darling?" Iris looks perplexed. "Let's come all the same," she says. Always he tries to draw her into the talk and seems not at all put out when her replies make sense only to her.

For as Bayley writes in his spellbinding *Elegy for Iris* (St. Martin's) as one of the last books Bob Weil edited there before he decamped for Norton in November, the important thing is not *what* she com-municates, but that she still does so at all; and occasionally she man-ages a flash of extraordinarily vivid insight, as when she described her current plight as "sailing into darkness." Bayley paints a picture of a long, mutually supportive marriage in which the essential closeness, rooted in a primordial level of childlike warmth and contentment, has scarcely been affected by the loss of Iris's amazing mind.

And it *was* an amazing one. Bayley recalls how she would say of a new novel, "Finished it!" before she had put a word on paper. "But it was all there already in her head, as a sort of metaphysical vision, and only had to be written out," he says. "You could do an essay on the metaphysics of the novel, using Iris as an example." Among the books she created over the years, however she managed it, were several prize-winning ones, like *Flight of the Enchanter* (1956), *A Severed Head* (1961), *The Black Prince* (1973), *The Sacred and Profane Love Machine* (1974), *The Sea, The Sea* (1978); she was made a Dame Commander of the British Empire in 1986, an honor bestowed on but a handful of writers.

The idea that Bayley should do a book about Iris's plight, and their previous life together, came from Weil, who had long been a friend of Bayley's, and his publisher in the U.S. "It was just about a year ago he suggested it. It was a short book, and it came quite easily." Bayley's story first caught the attention of American readers in a lengthy excerpt that ran in the *New Yorker* last summer, and was, for many of them, the first intimation of Iris's situation. "Tina Brown wanted to run it before she left, so she rushed it out, and the *Sunday Times*, which had first serial rights here, was so cross it withdrew its original offer," says Bayley, without apparent regret, having seemingly rather enjoyed the scrap.

"What are you doing now?" says Iris, gazing fixedly at the visitor; she has an air at once distraught and faintly reminiscent, as if she is trying to recall something just beyond her grasp.

"Would you like a biscuit?" asks Bayley, turning to find some. "Two," says Iris firmly, a clear connection established at last. He brings her biscuits and an orange drink—probably of the kind he describes in *Elegy*, in which some of Iris's beloved red wine is mixed in, both to please and to help calm her.

Bayley continues to talk, dazzlingly and amusingly, about the English literary scene, in which he still plays a very active role, though he retired as Wharton Professor of English at the university 10 years ago. He remains highly productive as a critic, appearing often in the *New York Review of Books*. "Bob Silvers suggests things, and I do them," is how he puts it, with that studied English diffidence that can seem at once charming and an attempt to hold serious conversation at bay. He hasn't begun work on another book, he says, though "Bob Weil has an idea I could do something on Leo Tolstoy." (Russian literature is an area of special expertise and interest.)

As for a memoir, *Elegy* is it. "I could only do it under Iris's wing. I couldn't make my own affairs sufficiently interesting." He picks up a copy of the English edition, which has already appeared, to admiring notices and a flurry of interview attention, and has achieved a degree of bestsellerdom. Turning to a picture of Iris as a younger woman, he shows it to her, and says, "You look just like your picture, darling." "How exciting," says Iris, without animation. Her eyes close and she seems to nod off.

As to how the book will be received in the States, Bayley is at once eager and skeptical. "We shall see what we shall see," he says. Weil has already received a personal call from Knopf's Sonny Mehta telling him how much he admired and was touched by the book. "Hmm," says Bayley. "Let's hope he'll say that in public."

Elegy describes with great skill and grace the odd mid-1950s courtship between the young graduate English instructor and the professor six years his senior who was already making a name for herself by her brilliance and her mysterious lifestyle, which involved distinguished lovers in London and a rather raffish Bohemian set. Child called to child in the pair, however, and a nude swim they took together in the river Isis confirmed their relationship. Bayley, with his own (if lesser) role assured as a pillar of the Oxford establishment, seems not to have felt threatened by his wife's much greater international fame.

He penned some notable books of criticism—*The Romantic Survival, The Characters of Love*—which, he says, "seem rather old-fashioned now." Then, after his retirement, he wrote a trilogy of novels revolving around an odd but alluring Australian heroine—*Alice, The Queen Captain* and *George's Lair,* which were published by Duckworth in England, but have not appeared here. Last year at St. Martin's Weil brought out *The Red Hat,* a beautifully crafted mixture of suspense and fantasy based on an expedition by a group of English intellectuals to The Hague to see a Vermeer exhibition, in the course of which a young woman mysteriously disappears. But he is equivocal about whether he intends to write any more fiction. "Perhaps I might do something a bit autobiographical, about ways Oxford has changed yet stayed the same."

But the combination of his own continuing work and looking after Iris takes up a great deal of time. "It's hard to find things to do with her." She used to enjoy passively watching television—the Teletubbies, when they began, were a favorite—but that seems to have "worn out its welcome." They take shopping trips in their little car and are sometimes invited out, although social gatherings tend to make Iris anxious. A big centenary dinner being given at London's

Dorchester hotel by Duckworth, Bayley's publisher, was looked forward to as a special treat: "They're being very kind and sending a car for us."

His conversation tends to revert to Iris whenever he feels, as he often does, that he has said enough about himself. Now he recalls with pleasure the time Iris visited the U.S., to receive the Medal of Honor for Literature from New York's National Arts Club in 1990. Ed Victor, who had recently become her agent ("I think they'd tended to keep her royalties back a bit, and she did much better after Ed took over," says Bayley) showed Iris the neighborhood where his father had been a fish salesman. "Ed's father told him to leave the States, and make a better life for himself in England," Bayley exclaims, delighted at the way the story stands the common wisdom on its head.

Among Iris's disciples as writers, says Bayley, was A.S. Byatt, who "sat at her knee" (and who later wrote a book about her work) and A.N. Wilson. Iris herself had been a great reader of Tolkien's *Lord of the Rings.* "You read and reread it, didn't you, darling?"

There is talk of the Booker Prize, then upcoming, which Iris had won (for *The Sea, The Sea*) and for which she had several times been a runner-up. "Yesterday," says Iris. "No, no, two weeks from now," says Bayley. "Do tell us," says Iris eagerly.

Bayley himself had been chair of the Booker judges several years earlier and recalls the occasion with great glee. "That nice man, Martyn Goff, who runs it, said he had never had such an incompetent chairman, and the whole thing was an utter disaster. That Scottish writer with all the bad words [James Kellman] won, and everyone was cross. Everything always seems to go wrong, but I suppose it's all good publicity." Bayley appears to take a perverse pleasure in his mistakes. The novelist and biographer D.M. Thomas had been a pupil of his, "and when he showed me *The White Hotel* I didn't like it at all, and urged him not to publish. Fortunately," he chortles, "he took no notice."

A biographer, Peter Conradi, is currently at work on a sort of official biography of Iris, and Bayley is helping as best he can to find old reviews and her diaries. Conradi is described in *Elegy* as being almost obsessively neat, and it is possible that on his occasional visits to the Oxford house he does some tidying up; otherwise it is difficult to see how the old pair could keep their heads above the flood of old newspapers, discarded clothes and previous meals.

As Bayley escorts his visitor to the door, with Iris hesitantly following along, her eyes wondering who could be this visitor who has spent a couple of hours chatting with her husband, notebook in hand, an impulse strikes the intruder. "Do you think she'd mind if I kissed her good-bye?"

"I think she'd like it very much."

He brushed his lips against the soft cheek of the elderly author of books that had meant so much to him for so many years.

"Thank you very much," said Iris Murdoch doubtfully.

JOHN F. BAKER
December 14, 1998

BILL BRYSON

Bill Bryson's office in his spacious Hanover, N.H., home surely reflects this ex-expatriate's rich career: the shelves hold copies of his books on travel and the English language, and on the walls hang posters for those books. On the coffee table lie books he's reading and sober magazines like the *Economist*. A family room by night, the space houses a pool table and a giant-screen TV.

But the room also boasts flagrant evidence of Bryson's curiosity, wanderlust and eccentricity: a collection of matchbooks; photos rescued from junk shops; an inflatable version of Munch's *The Scream*. Is that spilled coffee on his computer? Nope, it's a plastic novelty look-alike. And that stuffed grizzly bear, looming seven feet high? Well, that's a gift from his wife, Cynthia—and also an apt tribute to Bryson's latest book.

In his adoptive Britain, Bryson reached bestseller status with wiseacre travelogues that retraced earlier trips to the American heartland (*The Lost Continent*), tourist Europe (*Neither Here Nor There*) and the Britannia he loves (*Notes from a Small Island*). In the United States, he's best-known for excursions into the lore of the English language, in *Mother Tongue* and *Made in America*. That should change. When Bryson moved back to the States three years ago, the local countryside inspired a new quest: a trip hiking the Appalachian Trail that became the subject of *A Walk in the Woods: Rediscovering America on the Appalachian Trail* published by Broadway Books.

That grizzly honors some comic paranoia, one Bryson frothed up by reading, in preparation for his trek, a book about bear attacks. A mild-mannered red-bearded chap who obediently leaves the house to puff on his pipe, Bryson on the page becomes a more picaresque character, bemoaning modernity, reveling in tackiness and wielding a lusty, often caustic wit.

Bryson explains: "The voice you're reading is me, but it's only part of me," the part that emerges less while traveling than when re-creating the experience. In jeans, a sweatshirt and wire-rim glasses, Bryson, 46, looks more like a putterer than a hiker.

Indeed, Bryson devised, as he wrote, a number of rationalizations: the hike would get him fit, put him in touch with a fading wilderness and help "reacquaint myself with the scale and beauty of my native land." Not to mention the contract he garnered from his British publisher. So Bryson unearthed Stephen Katz, a childhood chum from Des Moines, Iowa, who was a maddening presence during his European jaunt (as described in *Neither Here Nor There*). Katz—who once "single-handedly ensured that Iowa had a thriving drug culture"—serves as a Falstaffian sidekick for much of the book.

The team's misadventures, not all self-inflicted, include encounters with insufferable hikers, oddball Americans off the trail and landscapes natural and artificial. But the trail, some 2000 miles long from Georgia to Maine, proved too tough. "Initially, it didn't seem an impossible task," Bryson asserts. "But your expectations cannot match reality. What I didn't allow for is that the drudgery and unbelievable scale make it more a mental exercise than a physical one."

So the undynamic duo gave up after 500 miles and six-and-a-half weeks, reaching Virginia only after hopscotching part of the Trail. Katz went home. Bryson had his own obligations: "It was a real problem. Not only had I kind of lost the *raison d'être*, but I'd lost my comic foil, Katz." So Bryson returned to hike parts of the trail in segments, veered off to explore the area around it and drew more on trail lore and wilderness reflections to flesh out the narrative.

Bryson hastens to cite "the feeling of elation when I went to the Berkshires and got back on the trail." That epiphany allowed Bryson to write, not unfairly, that his trip taught him "a profound respect for wilderness and nature and the benign dark power of woods." Even if he and Katz didn't finish the trek, he concludes, they tried.

Bryson says he's not a travel writer: "I stumbled into this genre." Coming of age in Des Moines, he seemed destined for journalism, the family profession. But the region pushed him outward, as recounted to comic effect in *The Lost Continent*. "Much as I resented having to grow up in Des Moines, it gave me a real appreciation for every place in the world that's not Des Moines," Bryson adds.

Still, his hometown laid the seeds of his career. His sportswriter father bequeathed a love of language (and supplied baseball terms to H.L. Mencken's *The American Language*) and shared his P.G. Wodehouse and Robert Benchley books with his son. The *National Geographic*—especially pieces on Europe—shaped young Bill's vision of the outer world.

So, after two years at Des Moines' Drake University, Bryson backpacked through Europe, thinking he'd go home and rise to a journalism career, perhaps in Chicago. Instead, he found a job at an English sanitarium ("It is an interesting experience to become acquainted with a country through the eyes of the insane," he writes in *Notes from a Small Island*), met a lovely nurse named Cynthia and went home to finish college.

But Britain beckoned. After graduation, Bryson found a series of copyediting jobs (ultimately, at the *Times*) and began freelancing. His copy editor's eye led him in 1984 to produce what he calls "a poor man's version" of Theodore Bernstein's *The Careful Writer,* called the *Penguin Dictionary of Troublesome Words* (published here by Facts on File).

Travel articles spawned his first travel book, *The Palace Under the Alps,* a guide to unusual European spots published here in 1985 by Congdon & Weed and, as Bryson puts it, "instantly remaindered." The publisher, vainly seeking a veneer of class, listed the author as William.

Bryson quit his day job in 1987, just as he won two book contracts. In *The Lost Continent,* he retraced family vacations and aimed to explain Middle America to curious Brits. *Mother Tongue,* an informal history of the English language, allowed Bryson to turn library research into entertaining narrative.

The Lost Continent earned Bryson a piddling $3500 advance from Secker & Warburg, but its savage take on American tackiness made it a British hit. Harper & Row paid Secker & Warburg $350,000 for the American rights. The book sold decently but not well here, and some reviewers chided Bryson for cheap shots, like giving small towns such fictional names as "Dry Heaves," New Mexico.

After *The Lost Continent,* Bryson found an agent, coincidentally a long-lost Des Moines friend, Jed Mattes, who saw a Bryson piece on Iowa in *Granta* and contacted him from New York. Mattes's London affiliate, Carol Heaton, now reps him in England.

Following the stellar U.K. sales of *The Lost Continent,* Bryson's editor at Secker & Warburg, Dan Franklin, wanted more, so Bryson "picked up where the story left off," in Europe. *Neither Here Nor There* gave Bryson the chance to observe that Norwegian TV "gives you the sensation of a coma without the worry and inconvenience." The book, published in the U.S. by William Morrow, again did better there than here.

Bryson actually has spent more time in the library than on the road. He returned to language in *The Penguin Dictionary for Writers & Editors*, published in 1991 in the U.K., but not here. And he extended himself with *Made in America*, which uses the evolution of American English to slalom through American history and culture.

Bryson, who acknowledges that *The Lost Continent* lacked balance, found a mellower voice in *Notes from a Small Island*, published here by Morrow in 1996. This affectionate valediction lauds British eccentricity, endurance and genius for adversity: "They like their pleasures small," he writes.

As an outsider, Bryson felt sympathy for the battered British psyche, and the Brits loved him back. Titled there as *Notes from a Small Country*, the book became a huge hit in paperback, selling nearly a million copies. It's even turned Bryson into a TV personage, as he returns to Britain this summer to retrace his steps for the camera.

With Franklin gone from Secker & Warburg, London agent Carol Heaton sold *Small Country* for a reported £300,000 to Transworld, BDD's English wing, where Bryson works mainly with Patrick Janson-Smith. (It became a Doubleday hardcover and a Black Swan paperback).

Bryson has long written mainly for a British audience, though less so in the case of this new book. *A Walk in the Woods* has been a British bestseller, but reviewers were puzzled, he says, by the "fairly alien" topic and lack of "nonstop yuks." The American version has been tweaked accordingly. Broadway editor-in-chief John Sterling encouraged Bryson to beef up his conclusions and to divide the narrative into two distinct parts.

With a $150,000 investment in promotion alone, Broadway is proclaiming this as Bryson's breakout book here. Indeed, advance reviews have been good, and Bryson will appear on *Good Morning America*, *Sunday Morning* and *Charlie Rose* to promote it; it's been selected as Book of the Month Club and Quality Paperback Club alternates.

If *A Walk in the Woods* may not be vintage Bryson (British reviews noted that it lacks the previous plethora of strangers serving as comic foils), it does show the author more than ever combining his two modes: picaresque traveler and lore-gatherer.

For five years, he reflects, he alternated between lighthearted travel books with more serious language books. He's keen to return to research. One book might be a popular history of the earth, a topic spurred by his mountain musings.

But he's already signed with Transworld to Brysonize Australia, a country he's visited several times. He'll start early next year: "It fascinated me," he says, citing the strong colonial legacy mixed with Yankee extroversion and outdoor style—not to mention the sturdy local culture. It doesn't hurt that the Summer Olympics (in Sydney) will focus attention Down Under in 2000. Bryson's hybrid nature—revealed by his not-quite-British accent—makes him a valuable cultural translator. Yet he admits confusion about his national identity. "With every passing month, it becomes harder. I'm definitely an American, because I grew up here. But I've lived very happily in Britain," he adds.

Bryson says he's "still completely confused" about the contrast between British and American senses of humor, noting that British TV comedies both sophisticated and sappy have found success here. He does allow that "there's a greater element of cynicism in British life, generally" and that humor "is a more widespread trait." As he once wrote, the British have "a natural gift for making excellent, muttered jokes about authority without ever challenging it."

Despite Bryson's Anglophilia, he says his wife and four children love Hanover so much that their New World venture, initially aimed to be a five-year sojourn, may continue indefinitely: "We'll have to spend our time in both places."

Bryson, who has no association with Dartmouth College, chose a congenial college town because, as he wrote in *The Lost Continent*, such locales mix small-town pace with urban sophistication. People are friendly, he says, and it's an easy place to live, the contrast accentuated by the family's last abode in a tiny Yorkshire village some 12 miles from the nearest market.

Not that Bryson has lost his ties to Fleet Street. Asked by an editor at the *Mail on Sunday* to write a weekly column, Bryson reluctantly agreed. "I found I really enjoyed it, and it gave me a reason for being here." Bryson describes "Notes from a Big Country," as a weekly "letter" ranging from the farcical (haircut trauma) to the serious (the death penalty). And yes, Transworld will soon collect those columns for a book.

Bryson says he's running out of column topics, but his files include clippings sorted into categories, from "Beer" to "Zero Tolerance," not to mention a grab-bag Bryson dubs, with British lexical precision as "Good Oddments." For Bryson, it seems, the world offers a never-ending supply of such oddments.

NORMAN ODER
May 4, 1998

CALEB CARR

On a hard block on Manhattan's Lower East Side, within shouting distance of a Hell's Angels clubhouse and squeezed between worn tenements, stands the building that Caleb Carr calls home. Carr's one-bedroom walk-up occupies the top floor rear of the five-story brownstone. On the day that *PW* visits, Carr's rooms are in shadow. Daylight, curtained by rain clouds, casts only a murky light over the armchairs, heaped books and antique prints that crowd the tiny living room. Quiet and still, the apartment seems the perfect redoubt.

Carr's appearance mirrors the seclusion of his home. He seems dressed for himself alone, in a casual dark shirt, wrinkled khakis and white socks, no shoes. He is 42, but a teenager's long hair frames his pale, handsome face. Although he flicks on a lamp to cut the gloom, its glow scarcely penetrates his rimless spectacles, and his eyes remain hidden.

It is difficult at first to reconcile this cramped apartment on this mean street with the fame and fortune (including a two-book contract worth upwards of $1 million) that came to Carr after his second novel, *The Alienist,* ripped through hardcover bestseller lists three years ago. It is difficult to reconcile this charming man, who serves us peppermint tea, laughs easily and sometimes stammers as he speaks, with the raw violence that invigorates his novels and books of military history. As Carr folds his lanky frame into the armchair facing ours, it occurs to us that Dr. Laszlo Kreizler, Carr's fictional psychologist-hero, who returns in *The Angel of Darkness,* (Random House) and who solves mysteries by delving into suspects minds and cruel childhoods, might have a field day with his creator.

"There was a lot of alcoholism and fairly violent behavior in my household when I was a kid," Carr admits. He is reluctant to elaborate, but he allows that much of the violence was directed toward him. The household, based in Greenwich Village, consisted of Carr's two brothers, his mother and his father. Lucien Carr, a UPI journalist famous for introducing Jack Kerouac, Allen Ginsberg and William Burroughs to one another and infamous for stabbing dead a homosexual suitor in 1944 and serving two years in prison as a result. Carr remembers the Beats fondly, but insists that the Beat movement "was not something that philosophically I was a part of."

Carr's earlier years seem in fact to have been dominated by the urge to flee his parents' rough-and-tumble ways, often into the past, where his aristocratic family tree flowered; one relative, Dabney Carr, was Thomas Jefferson's brother-in-law. As a child, Carr escaped into "boy adventure-story stuff." As an adolescent, after his parents divorced, he became passionately interested in military history, which he refers to as the study of "organized violence."

He also fled into the street, where his escapades gained him a reputation as a troublemaker. "What I was doing," he says, "was the more traditional sorts of mayhem, like setting off cherry bombs and throwing water balloons." He excelled at his studies but was rejected by the four colleges he first applied to. Years later, Carr learned that his high school, the exclusive Friends Seminary, had labeled him "socially undesirable."

"I felt very betrayed by that," Carr says, shaking his head. Still, at Friends, he caught the writing bug and turned out "long papers, tons of history. In those days I had a lot more trouble expressing myself verbally, and I think writing was a natural way to put out a lot of emotion."

Carr wound up at Ohio's Kenyon College but returned after two years to Manhattan, where he enrolled at N.Y.U. While earning a degree in history, he wrote a novel, *Casing the Promised Land,* an earnest story of young men in the big city. He sold the unagented manuscript to Harvey Ginsberg at Harper & Row, which published it with little fanfare or sales in 1979. During the next several years, Carr clerked in bookstores, played in a rock band, experimented with a theater group, "kind of bumming around, trying to figure out what I was doing." He also did research for the prestigious journal *Foreign Affairs* and edited a book for its managing editor James Chase. The two went on to collaborate on *America Invulnerable* (1988), a study of our government's historical obsession with national security that Chase's agent sold to Summit Books.

Positive reviews encouraged Carr to write again on his own. During talks with ICM agent Suzanne Gluck, a friend from high school, he determined to undertake a biography of Frederick Townsend Ward, an American soldier-of-fortune who in the mid-19th century found both glory and bloody death in China. Gluck sold *The Devil Soldier* to Atlantic Monthly editor Ann Godoff. When Godoff moved to Random House, Carr and *The Devil Soldier* went with her. Godoff remains Carr's editor, Random his publisher and Gluck his agent. *The Devil Soldier* sold modestly but earned strong notices that established Carr as a respected military historian.

Seeking to delve more deeply into the roots of violence than nonfiction might allow, Carr turned to fiction. "I think it was a logical step to get more involved in the psychology of violence," he says. To do this, he conceived of writing a series of novels detailing the grim cases of a *fin de siècle* Manhattan psychologist and his circle, with each case narrated by a different acquaintance of the alienist.

"I got the idea from Wilkie Collins," Carr explains. Collins's classic 1868 novel *The Moonstone* explores a central mystery from multiple points of view. "Well, I thought, what about different stories from different points of view?"

The alienist himself was inspired by Sherlock Holmes. "I wanted to create a character," Carr says, "who could solve all the cases Holmes wouldn't have been able to solve. Holmes's point was that he didn't need to know the personal backgrounds of people. He could figure out a case from the circumstantial evidence. But there are a lot of cases where there's not enough circumstantial evidence, and you have to crawl inside people's heads to solve them."

These literary antecedents are important to Carr. "Jules Verne, H.G. Wells, Conan Doyle—that's the tradition I see myself following. I want to write a good story and good characters, but I also want people to learn something when they read the books. I think we've lived through enough of fiction being author-specific, all this confessional literature. I think people more and more are demanding that books plug into something more universal in terms of experience, in terms of lessons to be learned." When asked what contemporary writers he likes, Carr praises Michael Crichton and especially *Jurassic Park*, which Carr declares "a landmark piece of modern fiction. He's one of the writers who inspired me to believe that you could write popular fiction that had a lot of educational information in it."

Carr confesses a sense of mission about his writing. "I feel a tremendous sense of social responsibility. I think that came down to me from my family, from a certain blue-blood tradition. You're supposed to care; you're supposed to do something."

To convince Random to advance him money for a novel, Carr indulged in an inspired literary escapade. "I mocked up a proposal as a nonfiction book. I made up this tale, and made up phony quotes and phony sources, even doctored up a photograph of Teddy Roosevelt in his office." Carr sent the proposal to Gluck. "She was fooled. Then we took it to Ann. She said, 'Why does nobody know about this story?' I said, 'Well, the basic reason is, it never happened.' After she got over her slight shock and indignation, she got really enthusiastic. Only she said, 'We're not going to try this with Harry [Evans, Random's publisher].' "

Carr received a $65,000 advance for his tale of how Kreizler, Roosevelt (then New York City's Police Commissioner) and other carefully calibrated figures, historical and fictional, solve the mutilation-murders of boy prostitutes in Manhattan's lower depths in 1896. Applying the discipline of nonfiction to fiction, he devoted "seven to eight months" to "pure research" and plotting. Carr points to a wall of the room. "From the corner of this room all the way across the wall, *The Alienist* was plotted out on tiny strips of paper." After an equal amount of time spent writing, he turned in the manuscript.

Shortly before publication, film rights to *The Alienist* sold to Scott Rudin at Paramount for $500,000. But the book "did not get heavy promo until it started to sell," Carr reports. "Random House will sometimes deny that, but the fact is the book started to sell for two reasons: the cover [an enigmatic sepia-toned photo that is nearly duplicated on *The Angel of Darkness*] and word of mouth." It's no surprise to learn that Carr helped design that cover. The attention to detail that invests his novels with such verisimilitude speaks of someone with market savvy, who keeps a tight rein on all of his endeavors. Carr's author photo for *The Angel of Darkness* has him ruminating next to a grinning skull; given the lack of pretension he exhibits in person, it must be seen as an exercise in pure pose.

Generally enthusiastic reviews propelled *The Alienist* to number 4 on *PW*'s hardcover bestseller list, where it hovered for nearly half a year (the 1995 Bantam paperback edition reached number 2 on *PW*'s mass market bestseller list). Carr's new contract with Random called for two further "historical novels." The first is *The Angel of Darkness*, which follows Kreizler's pursuit of a female serial killer. While *The Alienist* is narrated in the cool, cultured tones of a *New York Times* reporter, the sequel finds voice through the hotter, more ragged words of a former, and formerly abused, street urchin with whom Carr strongly identifies. "For all the fondness I have for *The Alienist*," he says, "I'm more fond of this book because it's a more personal narration."

In spite of vigorous advance sales, Carr worries about the novel's fate. "It's more of a mystery and less of a thriller," he points out. And "then there's the whole sophomore jinx thing. I know people are lying in wait to jump on it. Even your review, which was basically nice, had a bit of a pissy quality to it." Exhibiting the forthrightness that has him answering some questions before they're fully asked, Carr makes clear that he's willing to debate us about *PW*'s review. "I like a good fight," he says with a smile.

"But in the end," he continues, "despite all the hype and expectations, did I write the book that I wanted to write? I did. I cut myself off and lived in my little 19th-century world here. That's how I did it."

Carr escapes that world often, seeing friends and working on varied projects. He publishes the occasional article in *MHQ: The Quarterly Journal of Military History,* to which he is a contributing editor. He has recently written a two-hour pilot for *The Osiris Chronicles,* a futuristic TV series. He has also written the first draft of a screenplay of *The Devil Soldier* that now, after rewrite, is close to production with John Woo directing and Tom Cruise starring. The film version of *The Alienist,* meanwhile "nowhere," despite "millions of dollars" spent to develop a viable screenplay, he says.

Carr clearly cherishes his tucked-away apartment, however, not only for its proximity to the setting of his novels but for the privacy it affords. The solitary life suits him. He keeps what he calls a "punishing" schedule, writing up to 12 hours a day on a laptop computer, sleeping little, working mostly at night. He has lived with a woman only once ("It didn't last long. She felt that there wasn't any room for another person in my private world—which may be true"). In the familiar safety of this world—the building, it turns out, is owned by his aunt and uncle, who share it with several tenants—and in what he has created there, Carr seems to have made peace with his childhood demons through the classic method of transfiguring them into art.

"By writing these books," Carr says, "I grew to understand a lot more what went on in my own life, how violence in childhood affects a person. As a young person, I felt alone and unheard. But through the process of writing, especially when a book is successful, you feel like somebody's listening. You're not a voice in the wilderness."

JEFF ZALESKI
September 15, 1997

MICHAEL CUNNINGHAM

MICHAEL CUNNINGHAM HAS been climbing the walls, though it's not a manifestation of nervousness: he's just writing. In the tiny sixth floor walkup in Greenwich Village, which he used to call home but now calls his studio, there is text all over one wall of the kitchen. "It's Flannery O'Connor, at the moment," he says, greeting his visitor barefoot and in black jeans and black T-shirt. The text, in Cunningham's flowing hand, is scrawled in white chalk over what he calls "black chalkboard paint." On the wall opposite, a quatrain of verse, fashioned out of one continuous length of picture wire, hangs from screws.

The teeming textuality of Cunningham's very workspace seems a fitting interior for a discussion of his new novel, *The Hours*, which skillfully interweaves three novellas inspired by a classic text of modernism, Virginia Woolf's *Mrs. Dalloway*.

Cunningham, a lean six-footer, swivels in his desk chair on the balls of his feet, gracious, but with the pent energy of a writer accustomed to working in his space, not talking. Still the topic of Virginia Woolf brings a certain quietude.

"My introduction to Woolf's work," he remembers, "was in high school, where a very rough, difficult, slightly crazed girl with teased hair and long fingernails, who used to hang around behind the gym and smoke cigarettes, proclaimed her to be a genius." Cunningham, "not an especially bookish kid," in his view, picked up *Mrs. Dalloway* at the local bookstore, "and the book just nailed me; I've thought about it almost constantly ever since."

Some 25 years later, Cunningham understands Woolf in the context of the century's literature. "Woolf and Joyce," he notes, "were of course the great heroes of modernism. They were interested in using the most idiosyncratic, poetic language possible to get to the heart of human experience, which, by Woolf's lights, was contained in every atom of human experience. One of the great accomplishments of

Mrs. Dalloway was Woolf's insistence that everything you need to know about human life can be contained in two people having coffee together."

In *The Hours,* named after one of Woolf's early working titles for *Mrs. Dalloway,* Cunningham tells three stories, each deceptively small in scale, concerning a single day: Woolf on a morning outside of London in 1923 as she tries to overcome family distractions (her sister Vanessa's unscheduled visit, husband Leonard's prickly self-absorption) in order to work on what would become *Mrs. Dalloway*; the melancholy tale, set in 1949, of one Laura Brown, an unfulfilled housewife in suburban L.A., who escapes her little boy and the day's cooking chores (it is her husband's birthday) for a session in a hotel bed, which she spends reading *Mrs. Dalloway*; and a June day in the life of Clarissa Vaughan, a 50-something lesbian who lives in Greenwich Village and who is called "Mrs. Dalloway" by her dearest friend Richard, a writer, dying of AIDS, for whom she is planning a party. The subtle interactions of these narratives, and each one's mirroring of scenes right out of *Mrs. Dalloway,* adds a dimensionality to *The Hours* that makes it much more than the sum of its parts. And readers mesmerized by Cunningham's attention to quotidian detail will gasp when, out of the blue, the stories cohere in a moving, final tableau that evokes a familiar Cunningham theme: family.

"I'm probably not, by any means, the best or most reliable authority on what I'm writing about from book to book," says Cunningham, sipping black coffee and smoking. "But when I look back at what I've written, the whole question of family just jumps out, as I think it would to anybody who's read my books. I do seem to have some kind of fixation on the whole notion of family, which is something of a surprise to me.

"But as I was writing this book," he continues, "I thought, well, finally I'm not writing about families anymore. Finally I've put *that* behind me. And guess what? As it turns out, here, once again, is the specter of the queer, extended, post-nuclear family."

Cunningham's path to becoming a writer was neither more nor less conventional than most, replete with the standard stopovers and uncharted byways. Born to a family that enjoyed increasing prospects in the prosperous fifties, Cunningham lived in Ohio, in Europe (where his father's advertising career brought them) and then moved to California at the age of 10. His mother kept the home, and Cunningham and his younger sister, like an entire generation of American kids, were raised on rock 'n' roll and rebellion. Cunningham went on to Stanford University, saw himself as a painter for a while, and, hearing about the Iowa Writer's Workshop, sent some stories.

"I went to Iowa in 1978, with real trepidations about whether I wanted to be a writer, whether I could *be* a writer. I didn't have a great deal of determination at that point. But to some degree a decision about my seriousness got made when I got in. I found myself among 60-plus people, some of them extremely talented, who were just about willing to commit murder over a paragraph. It's a very competitive place but I *loved* it. And something about it made me snap to."

Cunningham's teacher there was the novelist Hilma Wolitzer— "wonderful and hugely encouraging," he says. He recalls those early days with a certain relish because, for a brief moment, it all seemed so easy. "I had a streak of luck at Iowa: a story in *Atlantic Monthly* and another in the *Paris Review,* which led me to the entirely false conclusion that if writing wasn't exactly easy, well, it was going to be easy for me. I would just write things and publish them. Boy, was I mistaken!"

Hearing Cunningham relate his stories, it's apparent that one of his gifts is an immediate and total immersion in the emotions he is describing. If it weren't early morning, one has the feeling he would be reaching for a stiff drink as he revisits how things somehow ran off track. He is fairly shouting now.

"And I sent stories that were every bit as strong to the same people who had published the others, and I started getting them back so quick I doubted they were even being read. I thought, c'mon, can this be?"

Fortunately, Cunningham's agent, Gail Hochman, saw him through the rough patches. Hochman has represented Cunningham since his MFA days. "She came out to Iowa to show the students what an agent looked like. 'Like this!' she said," and Cunningham spreads his arms in a kind of diva turn, then hops up to catch the whistling kettle.

"I showed Gail a couple of things, and she agreed to represent me. Thank God! And she heroically returned all my calls and dropped me an occasional encouraging letter for years when *nothing* was happening."

The "when nothing was happening" was a period of 10 years that followed the publication of Cunningham's first (and now commonly forgotten) novel, *Golden States*, published by Barbara Grossman at Crown in 1980. He now admits he was never very fond of the novel. "I was approaching 30," he explains. "I was working in a bar, and I thought, I'm fast on my way to being a 50-year-old who once had a story in the *Paris Review*. So I managed to finish this novel. Barbara published it beautifully, and it got very nice reviews and sold seven or eight copies."

Wanderlust followed: "I was working either as a waiter, a bartender, moving around a lot, falling in love a lot and going wherever it took me, to Nebraska for a while with a woman, to Greece for a while with a guy." But all the while, Cunningham was working on what became his breakthrough book, *A Home at the End of the World*. And it all began at the *New Yorker*.

In 1988, in order to prove to a new lover (Ken Corbett, with whom Cunningham has been ever since) that the writer's life was misery, he sent a chapter from his work-in-progress to the *New Yorker*. "Watch," Cunningham told his new beau, "how fast this comes back. You think it's good? Watch."

And it did come back, but with a long memorandum from editor Dan Menaker. "Love the story, love the story, love the story, *but* . . ." is how Cunningham summarizes the letter. "And there was a handwritten note attached: 'Call me, or I'll call you,' And he did."

The *New Yorker*, published the story, after some revisions, under the title "The White Angel." And it created a sensation. Cunningham still seems a little amazed that of all the things he had sent to the *New Yorker* ("I began to believe that Menaker's sole job there was to reject Michael Cunningham submissions"), they published one "about a nine-year old and acid and sex and violence in cemeteries.

"When the story appeared, Gail started getting calls from editors all over the place. 'Can we see the novel?' But my very favorite was a call from Roger Straus, who didn't say, 'We'd like to see his novel' but rather, 'If he can write something I like this much I have faith that he can write a whole book. And we'd like to publish it.' "

Lucky for Cunningham, because he didn't have a novel yet. It took him another two years to finish *A Home at the End of the World*, which charted, in alternating voices, the passage into manhood of two boys from Cleveland (one of whom is gay), the fate of their families and their ultimate discovery of new arrangements in which to love. The book's exhausting intensity and poetic prose garnered glowing reviews, and established the author at FSG. "There is a sort of unspoken understanding at Farrar, Straus," says Cunningham, "that they are your publishers; that doesn't necessarily mean they are going to publish everything you write, but if you write another book and they like it, they'll publish that one, too."

Flesh and Blood followed in 1995, and it was here that Cunningham's concerns for honoring a new kind of family perhaps burned the hottest.

The 485-page *Flesh and Blood* "was a much bigger book than any I'd done before. It spanned 100 years, and I had really wild ambitions for it. The book was written while a lot of people I loved and admired were dying. My desire to write the best book I possibly could was all tangled up with my desire to write a book that would contribute in some way to the battle for a cure for AIDS.

"I think my interest in the post-nuclear family, which might include, say, a biological mother, a same-sex lover and the drag queen who lives downstairs, probably comes from being a gay man living through the AIDS epidemic. Everybody writes about what they know, obviously. I've lived through an epidemic that involves seeing all kinds of things, maybe one of the most significant of which is seeing nonbiological families come through in the way that biological families might not."

Flesh and Blood met with mixed reviews, some welcoming the brash revision of family dynamics, others contending that Cunningham the artist had become a gay populist. But Cunningham knew what he was doing by stretching the family saga formula.

"I very much wanted the book to be accessible to a wider range of people, by which I don't mean 'gay' people or 'straight' people but people who didn't read an awful lot. There are not a lot of books you can take to a sick 28-year-old man who doesn't have a lot more books to read. I mean, you can bring him Dostoyevsky, but will it be read? I wanted *Flesh and Blood* to have some of the easier virtues of a pulpier kind of book. There were things I would do differently now, but I was pleased with the real range of responses it got.

"I have a friend who said something to me that struck a chord," he continues, "She said that we seem to be at a point where it's fine for gay people to write about other gay people, but don't go messing around in the family album, don't go writing about straight people and housewives and the like. Because then you've crossed some kind of line."

Cunningham's friend may be right; which is not to say that he's heeded her words. In *The Hours*, he writes about straights and gays and lesbians and teenagers and housewives and a great figure of Western literature—and, deftly, brings them all together in a tale about love accommodating difference. So, clearly, the family album is still under revision, just as the words on Cunningham's kitchen wall will no doubt be erased, replaced by a new text with a new relevance for a new day.

MICHAEL COFFEY
November 2, 1998

EDWIDGE DANTICAT

ASK EDWIDGE DANTICAT too personal a question and the soft-spoken 29-year-old writer becomes flustered, nose scrunched in distress, polite smile suddenly frozen. A scrupulous hostess who serves guests spring water from a small enameled tray in her parents' living room in Brooklyn, the baby-faced Danticat can, without saying a single word, make an interviewer feel that some unwritten code of journalistic chivalry has been breached.

To find Danticat so guarded is surprising, considering the intensely personal nature of her writing. This is, after all, the woman who in her critically acclaimed first novel, *Breath, Eyes, Memory* (Soho, 1994), described a young Haitian torn between her love for her mother and her sense of betrayal, particularly over the Haitian practice of "testing," or monitoring a daughter's virginity. (Danticat received hate mail from Haitian-Americans for outing the custom). The stories in Danticat's collection *Krik? Krak!* (Soho, 1995) candidly examine not only the painful social legacy that Danticat left behind in her homeland of Haiti, but also the delicate, sometimes agonizingly twisted ties that bind an emigrant daughter to her heritage. Her new novel, *The Farming of Bones,* also published by Soho, exposes the 1937 Haitian genocide at the border of the neighboring Dominican Republic, an episode that still haunts the Haitian community.

So why the reticence? Blame it a little on natural shyness, hinted at in the obviously autobiographical epilogue of *Krik? Krak!*; blame it also on Oprah, who selected *Breath, Eyes, Memory* for a recent "meeting" of her book club. Since her television appearance, Danticat says, she has been trying to "stay low." In its wake, the novel shot to the number one slot on the *PW* paperback bestseller list, Vintage took its edition back to press to bring the total in print to 600,000 and Danticat's agent, Nicole Aragi, at Watkins, Loomis, has been inundated with calls.

The lyrical, folklore-steeped *Breath, Eyes, Memory* has many of the themes common to an Oprah pick: a troubled mother-daughter relationship and a present deformed by a shameful past. It tells the story of Sophie Caco, the daughter of a rape victim, raised in Haiti by her aunt until her mother summons her to New York when she is 12. There, Sophie struggles to appease her mother's demons, but at 18 finally flees into the arms of the family's next-door neighbor, a Louisiana-born Creole jazz musician. When marriage and motherhood cannot soothe Sophie's troubled soul, she makes a pilgrimage back to Haiti to seek solace—and a measure of self-knowledge—with her aunt.

Though she received "the call" in March, Danticat met Oprah previously when she worked as an extra on the talk show hostess's forthcoming adaptation of Toni Morrison's *Beloved.* "Being on *Oprah* doesn't turn your life upside-down—it's been pretty calm for me, thank God," she says. Nonetheless, she has been trying to stop giving interviews in her parents' home, where she lives part-time but whose silver-flock-wallpaper and beige-carpet decor, she notes delicately, is not her own. Since January, she has been subletting a studio in a Haitian community outside New York. "I just feel you need a little safe place sometimes, some place that you have just for yourself," she explains.

Danticat may find her much-cherished privacy increasingly difficult to hold on to. The first African-Haitian female author to write in English and be published by a major house, she captured the attention of the national media in 1995 when *Krik? Krak!* garnered a National Book Award nomination (the title is the traditional opening call-and-response at a Haitian story-telling session). One year later, she was selected as one of the 20 "Best Young American Novelists" by *Granta.* Paperback rights to *The Farming of Bones,* which is a QPB selection, have sold to Penguin for $200,000. Danticat's low profile, it seems, is in imminent danger of being blown for good.

Danticat's personal background is as turbulent as one might expect from her writing. Born in 1969, in Port-au-Prince, Haiti, Danticat was separated from her father at age two, when he emigrated to the United States to work in a factory (he is currently a driver for a car service). Her mother, now retired, followed him when Danticat was four. Danticat and her younger brother, Eliab, were turned over to the care of her father's brother, a minister, who lived with his wife and grandson in Bel Air, a poor area of Port-au-Prince. At 12, Danti-

43

cat finally rejoined her parents in Brooklyn, but had to struggle to remake her family ties (for starters, she had two new younger brothers). She also had to learn English from scratch (the family still speaks Creole at home) and endure epithets from public school classmates who mocked her as a "boat person." "My primary feeling the whole first year was one of loss," she recalls. "Loss of my childhood, and of the people I'd left behind—and also of *being* lost. It was like being a baby—learning everything for the first time."

But what Danticat had already learned in Haiti would prove a more valuable education. As a child in Bel Air, she received an enduring lesson in the power of storytelling at the feet of her aunt's grandmother, a woman whose long hair, with coins braided into it, the neighborhood children fought to comb. "She told stories when the people would gather—folk tales with her own spin on them, and stories about the family," says Danticat. "It was call-and-response—if the audience seemed bored, the story would speed up, and if they were participating, a song would go in. The whole interaction was exciting to me. These cross-generational exchanges didn't happen often, because children were supposed to respect their elders. But when you were telling stories, it was more equal, and fun."

Danticat made her own first foray into storytelling at seven, when, after borrowing the Madeline books from an aunt who was a street vendor, she rewrote the stories with a Haitian heroine. In Brooklyn, she was penning articles for a high school newspaper, *New Youth Connections*, within a year of her arrival. An article she wrote in high school about her arrival in America and her reunion with her mother became the germ of *Breath, Eyes, Memory*. "I felt like I was stuck with more of the story," says Danticat. "I started writing it in fictional form, and adding things to it."

After graduating from Barnard College in 1990, Danticat worked as a secretary and applied to both MBA schools and MFA programs while writing after-hours at the office. When she was simultaneously accepted by NYU's Stern Business School and Brown's creative writing program, she chose the latter, not least because it offered a full scholarship.

Even before taking her MFA, however, Danticat had a publisher waiting in the wings. After leaving Barnard, she had sent 70 pages of what would become *Breath, Eyes, Memory* to Soho, a press she discovered in *Writer's Digest*. It was fished out of the slush pile by editor and v-p Laura Hruska, who eventually purchased the novel for a

$5000 advance. "They would send me notes and ask if I was done with the book yet. They were very encouraging," says Danticat. It wasn't until the spring of 1996, after the writer had negotiated the deals for her next two books herself, that she signed with Aragi, who had been courting her ever since reading the galleys for *Breath, Eyes, Memory* in early 1994. "She's a younger agent, and her list isn't so long that she doesn't take my calls," reports Danticat with characteristic modesty.

Danticat, who currently travels to Haiti as often as four times a year, has been researching *The Farming of Bones* since 1992. The novel takes as its historical background the reign of dictator Rafael Trujillo Molina, a period of rising Dominican nationalism and anti-immigrant sentiment (Haitians have been emigrating to the bordering Dominican Republic for work since the 19th century). In 1937, the anti-Haitian propaganda campaign flared into violence, resulting in the death of thousands of Haitians. An earlier story about a survivor of the massacre, "Nineteen Thirty-Seven," is included in *Krik? Krak!* But it wasn't until Danticat stood on the banks of the river Massacre itself, where the killings had taken place, that she fully realized that she wanted to make a novel out of the story. (The river is named after another 19th-century genocidal episode that had occurred on its banks.) "It was really strange to stand there—it was low tide, and people were bathing, and washing their clothes in the water," recalls Danticat. "There are no markers. I felt like I was standing on top of a huge mass grave, and just couldn't see the bodies. That's the first time I remember thinking, 'Nature has no memory'— a line that later made its way into the book—'and that's why we have to have memory.'"

The Farming of Bones is told from the perspective of Amabelle Désir, a young Haitian woman working as a servant on a sugar-cane plantation in the Dominican Republic in 1937. When the violence breaks, out, Amabelle is maimed as she flees back into Haiti, but her lover, Sebastien, is murdered. The novel is more overtly historical than Danticat's previous writings. One senses that its author has laid to rest some of the personal issues that loom so large during the passage from adolescence to adulthood. These days, Danticat is focused instead on a mission of writing for the benefit of her community. "The massacre is not as well-known here as it is in Haiti," she says. "But I wasn't thinking so much I wanted to popularize it with a larger audience as with younger people, like my brothers, who didn't know about it at all. It's a part of our history, as Haitians, but it's also a part of the history of the world. Writing about it is an act of remembrance."

Today impoverished Haitians still migrate across the border to the Dominican Republic to work in construction or sugar-cane harvesting (known colloquially as "farming the bones" due to the cane's toughness). To foster greater understanding between the two nations, Danticat organizes joint Haitian-Dominican community youth groups in the New York area with writer Junot Diaz, who grittily chronicled Dominican immigrant life in his 1996 short story collection, *Drown*. ("Junot and I were paired so much for readings that it would have been tragic if we didn't like each other," recalls Danticat with a laugh.) As part of a 1997 three-year grant from the Lila Acheson Wallace Foundation, Danticat also works with the National Coalition for Haitian Rights.

Danticat has no concrete plans yet for her next book project, and Aragi says her client has no thought of cashing in on her current status as a hot property by rushing to sign a hefty contract with a larger house. Says Danticat: "I feel really comfortable with Soho. I like the size." But she grins and makes a zipping motion with her fingers over her lips when asked if she intends to remain with them for her next project. "I always felt like I was a four-book writer, but I don't know when that fourth book will be written," she says. "I don't want to sign papers and feel like I have to produce something on demand."

It is difficult to imagine Danticat working to someone else's demands. She insists that her newfound role as mouthpiece for her community will not burden her as an artist. "The only pressure I feel is that I always have to explain to people that when I describe a character in one of my books, I'm only writing about this one, perhaps exceptionally twisted individual," she says. "My characters are not representative of the community as a whole. As a writer, it's the person who is different from everybody else who might be interesting to you." Just as, one might argue, it is the writer who is different from everyone else—who, like Danticat, has a unique personal and historical legacy to share—who is most interesting to readers.

MALLAY CHARTERS
August 17, 1998

MIKE DAVIS

MIKE DAVIS LIVES in a trim one-story house on a tranquil street in middle-class residential Pasadena. The onetime truck driver and current MacArthur fellow, who says he couldn't even compose a letter until he was 30, shuffles amiably across the porch to extend his hand in greeting to *PW*. At 52, he's dressed in youth's eternal uniform of blue jeans, T-shirt and sandals, without the storm clouds over his head that a reading of his fierce work would lead one to expect. His gray hair flips forward, his middle reveals a slight paunch and his face has the air of a slightly bemused choirboy. His wife, Alessandra, a painter born in Mexico, is on her way out the door to do battle with the government over a green card.

"I talk a lot," Davis warns his interviewer before leading us to a dining table generously set with breakfast treats. He has just returned from one of his frequent visits to Ireland, the permanent residence of his eight-year-old son (his daughter is away for the summer), and he rapidly pops off on topic after topic—the summer heat, this year's abundant crop of rattlesnakes in the nearby San Gabriel mountains, the unique reproductive capacity of coyotes, the fruitless efforts by the citrus industry early in the century to change the area's vegetation in the misguided belief that it could alter weather patterns. In person, Davis is much less fearsome than on the page, but the same sharp edge, intense delivery and idiosyncratic mixture of erudition and street talk that characterize his prose is evident in his conversation. His concentration is unwavering.

Davis is a historian by training, but this description hardly does justice to the books he writes: intricate patch-works of urban theory, literary and social criticism that pierce Los Angeles's urban and social sprawl. He is known for bringing a radical perspective to the culture of palm trees, freeways and unchecked urbanization that is so often seen as a garden of Eden, not an Eden run amok.

His writing style is an equally distinctive blend of heady ideas and incendiary, sometimes lyrical prose. Though he writes resolutely about L.A., he is always on the prowl for the keys to some larger theory, whether social, political, economic or scientific—or all combined. In the service of these goals, he hobnobs with academics and scientists, schoolteachers, former trucker buddies and hardnosed kids from South Central. He is widely credited with pointing out the gross social inequities that led to the Rodney King riots of 1992, but he dismisses the notion. "Any 10-year-old could have done that. It was no feat to predict them."

Davis has a devout following in Southern California, a reputation based primarily on his 1990 book, *City of Quartz,* published in hardcover by Verso and now available as a Vintage paperback. Many readers greeted it as a messianic text; the book belongs on any short list of must-read titles about life in the City of Angels.

Metropolitan Books has now published his eagerly awaited follow-up book, *Ecology of Fear; Los Angeles and the Imagination of Disaster.* It is an unsettling analysis of the relationship between natural and social catastrophe in an area where nature brings abrupt, violent changes, "with periods of boredom and inactivity followed by brief moments of terror." In Davis's view, the culprits are not earthquakes, wildfires, mudslides and coyotes that prey on household pets but rather shameful public policies that have transformed natural hazards into serious social ills. Going further and developing ideas first hinted at in *City of Quartz,* Davis analyzes how the "politics of disaster" have become "the moral equivalent of class warfare." It's a complex, fanatically researched and carefully presented thesis.

Davis was born in Southern California to Midwestern Irish-Welsh parents who hitchhiked west during the Depression. In the xenophobic suburbs where he grew up, he thought of himself as half-black, half-Jewish. As a boy, he conducted conversations in his head with an imaginary Russian pal, telling him what it was like to live in the Golden State. As he got older, his thoughts turned to social justice. "I came to consciousness when ordinary citizens were affecting the political process. I was an alienated, angry 16-year-old at a CORE demonstration in 1963. This changed my life in the best possible way."

After a short stay at Reed College in Oregon, he returned home to Southern California and became a community organizer, joined the Communist Party and worked as a long-distance hauler. He did a stint as a tour guide in Hollywood, which proved pivotal to his development as a dark guide to the city's secret history. "You'd buy a spiel from the other drivers and I thought, Why do that? I read all of Carey McWilliams [the Southern Californian historian who subsequently became editor of the *Nation*] as a way to develop a spiel, and got intimate with California history." (McWilliams's most notable book is the 1946 book *Southern California: An Island on the Land.*) At 30, Davis made a break with blue-collar life and resumed his undergraduate studies at UCLA, eventually specializing in labor history.

His early writing career took off during an association with the *New Left Review,* a Marxist journal published by Verso and based in London, where Davis was invited to edit and write. The six years he spent in the London office led to his first book *Prisoners of the American Dream,* about Reaganism and the American Labor movement, published by Verso in 1986. During those years, Davis also established Verso's Haymarket series to specialize in radical studies of American politics and culture. A forthcoming title is about the threat chain stores pose not only to independent booksellers but also to independent cultural production. As an independent press, Davis says, Verso is as threatened by conglomerates as independent booksellers. "We're quaking in our boots."

Davis's time in London completed his transformation into a serious scholar with important things to say about urban history. When Anna Deveare Smith was at work on her play *Twilight Los Angeles,* following the 1992 riots, she came to Davis for his views. Originally, he planned to write a community-by-community history of the "uprising," his preferred term for the L.A. rioting, but he stumbled over his own qualms. "Ethically," he says, "I couldn't use journalism to exploit other people's pain and suffering."

Tackling a book from a socio-ecological angle instead provided a new view of L.A. and enabled Davis to bridge the worlds of the riots and the university culture through a powerful new lens, one that historians had not used. "I had become disenchanted with science in the '60s, after John Hersey's book on Hiroshima. This new book gave me a way as a historian to do science." Unlike *City of Quartz,* which was written without grants, sabbaticals or teaching assistants, or as he wrote at the time "other fancy ingredients," *Ecology of Fear* was supported by a MacArthur grant. Davis was able to attend a conference on paleoclimatology in Utah, coming away with his head filled with thoughts on El Nino's truly destructive aspects, how it leads to synchronized droughts. He sees the germ of a short book, perhaps *The*

Secret History of the 19th century: El Niño, Famine, and Imperialism. His rallying cry for scholars, he says, is "Less Derrida and more Stephen Jay Gould!"

"Though huge and wonderful," the MacArthur fellowship didn't "address the huge capacity to spend money," he says. His wife doesn't have a job, his mortgage payments are relentless and he has to pay child support. Davis's holy grail is a regular full-time teaching job. "I've had utterly no luck finding this in Southern California." A prospect is blooming in the East, which he may reluctantly accept, if offered. He has cobbled together a teaching career at such places as the Cesar Chavez Center for Chicano Studies at UCLA, which he compares to CCNY in 1936 "with all those smart Jewish kids," and at the Southern California Institute of Architecture, a small, specialized school in West L.A. where he creates one-of-a-kind courses in urban theory, leading his students to metropolitan areas around the Southwest.

"I have more fun than a lot of people. I love getting off campus and into the field. We look for realities not depicted elsewhere." He describes a Tongan bingo parlor in an outlying area of L.A. that he recently visited. "The city never disappoints. You can never be current with it. There's always some reality out there waiting for you."

Being acknowledged now as a writer brings Davis enormous satisfaction. "I like the idea of crafting something and sending it out into the world as part of the bigger picture." Being a popular author is another thing altogether, and he says he's terrible at it. "I can't stand going on the road. I don't like TV, being on the radio, revealing my personal life." (He has been married five times.) He prefers researching and writing and resents time away from it. "I'm tired of myself talking."

In Metropolitan's Sara Bershtel, he says, he has "without question the best editor in the world." He also works with editor Tom Engelhardt and is equally appreciative. Originally, he had a contract with Knopf for *Ecology of Fear* but ran afoul of the editor-in-chief. "I went to Los Angeles to cover the riots for the *Nation*," he says. "But I stood Sonny Mehta up for lunch; no mortal should do that. Knopf never forgave me.

"With Metropolitan," he adds, "I've had the experience of a writer's dream with an editor who reads every word and questions everything." In the end, he says, he didn't go along with a lot of the advice but came out with a better book because of it.

Ecology of Fear was written during a six-month period at the Getty Research Institute after years of preparation. He spent 12 months immersed in urban disaster fiction for his chapter on "The Literary Destruction of Los Angeles," in which he explores why the city bears the brunt of the nation's primitive urges—why people cheer while L.A. is buried under rubble or otherwise self-destructs. For the chapter on tornadoes in the L.A. basin ("Our Secret Kansas"), he spent months reading five L.A. dailies published before 1950 and pored over thousands of weather pictures looking for photos of tornadoes. "I like the archeological aspect of it immensely." He maintains an active file system of upward of 15,000 files, with thousands more stashed away in his garage. "Not knowing when to stop research is my personal demon," he comments. The photos in the book took three months to find, and $5000 of his own money. "I'd rather have good photos than anything," he says, showing off two favorites: a man on the beach hunting for rattlesnakes and a California prison guard holding two dead killer African bees.

His next book, which Davis views as the last in a trilogy about L.A. and which is still unnamed, will be more people-centered than either *City of Quartz* or *Ecology of Fear.* He is interested in the influence of immigrant cultures, especially East Asian family capitalism, on L.A.'s economy. The trilogy, he explains, derived from a fantasy. Three great thinkers, Walter Benjamin, Fernand Braudel, and Friedrich Engels, each with a different understanding of history and society, meet in a bar. They talk, trade ideas, agree to take a look at L.A. Benjamin writes *City of Quartz.* Braudel writes *Ecology of Fear.* Engels writes the third.

Given the litany of gloom in his work, what does he hope people will get from it? Why offer up a worldview so catastrophic that there seems to be no way out? "Any political activist wants people to act," he says. "My 16-year old daughter gave the best criticism of my work I've ever heard. 'You think you're organizing by telling how bad things are,' she said. 'You've got to tell how they can change things.' The next one will be less about how bad things are," Davis says. "Its focus will be on the actors trying to effect change.

"I may sound dire and hopeless," he adds, "but I have a lot of hope for the next generation."

SUZANNE MANTELL
August 31, 1998

DON DELILLO

O NE MORNING LAST month, Don DeLillo emerged from the shadows of a well-protected life in an undisclosed suburb, arrived at his
publicist's office at Scribner and did something truly remarkable; he
allowed himself to be interviewed and photographed. The author of
11 novels depicting the power of corporate America and the dark
and insidious logic of consumer society, DeLillo is himself a most reluctant commodity. He avoids the limelight, grants few interviews,
never reviews books or teaches writing seminars and rarely speaks to
the media. His wariness at the invasive prospect of a magazine profile is not altogether unexpected.

DeLillo's new novel, *Underworld* finds himself at a peculiar turn.
Underworld (Scribner) is an epic history of the atomic age and covers more ground than anything DeLillo has attempted to date, from
a legendary baseball game in 1950s New York to the atomic testing
grounds of contemporary Kazakhstan. Writing with incandescent
heat, DeLillo depicts a family marked by the forces shaping the
American millennium—rising tides of weaponry and waste that
transformed the landscapes of New York City and the American
Southwest. Gordon Lish, a close friend of DeLillo, tells *PW* the
novel's subject is not simply baseball or the bomb, but "America itself
as an unstoppable mechanism, one whose glory is its onrush, its
power to assimilate everything in it."

The novel itself has been quickly assimilated by the publishing industry. In an auction that began on October 29 last year and closed,
aptly enough, on Halloween, hardcover and paperback world
English-language rights were purchased by Scribner editor-in-chief
Nan Graham for what is rumored to be $1.3 million, a deal that
made headlines in half a dozen magazines. It was optioned two
weeks later by Scott Rudin at Paramount, reportedly for another $1
million. Audio rights also went to Simon & Schuster, making *Underworld* a vertically integrated property of Viacom—a feat of corporate

packaging that conspiratorial-minded readers might say bears the ominous echo of DeLillo's own novels.

In person, the writer, too, appears to have stepped out of the pages of his fiction. A slim, unprepossessing man with owlish features, large boxy glasses and an unruly forelock of silvery hair, he speaks in long, analytical sentences sharply inflected by the accent of his working-class childhood in the Bronx. It is easy to imagine him as the protagonist of *Mao II* (Viking, 1993), the reclusive author Bill Gray whose distance from the publishing industry leads him to say: "The more books they publish, the weaker we become. The secret force that drives the industry is the compulsion to make writers harmless."

It is a sentiment that DeLillo does not disavow: "I don't think there's anything in the industry particularly, but there may be a mechanism in the culture that tries to reduce any threat to consumer consciousness. I don't think writers are exempt from this. On the other hand, it's not easy to think of a case where a novelist poses a significant threat.

There are writers who refuse to make public appearances. Writers who say 'no.' Writers in opposition, not necessarily in a specific way. But there are those of us who write books that are not easily absorbed by the culture, who refuse to have their photographs taken, who refuse to give interviews. And at some level, this may be largely a matter of personal disinclination. But there may also be an element in which such writers are refusing to become part of the all-incorporating treadmill of consumption and disposal."

The fact that a prestigious novel such as *Underworld* is subject to the same realities of the marketplace, the same P&L, the same lateral marketing plans that govern the rest of the trade, is a matter the writer, quite understandably, prefers not to discuss. "It doesn't impinge on me except to the extent I want it to, and as an element that feeds my work," he says. "I keep the greatest psychological distance I can maintain from all of this. I'm not part of it except in the sense that you and I are having this conversation. It's there. Writers write, publishers sell. That's probably a very old-fashioned conviction but I do maintain it."

In keeping with the principle that *Underworld* will market itself, Scribner will promote the novel in the most traditional and non-sensational fashion: 350 bound galleys have been sent to reviewers. A seven-city reading tour at libraries and literary centers is planned. There will be a *Vanity Fair* photograph, a *New Yorker* profile by

David Remnick, perhaps an NPR booking, but the author won't do TV.

Two decades ago, DeLillo was a critic's writer, his readership small and steadfast. In his first novel, *Americana* (Houghton Mifflin, 1971), a disaffected TV executive traverses the country in search of a national identity; his subsequent books also took the American character as their subject, each as a kind of postmodern, comic nightmare involving a separate arena of American life. There is college football and nuclear weaponry in *End Zone* (Houghton Mifflin, 1972), rock 'n' roll and the drug culture in *Great Jones Street* (Houghton Mifflin, 1973), science and mathematics in *Ratner's Star* (Knopf, 1976).

Beginning with 1985's American Book Award recipient, *White Noise* (Viking), a novel about academic life and industrial disaster, the author finally began his halting migration from the cultural fringe to the mainstream. More than 300,000 copies of *White Noise* have sold in paperback and hardcover (roughly the same number of copies of *Underworld* will have to sell for the book to break even). With backlist longevity has come an enduring reputation. He is now widely hailed as one of the stars of our literary pantheon. His personal tendency to eschew book publicity has proven to be the best kind of publicity, deepening the aura of intrigue surrounding his books.

DeLillo professes not to take much of an interest in reviews and scholarly critiques of his work. "Normally I look at the first wave of reviews. After that it's not what reviewers say that become a problem, it's just reading about myself and reading yet another summary of the book that becomes a bit difficult. There's a certain kind of soul-weariness that sets in."

In 1988, critics on the right condemned *Libra,* his novel depicting the life of Lee Harvey Oswald, for questioning the lone gunman theory of the Kennedy assassination—in the *Washington Post* George Will lambasted the book as "an act of literary vandalism and bad citizenship." *Underworld's* freewheeling cast of real and fictional characters may prompt other readers to question the novelist's fidelity to the record. "History is essentially the record of events," DeLillo explains. "Fiction comes out of another level of experience. It comes out of dreams, daydreams, fantasies, delirium. It comes out of hours of wasted time; it comes out of nightmares. It's everything in a writer's life that finally determines how and what he writes. And all of these things declare a kind of opposition to history. And there's a sense in which a novel may, as in the case of *Libra,* fill in gaps in history, in the sense that *Libra* proposes a specific conspiracy to fill the blank spaces of that particular afternoon in Dallas in 1963. There's a sense that fiction can rescue history from its confusion."

The novel as an art form, DeLillo says, "has moved to the margins and we cannot expect it to be anywhere else. From this sideline vantage, the novelist can assert an influence in a context that may be relatively narrow, but may be all the more forceful and incisive for this very reason. Maybe marginality sharpens the writer's responses and makes him more trenchant, more observant and more dynamic."

To an industry that often asks itself, who are the rightful heirs of Faulkner, Joyce and Nabokov, DeLillo is anything but marginal. He has become an emblem of literary greatness: a novelist whose books are so dense and rewarding that critics spend years unraveling their secrets. A symbol of integrity in a culture of publicity, he has broken his public silences to speak out in reaction to the *fatwa* against Salman Rushdie and other concerns. In an age of million-dollar publicity campaigns, DeLillo's popularity has spread at the grass roots level: through independent bookstores, in classrooms and across the Internet. As Nan Graham puts it, with DeLillo "you really do have the writer alone in the room writing for the reader alone in the room reading. More than with most authors by far, those two individual acts are united by the publishing industry with as little *Sturm und Drang* and politicking as possible."

DeLillo would rather not contemplate the perception that this novel represents, in the publishing argot, a "breakout book" (it must be said, this is not a term his publicist has used). "I've never thought about myself in terms of a career. When people ask me a question about my career, I answer, perhaps a bit facetiously, I don't have a career, I have a typewriter. I've never planned anything."

Even DeLillo's stripped-down working methods suggest a deliberate effort to hold the web of instantaneous marketing and news at arm's length. The novelist whom James Walcott has called "America's leading literary diagnostician" doesn't surf the Net or even use a word processor. DeLillo explains: "The physical sensation of hitting keys and watching hammers strike the page is such an integral part of the way I think and even the way I see words on the page that I'd be most reluctant to give it up. That is, there's a sculptural quality, to me, of letter-by-letter, word-by-word, linear progress across a piece of paper as I type and as the hammers hit the page. It's more immediate. It's more physical. It's actually sensuous."

DeLillo's life is, in a sense, a great American story, but one he is not eager to discuss at any length. The son of Italian immigrants, he grew up in a two-family house in the Bronx with a sister, grandparents and cousins, a few blocks away from where Lee Harvey Oswald, who was three years younger, lived with his mother in the mid-1950s. (The two never met.)

It wasn't an environment that encouraged writerly introspection, nor was DeLillo captivated by literature and language. "I did not start reading regularly until I was in college," he says. "My memories of high school are of getting home as fast as I could so that I could go play basketball in the schoolyard."

Underworld revisits DeLillo's own knockabout years in the Bronx in chapters depicting his protagonist, the waste management executive Nick Shay, as a fatherless street punk who kills a man in a pool hall basement. "I know the streets that he came from, and that entire environment and that language is just second nature to me," he says. "And it was an enormous pleasure to return to this material after all these years. The first things I wrote were short stories about the Italian Bronx. I didn't write very many of them at all. But it's been a long time between those stories and this novel. And I needed a certain number of years in order to see it clearly and understand how to write about it, which I did not understand when I was 21 years old."

DeLillo went to Fordham in 1954, then joined the advertising firm of Ogilvy and Mather, writing spots for accounts like Sears Roebuck and Zippo lighters. Throughout the 1960s, he placed short stories in literary journals like *Epoch* and the *Kenyon Review*. He'll say little about this transitional period of his life and the slow gravitational pull of writing. "It was very, very gradual," he says. "I didn't realize until I was two years into my first novel that I could be a writer. Suddenly I just had a feeling. Call it an experience. And it was the first indication that I ever had that I was possibly good enough to do this on a regular basis or for an extended amount of time."

DeLillo attributes his fascination with the deep, apocalyptic undercurrents of rituals like sports and shopping not to personal circumstance, but to the historical context of his fiction: "For the last 35 years or so, there have been two levels of violence—the clear, vivid overarching threat we've faced until recently of a nuclear exchange.

And the other is something which I think began to flow from the Kennedy assassination and the social disruptions of the 1960s—a sense of randomness, uncertainty, ambiguity that includes violence, among other things. This is part of our psychic weather."

DeLillo adds: "I became a writer by living in New York and seeing and hearing and feeling all the great, amazing and dangerous things the city endlessly assembles. And I also became a writer by avoiding serious commitment to anything else."

Since his second novel, DeLillo has been agented by Lois Wallace, who does not sign the author to one house for more than one novel at a time. But his résumé of editors reads like a *Who's Who* of the publishing world: Philip Rich edited his first three novels at Houghton Mifflin, Knopf's Robert Gottlieb—"with the substantial assistance of Lee Goerner"—edited *Ratner's Star, The Players* (1977), *Running Dog* (1978) and *The Names* (1982).

His next three novels were published by Viking. "In each case at Viking, after I published a novel, the editor left. I got along very well with all of them and I'm still friendly with all of them. But this is something that happens in the business. I didn't consider it an enormous problem." Elizabeth Sifton was the editor of *White Noise*, Gerald Howard edited *Libra* and Nan Graham edited *Mao II* (1992).

Protected by a cadre of editors, agents and friends who reveal few details about the author's character and whereabouts, DeLillo continues to produce new books and projects: he has written an original screenplay called *Game Six* and is widely believed to be the author of *Amazons*, a novel about a woman hockey player, written under the name Cleo Birdwell and published by Holt in 1980. But one wonders if it will soon no longer be possible for DeLillo to maintain the distance he seeks from the publishing machine and the public eye. As the first books in years from Pynchon and possibly Salinger have inspired journalists to invade the private lives of these authors with ever increasing zeal, it has been suggested that a writer's ability to shield himself from the media is a dead art. DeLillo doesn't agree. "Surely the media has become stronger than ever, and surely there is this urge, as I say, almost an automatic mechanism that will try to absorb certain such reluctant entities into the weave. I don't think it's necessarily an artifact of the past. I hope that writers will still refuse to submit."

What is the Underworld? A zone where information, desire, crime and capital circulate beneath the manifest events of daily life, and where wealth and power stake a dangerous, hidden claim on the American mind? Asked why he found this title appropriate, DeLillo says: "While I worked on the book, I gradually compiled a number of titles. I first hit upon *Underworld* when I started thinking about plutonium waste buried deep in the earth. Then about Pluto, the god of the dead and ruler of the world. New connections and meanings began to suggest themselves, and I recall drawing a circle around the title *Underworld* on a page filled with prospective titles."

Can it have escaped the novelist that Pluto is also the god of money? As DeLillo emerges from the literary underground, he may find that his place in the big business of literature and celebrity isn't quite as marginal, or as oppositional, as he would like it to be. It is a predicament that may well provide the grist of his next sublime journey into the secret life of contemporary America.

JONATHAN BING
August 11, 1997

DOROTHY DUNNETT

MANY OF HER readers probably picture Dorothy Dunnett, hailed by the *Washington Post* as "the finest living writer of historical fiction," living in the kind of castle pictured on the covers of her books. But although she lives in Edinburgh, a city steeped in romantic history with a skyline dominated by the ancient castle where Mary, Queen of Scots, who appears as a child in Dunnett's novels, gave birth to the first king to unite Scotland and England, Dunnett's home is a sandstone semi-detached Victorian villa about 10 minutes from the city center.

She has lived here since 1956, and the first impression, as one steps into the hallway, is of a period grandeur. The rooms are spacious, decorated in strong colors, and there is a handsome staircase lined with family portraits, painted by Dunnett herself, that include a dashing, full-length likeness of her husband, Sir Alastair Dunnett, wearing his kilt. Sir Alastair, who edited Scotland's leading newspaper, the *Scotsman*, for nearly 20 years, was also a director of Scottish Television and chairman of Thomson Scottish Petroleum. He was knighted for his services to journalism and Scotland in 1995.

Lady Dunnett is a young-looking 74, smaller and slighter than in her publicity photographs, with silver curls and a pretty face that lights up with an infectious sense of humor. Her voice has the kind of soft lilt that endorses the view that Scots speak the best English in the world, and her hospitality is traditionally Scottish: not a cup of tea but a generous slug of a fine malt whisky (she is one of the judges for the Glenfiddich Awards for Living Scotland).

Dunnett's latest book, *Caprice and Rondo,* (Knopf) is the seventh in The House of Niccolò series, which chronicles the life and times of merchant-adventurer Nicholas de Fleury. The books are set in 15th century Europe, and she is currently working on the eighth and final title, which is due to be published in time for the millennium, when readers from all over the world plan to celebrate the completion of the series with a banquet in the Grand Hall of Stirling, another royal castle featured in Dunnett's novels.

The Niccolò series forms a pendant to the earlier Lymond Chronicles—reprinted in a splashy trade paperback set last year by Vintage. The six novels in the Lymond Chronicles, first published in the 1960s, established Dunnett's reputation as a witty, stylish writer of romantic historical fiction that blends the pageantry of Renaissance Europe with the adventures of a fictitious buccaneering Scottish nobleman, Francis Crawford of Lymond. Action-packed stories with a cast of hundreds of historical figures and backgrounds ranging across Europe from Scotland to Russia, the novels are remarkable for their historical accuracy and an attention to detail that any academic historian might envy.

Dunnett's background was solidly middle-class. "My parents were not particularly academic. My father was a mining engineer," she says. Although she was born in Dunfermline, a small town not far from Edinburgh, the family moved to Edinburgh when she was about three. Dunnett grew up in Edinburgh and went to James Gillespie's High School for Girls (later immortalized as the Marcia Blaine School by Muriel Spark in *The Prime of Miss Jean Brodie*). Although not a classmate of Spark (Dunnett is six years younger), Dunnett agrees that the teaching was first rate. "I got a solid grounding in Latin that has proven invaluable in my research. I have no problem with medieval Latin and Romance languages."

But Dunnett is not a trained historian. In fact, history was her least favorite subject at school, and she was not attracted by the idea of going on to university. "Instead," she recalls, "I took a job as a press officer in the wartime Ministry of Information, which gave me time to go to painting classes in the evenings." It was to prove an inspired choice when she married her boss, Alastair Dunnett, in 1946. The job also honed her powers of observation. "It was working with Alastair and meeting his journalist colleagues that gave me an invaluable insight into how men's minds work," she says.

Dunnett continued to study painting when they moved to Glasgow in 1946 and soon found that she had a facility for catching a likeness that enabled her to become a successful portrait painter. She still undertakes the occasional commission, and her painter's eye for colors enlivens her descriptions of people and places. But the painting studio in the back garden of her house has long since been converted into a writing studio.

It was not, however, until her late 30s that Dunnett began writing. "I shared with my mother a fondness for historical writers like Alexandre Dumas, Raphael Sabatini and Baroness Orzy [of *The Scarlet Pimpernel* fame], and I particularly enjoyed stories with a highly articulate central heroic figure, lots of action and touches of humor," Dunnett explains. "After a while, I seemed to have read everything in the genre, and it was Alastair who suggested that perhaps I should try writing a historical novel of my own.

"I wanted to create a fascinating central character and give him a setting that no one else had used," Dunnett continues, "Sixteenth-century Europe appealed to me as a glamorous, exciting, gorgeous period, rich in fascinating figures like Suleiman the Magnificent, Ivan the Terrible and François Premier, but I soon realized why the period had not been used—it was very difficult and complicated to research."

Dunnett's first effort required a huge amount of background reading, but Edinburgh proved an ideal base with its renowned National Library of Scotland, of which Dunnett is now a trustee. "But these were the days before photocopying, so I had to spend long days in the library, and I've still got dozens of notebooks full of painstakingly copied material dating from my early research," she recalls.

The historical tapestry Dunnett had chosen as her subject meant that the books would inevitably be long, and when she submitted *The Game of Kings* to Hutchinson, a leading fiction house at the time, she sent the first half only. Despite an enthusiastic reader's report, the publisher was alarmed by the length and wanted cuts. A further five publishers all said the same thing, but Dunnett was not prepared to give in. Then her husband—who seems to have always ridden to her rescue—suggested she try an American publisher, as they seemed to welcome longer books. He had met Lois Cole, then an editor at Putnam who had worked with Margaret Mitchell on *Gone With the Wind*, and he sent her *Game of Kings*. Cole's response was gratifyingly immediate: she sent a contract by return mail with the message: "We want this, we want its successors—but you'll have to cut it."

Offered real commitment, Dunnett was willing to make cuts. She found Cole to be a splendidly sympathetic editor who shepherded her first two books, introduced her to the museums and art galleries of New York and left her a French dueling sword in her will. It's an evocative souvenir, a 16th-century French short sword with an ivory handle.

Publication in the U.S. was swiftly followed by publication by Cassell in the U.K. Dunnett has since had a number of British publishers, and all her historical novels are currently in print with Michael Joseph/Penguin. Her books have always been popular, with sales steadily increasing over the years; there's also a keen trade in second-hand copies. The new books are first published in London, and Dunnett works closely with freelance editor Richenda Todd, who has a sharp eye for any factual mistakes and inconsistencies, and with Susan Ralston and Robert Gottlieb at Knopf. "Bob is the most famous editor in the world," exclaims Dunnett. "And I feel very flattered that, although he now looks after a very small stable of authors for Knopf, he's promised that he'll always edit me." The research and writing for each book takes about 14 months, with the finished manuscript flying between Edinburgh, London and New York for any small queries to be ironed out.

The books are meticulously plotted. "I use menu cards for the characters and record in tiny, tiny writing the main details as I accumulate them," Dunnett explains. "I keep them in a shoebox, and before I start writing a chapter I spend a couple of days combing out everything I need. When I go away"—her latest book took her to Poland and the Ukraine—"I take masses of photographs and note down details of the smells, sounds, language, flowers and climate, then I fish these out and see what's relevant to a particular scene. Once everything is clear in my mind I start writing, and I'll do half a chapter (about 2500 words) one day, and the second half the next."

All the battles are carefully designed. If a character sets out on a journey, she works out every stage in detail, calculating how long it will take by ship, on horseback, by sledge, though most of this information never makes it into the book. Dunnett owes much of her knowledge of the sea to her husband, an avid sailor who put her into boats and also took her on riding holidays. Dunnett's sailing experience became the basis for a series of contemporary thrillers about an undercover agent, posing as a portrait painter named Johnson Johnson who owns a yacht, which she started when she was halfway through the Lymond series and wrote under the name Dorothy Halliday.

Nowadays, Dunnett tends to work in her studio late at night when she can be sure of not being interrupted by phone calls, faxes or e-mail. The old Olivetti typewriter on which she wrote *The Game of Kings* has long gone. Today she has a laptop and a desktop computer—which offer access to the various Dunnett Web sites that attract hundreds of postings a day (though she notes that some are accessible only by passwords she herself doesn't know).

Much of her time is taken up with interviews, various Scottish projects of which she is an enthusiastic patron, readers' queries, plans for promotional tours, revisions for new editions and approving new jackets. Her stamina is impressive. She likes to socialize in the evenings, so it is often quite late before she is able to slip away to her studio. She works through the night until dawn and compares her routine to the evening shift on a newspaper. "It's all part of the job. Most writing days, I don't get up before 11 o'clock, so I have nearly eight hours' sleep, even if at rather unconventional hours."

Dunnett admits that she enjoys teasing her readers by setting up links between characters and events that keep them guessing to the very last page. "I'm currently playing a guessing game with the Lymond and Niccolò series. Although there's a time gap between them, the central families are common to both, and readers are trying to work out the connections and in particular which family turns out to be the ancestors of Lymond himself," she says.

Such gambits have earned her a steadfast readership. Since 1984, her readers have kept in touch via a quarterly magazine called *Marzipan and Kisses* in the U.S. and *Whispering Gallery* in the U.K. Despite the predominantly male character of the novels and the military action, her readership seems to be largely female, with the books offering strong plots and absorbing worlds into which to escape.

Dunnett's studio—with its collection of foreign editions, files, maps, tapes, a printer, a photocopier—is businesslike and solitary, a reminder of the lonely, dedicated hours that must be spent by any successful writer. At one end, a door opens into the garage, and she says that readers often ask what kind of car she drives. Aware that her car was perhaps too ordinary, she asked one of her two sons to find her something more adventurous. And he did.

The fans are fond of Dunnett quizzes, so what sort of car would Francis Crawford be driving if he were alive today? The answer has to be the same as Lady Dunnett: a gleaming scarlet Porsche.

JEAN RICHARDSON
May 11, 1998

FANNIE FLAGG

H ER ORIGINAL NAME was Patricia Neal, but when Fannie Flagg's father marched the aspiring actress down to the local Birmingham, Ala., chapter of Equity at age 17, they told her the name was already taken by a famous actress. "Take a name that is really spectacular," her father told her. "One that no one will forget." Flagg has been reinventing herself ever since. A comedienne, actress, TV personality and author of 1981's *Coming Attractions* (reprinted in 1992 with a new title, *Daisy Fay and the Miracle Man*); *Fried Green Tomatoes at the Whistle Stop Cafe* (1987); and most recently *Welcome to the World, Baby Girl!* (Random House) Flagg has a knack for creating indelible characters.

Fried Green Tomatoes, set in Depression-era Alabama and in a contemporary nursing home, spent 36 weeks on the *New York Times* bestseller list after it was published in 1987. The novel depicts two women who run the Whistle Stop Cafe and the characters who depend on them, body and spirit. The book had a second life as a film starring Jessica Tandy, Kathy Bates, Mary Stuart Masterson and Mary-Louise Parker, released by Universal Pictures in 1991. The movie won rave reviews, a cult following and an Oscar nomination for the screenplay that Flagg wrote with Carol Sobieski. Flagg also received a Grammy nomination for the audiotape she recorded for Random House Audio.

"The core of the story," wrote Jack Butler in the *New York Times Book Review,* "is the unusual love affair" between Idgie Thread-goode and Ruth Jamison, the capacious, kindhearted founders of the Whistle Stop Cafe. The two set up such a hankering in the American public for small-town life that Erma Bombeck wrote of the novel, "this book is so much fun it makes me sick I missed the Depression."

Fans who have waited 11 years for Flagg's new novel won't be dismayed. *Baby Girl* has the same small-town spirit of *Fried Green Tomatoes,* if not the complex narrative structure, and is, says the author, a sort of sequel to her first novel. All three books are powered by nostalgia for home, for simpler times and for community. They are also, Flagg admits, partially autobiographical. In *Baby Girl,* Dena Nordstrom, a wholesome Midwestern girl, moves to New York where, much like Diane Sawyer or Jane Pauley, her career as a television interviewer takes off. Dena goes as far as she can with big-city success, but there are a few unanswered questions about her past, and she is, almost without knowing it, homesick for her grandmother's house in Elmwood Springs, Iowa, where she felt secure as a child. The town is described for us by one of the last of the radio homemakers, a talk-show hostess who offers her faithful listeners everything from recipes to local gossip.

A down-home, screen-porch sweetness radiates from Flagg when she meets a journalist at a restaurant on the Pacific coast, midway between Los Angeles and her house in Montecito, just south of Santa Barbara. The restaurant is a sleepy fixture that seems to cater to an older, golf crowd. A wedding reception in one corner sends white sparks across the room, from flashbulbs, the gowns of bridesmaids and the smiling guests.

On the final day of a heat wave that has most of Southern California unbuttoned and disoriented, Flagg is cool and welcoming in a simple sleeveless dress with a single strand of pearls. Her blonde hair is cut short and round, horn-rim glasses perch on her nose. If she has the porcelain fragility sometimes associated with Southern women (a fluttering nervousness about such things as the flying she'll have to do on her forthcoming book tour), Flagg is also refreshingly forthright and expresses a generous interest in the lives of other people. She has left six houseguests visiting from Birmingham watching Mark McGwire on her TV at home.

"It could be an Alabama house," she says proudly of her home in Montecito. "I came to Santa Barbara to visit in 1975, walked into a real estate office and said to the man, 'I want a white house with a porch that wrapped around to the side. You probably don't have anything like that, now do you?' Well he did, and I've been there ever since."

Born in 1941, Flagg grew up in Birmingham. Her father went to war with the Army in 1942 and came back in '44, after which he tried various money-making schemes, including running a malt shop, with mixed success. Flagg began acting when she was 14, joining a theater group in Birmingham. Friends in the group called her Baby Girl because she was the youngest. Flagg was also dyslexic. "I always wanted to write but acting came so much more easily," she says. "I didn't pursue writing because I always assumed and was told that if you can't spell you can't be a writer. I'd get Cs and Ds in creative writing. It was so embarrassing." Flagg whispers as she discusses her grades, and then catches herself, whispering, as if 40 years later, they still embarrass her. "To have gone," she says, "from being a girl who could not spell her name to an author with her own books on a library shelf is the most rewarding thing that has ever happened to me."

Fannie, then Patricia, went from high school in Birmingham to the Pittsburgh Playhouse, a drama school, and then right into a job as a co-hostess on a morning TV show in Birmingham. "There was nobody famous in Birmingham, so we'd interview men who worked in the zoo and women from the garden club." She stored all of it away for future material.

In 1964, Flagg went to New York to write for *Candid Camera.* After a few months, Alan Funt put her on the show, where she stayed for five years. She made comedy albums in the late '60s for RCA Victor, went on to act in several TV shows, including *The Dick Van Dyke Show* and *The Love Boat,* and was a regular on the game show *Match Game.* She also appeared in such films as *Five Easy Pieces* and *Grease* and continued to do theater. In 1980, both of Flagg's parents died, three months apart. That same year, Flagg was playing the lead role on Broadway in *The Best Little Whorehouse in Texas,* when she had an epiphany. "I was sitting in the dressing room, covered with makeup in a low cut gown and I thought, 'I am so unhappy.' I stopped then and there and decided to be a full-time writer."

She had reason to be confident in her writing abilities. In 1981, Morrow published *Coming Attractions.* It spent ten weeks on the New York Times best-seller list. Around this time, she also began work on *Fried Green Tomatoes.* Flagg went on to write not only novels but her own screenplay. When Sobieski, the original screenwriter on *Fried Green Tomatoes,* felt ill, producer Jon Avnet called in Flagg to finish it, a process that took three years. Adapting her own work for the screen and writing by committee proved more trying than Flagg had expected. "You know your own characters so well, and other people are telling you what they would and wouldn't do. I wouldn't do it again. If I'm going to go down in flames I want to do it in my own voice."

Still more bizarre was the production itself. "I went down to Alabama to watch them filming," Flagg recalls. "I visited the set on a Sunday, when no one was around. I walked into the cafe they had created and it was the strangest thing. Like being a painter and walking into your own painting. All these things that were in your head all of a sudden are real. It's like walking into your own brain. I've never gotten over the fact that an idea can end up in a book, a thing you can carry around, much less a whole movie!"

Flagg needs a lot of isolation and solitude to write. Her new book proved particularly difficult because the success of *Fried Green Tomatoes* was so stunning. "I often don't know what my books are about when I'm writing," she says. When the U.K. rights to her new book were sold to Chatto & Windus in London, the British publisher sent Flagg a synopsis. "I was so delighted," she says, "to know what it was about!"

Flagg's dealings with publishers have not always been so easy. In 1985, she says, "I was in a motel in Monroeville, Alabama doing research for *Fried Green Tomatoes,* when my agent [Wendy Weil] called and told me that Morrow had turned down the book. I was devastated because I had quit acting and had no salary coming in." Eventually, Martha Levin, then rights director at Random House, brought the book to the attention of editor Sam Vaughn, who acquired it. As the editor of both *Tomatoes* and *Baby Girl,* Vaughn has been "so protective," says Flagg. "I started *Baby Girl* in 1987 and felt no pressure to finish or to write some version of *Fried Green Tomatoes* over again."

Flagg toyed with various plots for a few years before deciding that she wasn't quite finished with some of the autobiographical themes in her first novel. What would happen, for example, to that small-town girl once she reached the big city? In a small bookstore in Fair Hill, Ala., Flagg spotted a book on radio homemakers in the Midwest in the 1940s. She befriended one of them, Evelyn Birkaby in Sidney, Iowa, and began research on the new book. "This seemed so romantic to me, that sweet Midwestern life. I have, like most people, a homesickness, a longing to go back to a little town in 1948 and not have the pressures of the modern world. It's a longing to go back to a home that may nor may not have existed, a kind of innocence. Better to long for that than money and success!

"It's very seductive," Flagg adds, "to say, I had success with one book, why not stop? Eudora Welty always said she wrote so easily until she had some success. Then she began rewriting again and again, after she realized that someone would actually read it. Publishing can be too intertwined with show business. I left show business to enter a different world."

Flagg guards her privacy, but she is also surrounded by friends, many of whom appear in her novels with real names, like Norma and Macky, central characters in the new novel and two of Flagg's best friends from Alabama. Does Flagg consider herself a Southern writer? "No, I think I'm an American writer. I was surprised and delighted to see that *Fried Green Tomatoes* touched people all over the world. And I am in love with the American character." The people who interest Flagg the most are those "living quiet lives, nurses and firemen and those people who never get recognized. They don't really have a voice. In the South, we hear about the very poor or the very wealthy. There aren't many people writing for middle-class America."

Flagg gives her interviewer a copy of the cookbook inspired by *Fried Green Tomatoes*, published by Fawcett in 1993, and points out her favorite recipe for coconut cake. "I'm on a diet," she mourns, "in preparation for the book tour." For lunch, she has eaten only one half of a papaya, a great disappointment to Emma, our waitress. In fact, as it turns out, the entire staff in the restaurant is in the kitchen working up the nerve to come out and meet the author of *Fried Green Tomatoes*, whom they recognize from her days on TV. They catch her in the driveway, where a photographer is shooting portraits of the bride and groom whose reception has provided such a memorable backdrop to our interview. As the bride smiles for the camera, Flagg, the all-American actress, bestselling novelist and self-invented voice of middle America, shakes the hand of a particularly avid fan. "It's really you!" he says, a little breathless. "Yes," she says. "And who are you?"

SUSAN SALTER REYNOLDS
September 21, 1998

MARIA FLOOK

I'M NOT A writer who begins with ideas," says Maria Flook. "I begin with affliction—the affliction of obsession." Flook's own affliction is the disintegration of her family, which she chronicles in *My Sister Life: The Story of My Sister's Disappearance* (Pantheon). The book, which opens in 1964 and closes in the present, is not only a study of a childhood gone awry but also a meditation on the endeavor of balancing private pain with artistic activity. In one of its final scenes, Flook's older sister, Karen, 24 and a former child prostitute, discovers that Flook, a promiscuous 22-year-old pill addict and single mother, is applying to M.F.A. programs. Karen turns to her little sister and poses a harsh question: "You lead a double life, you know that? Which part is bullshit?"

Judging by her books and her life, the answer is neither. Flook's artistry and her experience exist in an intense symbiosis; donning an artist's objective eye permits Flook to keep a troubled past at bay.

In person, this dichotomy makes Flook something of a chameleon. A slender, conservatively dressed 45-year-old, she greets her interviewer holding an immaculate manila envelope that contains her past reviews and a copy of her first volume of poems. Flook is the author of two novels (*Family Night*, 1993, which won a PEN American/Ernest Hemingway Special Criterion, and *Open Water*, 1995); a collection of short stories (*You Have the Wrong Man*, 1996); and several books of poetry. She has an anxious, watchful air that is countered by a raw, forceful speaking voice and an unassuming candor. Speaking with us over dinner at a Provincetown, Mass., restaurant and, the following morning, at the home in neighboring Truro that she shares with her husband, John Skoyles, and 11-year-old son, Harry, she hopscotches among topics, giving her intellectual curiosity free reign. Her ebullience makes it easy to imagine why she grew impatient with the confines of poetry, her first literary calling ("I'm a storyteller. Poems don't give you enough elbow room.") As she mixes tales of schmoozing at a glitzy sales conference party last year with anecdotes of waitressing in strip clubs and scoring heroin (Flook has been sober and drug-free for a long time), she alternately suggests a less louche Marianne Faithfull and your favorite Woodstock mom.

Though she jokingly complains about magazine editors' requests for "tales of a junkie mommie," Flook's identification with—and allegiance to—America's fringe population is clear from both her persona and her work. Holly, the protagonist of *Open Water*, is a chambermaid living in Newport, R.I. On probation for setting fire to her ex-husband's bed, she falls in love with a thief and morphine addict modeled on one of Flook's ex-boyfriends. The short stories in *You Have the Wrong Man* are peopled by transvestites and adulterers, alcoholics and cons. "I write about people in peril, people struggling," says Flook. She does so with a bone-deep affection that is singular, outlining her knockabout characters' capers and quirks without judgment in her simple yet rich prose.

My Sister Life locates the source of Flook's anti-mainstream bent in her chaotic personal background, and in her close tie with Karen (Karen, who never graduated from high school, is currently married and works at a casino in a city that Flook declines to identify). "The tragedy of my family's disintegration is the core source of my art sensibility," says Flook. "It made me a witness—I began to notice the world from an artist's point of view, and that's what saved me." The book follows the two sisters from childhood into their mid-20s. Besides documenting their troubled home life, it describes the gradual emergence of Flook's artistic sensibility and also provides a portrait of a suburban culture buckling under the onslaught of the 1960s. In an unexpected twist, Flook narrates half of the memoir from Karen's perspective, describing her sister's fugitive life with a vividness and verisimilitude all the more startling because it is wholly imagined.

Flook seems to have relished the task of capturing her sister's droll, more plainspoken adolescent voice, although she admits it was a technical challenge. "I had to remember what it was like to be 14— Karen's got this real understanding, coupled with an innocence," she reports. "She has a lot of street savvy, and a lot of interior savvy—it's an intelligence that's remarkable, that comes from austerity of living." To aid her, Flook drew on her decades of informal phone "interviews" with Karen and also on her sister's letters to her. "People are going to wonder how I could re-create my sister's voice with license," says Flook, who adds that she wrote the book "with more authority" than any book she had previously written. "I'm so impregnated with this story, it's almost like it's in my marrow."

Flook was born in Hamilton, Ont, in 1952, the second child of Ray and Veronica, pseudonymously surnamed Mitchell in *My Sister Life.* It was the second marriage for both, and her mother also had two children from her previous union. Between the ages of two and five, Flook lived in Italy, where her father had an engineering job with Fiat. The sisters later grew up in the affluent surroundings of suburban Wilmington, Del., where Ray ran a successful industrial supply company.

In *My Sister Life,* it is Veronica who plays antagonist to Flook and Karen's twin protagonists. Flook portrays her mother as an exceptionally beautiful narcissist determined not to brook any competition with her daughters for her husband's affections. "Veronica's enterprising sexuality overwhelmed our individual goals and spilled into family matters. Her erotic aspect emerged in her every routine and came more naturally to her than maternal duty," writes Flook. Flook credits this coldness, coupled with her father's passivity, with triggering Karen's early flight into indiscriminate sexual liaisons and her premature departure, at 14, from home. When Karen returned after two years, Veronica had her institutionalized. In the wake of Karen's departure, Flook, who was 12 at the time, herself began to unravel. She became a juvenile delinquent and a drug user, as well as sexually active, imagining that she was following in Karen's footsteps: "Perhaps Karen and I were twinned in a pernicious mutation—little remnants of her soul had entwined with mine—like a grafted branch," she writes.

In high school, Flook began to write seriously and became involved in the antiwar movement. Seven of her poems were accepted in a Random House anthology of "disaffected young writers." At 17, after also being institutionalized by her mother, Flook fled home for Providence, R.I., where she married a graduate student (whose name she still carries) who fathered her first child, Kate, now 23 and working as a school teacher in Minneapolis. Flook also took a bachelor's degree at Roger Williams College. After the breakup of her marriage in 1977, Flook earned an M.F.A. in poetry at the University of Iowa Writers Workshop, where her fellow students included Jane Smiley, Jorie Graham and Sandra Cisneros. Flook found the workshop "inhospitable to young writers," but that adversity helped galvanize her own creative commitment. Following her graduation, she came to the Fine Arts Work Center in Provincetown, where she held a seven-month fellowship. "That was a big turning point for me," she recalls.

"It was such a nurturing community here, and this town in winter is so desperately beautiful, and also so empty, you can turn to your work with this nourishment outside, but also without distraction." At the Center, Flook also met Skoyles, a writer and college administrator, whom she describes as having "been very supportive of my writing life. He also has an incredible literary mind that I can draw upon." The two were married in 1984.

In early 1982, Flook sold her poetry collection *Reckless Wedding* to Houghton Mifflin, unagented, for an $800 advance, and it was published that fall. Ampersand Press, a small house affiliated with Roger Williams College, next published a collection of stories, *Dancing with My Sister Jane* (the title story is a fictional treatment of some of the material in *My Sister Life*). In 1984, she and Skoyles moved to Asheville, N.C., where Skoyles worked for the M.F.A. program at Warren Wilson College, and Flook taught English.

There Flook wrote the manuscript that became *Family Night*, which her then-agent, Cynthia Cannell, submitted to Pantheon editor Dan Frank on the recommendation of a friend. Frank's acceptance marked the beginning of an editorial collaboration that Flook describes in glowing terms. "Dan has been an incredible source of vision and nourishment to me. He doesn't flinch from my darkness and actually mirrors it with a different level of acute perception," she says. Since 1993, Flook has been agented by Kim Witherspoon.

My Sister Life is not the first work in which Flook has raided her family background for creative material. The figure of a vanished older sister has appeared previously in numerous stories and poems, and fragments of dialogue from her other books resurface, verbatim, in *My Sister Life* ("It's because it's been percolating in my mind all this time," explains Flook, who was unaware of the cannibalization before it was pointed out to her). The father-obsessed half-brother of the protagonist of *Family Night* was so closely modeled on her real half-brother, Alex, that he didn't speak to her for two years following the book's publication.

"My allegiance to my writing is stronger than any family tie I might have, except for with my young son," responds Flook when asked if she feels any guilt over making public her siblings' personal histories. "And it's not my doing. I don't decide what to do as a writer—it gets me." She reports, clearly pleased, that her sister's response to *My Sister Life* has been positive. "She's told me what a relief it is not to have to live alone with her story. It vindicates her that her story was important enough to put on a page," says Flook, who gave Karen a sizable portion of her $90,000 advance for the book. Her mother, who currently lives in a retirement community in Wilmington and is in frail health, has not yet read *My Sister Life*.

Flook is excited at the advance buzz surrounding *My Sister Life* but irritated that it is being compared to such other familial tell-alls as Kathryn Harrison's *The Kiss*. "It makes my editor and me really nervous. We wish this whole memoir craze would disappear and people would just look at it as a book. It has a much broader canvas—it's a portrait of an entire family, as well as of an era."

Flook, Skoyles and Harry settled in Truro in 1992, in a two-story house surrounded by scrub pines on the crest of a sandy hill, a 10-minute walk from the sea. There Flook writes for six or seven hours a day, three and a half weeks per month. During the fourth week, she critiques student work for the graduate writing seminars in the Bennington College M.F.A. program. The walls of her sun-drenched study, on the second floor of her house, are hung with pictures of her family and herself; behind her writing table is a neatly arranged bookshelf of her "research books." In the summer, she swims, takes her son's Labrador retriever, Chowder, for runs in the surrounding moors, and tends her garden. It's the kind of tranquil environment that seems ideally suited to permit the risky personal excavation work that Flook is called to undertake, both for the sake of her art and to achieve the emotional catharsis that she says brings her a measure of peace. "When I write about the past from the relative safety of my desk, I re-experience it, but within the cushioning framework of being an artist," she says. "I can't escape from my subject, because it comes from within, but I can find solace by addressing it as art.

"I'm interested in people who leave their safety zones in search of transformation," she continues. "You can't experience transformation without danger." Where willingness to face risk is concerned, Flook certainly seems ably endowed; it is this fearlessness that allows her to transmute family sorrow into literature, and to create an identity for herself supple enough to contain all her complexities.

MALLAY CHARTERS
January 12, 1998

ALLEGRA GOODMAN

MEETING ALLEGRA GOODMAN in person is a bit disconcerting. How can this vivacious and unpretentious young woman have accomplished so much so soon? Although *Kaaterskill Falls* (Dial) is her first novel, Goodman published her first short story as a freshman at Harvard and her first collection, *Total Immersion* (Harper & Row, 1989), the year she graduated. She received a $30,000 Whiting Foundation Writer's Award in 1991 and published her second book, the celebrated novel-like collection of stories, *The Family Markowitz* (FSG, 1996), a *New York Times* Notable Book of the Year, at the ripe age of 29. Not to mention the fact that Goodman and her husband, David, a computer science professor at MIT, are happily raising two young boys (Ezra, six, and Gabriel, two and a half)—and that she received her doctorate in English Literature from Stanford in 1997. If you happened to hear a faint groan on June 26, 1997, it was probably the collective exhalation of the members of Goodman's generation reading that morning's *New York Times,* which contained a glowing profile of the young phenom. This is the kind of article one wants to hide from one's own parents—who would probably be satisfied with simply one grandchild, one book, perhaps a master's degree.

The final straw was the reporter's observation that Goodman's home was "completely tidy." So a visitor is relieved to discover that the family living room in Cambridge, Mass., a year later, appears to have been struck by natural disaster. "How'd you weather the flood?" she asks cheerfully as she fetches a glass of juice, gesturing toward an array of damp mass market paperbacks splayed out to dry in front of the fireplace. As we settle in to chat, Goodman curls up on the couch and explains that David's science-fiction collection—along with a few hardback copies of *The Family Markowitz*—was soaked in the basement by the recent rain storms. In the author's presence, the sadly bedraggled volumes—carefully arranged in the hopes of possible recovery—strike the eye like a detail from her fiction. Chronicling a group of characters whose lives overlap at a summer community in the Catskills in the late 1970s, *Kaaterskill Falls* concludes with a generational struggle over an inheritance of treasured books, an irreplaceable collection of theology, literature, history and philosophy. And Goodman's earlier fiction also treats the lives of characters deeply immersed in the written word: with titles like "Variant Text," "Onion-skin" and "Oral History," her stories find a rich source of plot and metaphor in the acts of writing and reading.

It's easy to picture Goodman as the grad student she recently was, enthusiastically hashing out some critical problem around the seminar table—except that the topic of discussion now is her own fiction. Her green eyes radiate pleasure as she expresses confidence that the claims of popular, entertaining fiction and fine literature can be met simultaneously. "I think ultimately the most satisfying entertainment is the most intellectually engaging. It has to be done well, but I do think people respond to it. Some people bemoan the state of literary fiction today, but I think readers know good stuff when they see it." She cites a few favorite contemporary authors: Cynthia Ozick, Rebecca Goldstein, Gish Jen, Elizabeth McCracken. "I'm confident that ultimately people will go for the rich stuff rather than the thin, flimsy stuff." She laughs and draws an analogy between the pleasures of reading and eating: "My feeling has always been that people are going to eat Milk Duds, but they're also going to yearn for those rich, creamy, handmade truffles—and they're going to buy them."

The metaphor, although it may risk immodesty, seems altogether apt for *Kaaterskill Falls,* an ambitious, multi-layered, yet very accessible novel that she began writing and painstakingly revising a decade ago, even before starting the stories that went on to comprise *The Family Markowitz.* Goodman's enthusiasm for her own fiction is all of a piece with her passion for the written word generally, a passion that she traces to her childhood in a small conservative Jewish community in Honolulu. She observes that her mother, a geneticist, and her father, a philosophy professor (both taught at the University of Hawaii), "took me seriously. They encouraged me, they read my work. That's a tremendous gift that not every kid gets. And they listened. I would read my work aloud to my family. They were my little writer's group."

At 17, she wrote "Variant Text," which she sent to the Jewish intellectual journal *Commentary* the summer after graduating from high school and saw into print by the end of her first year at Harvard.

Encouraged by Marion Magid, the magazine's managing editor at the time, Goodman continued publishing fiction in *Commentary* throughout college. "When she first sent me a letter beginning 'Dear Ms. Goodman,'" she recalls, "I thought, 'Does she know how old I am?'" The editor very likely did not. After all, how many 17-year-olds could so convincingly write about a self-involved Shaw scholar living in a sprawling, poorly heated Victorian house in Oxford, England, with his wife's parents for the sake of convenient grand-parental baby-sitting; about a series of minor doctrinal disputes; and, most startlingly, about the genial disarray of domestic life as conducted by distracted intellectuals? This didn't sound like the work of teenager.

Impressed by the fiction in *Commentary*, agent Irene Skolnick contacted Goodman when she was a junior in college and, says Goodman, "quickly sold" *Total Immersion* to Ted Solotaroff at Harper & Row. (The collection, containing several new stories, will be reissued in paperback this year by Delta.) In 1991, Goodman published her first story in the *New Yorker*, the magazine that these days seems to trade off with *Commentary* for the rights to her fiction. Goodman remarks on her good fortune in editors, raving about Robert Gottlieb, Chip McGrath and now Roger Angell at the *New Yorker*, and about Jonathan Galassi, who edited *The Family Markowitz* at FSG. "I feel like I've had the last of the old-fashioned editors. They don't make 'em like this any more," she says.

Kaaterskill Falls, which Goodman had been rewriting all that time, was edited by Susan Kamil at Dial. (On leaving FSG for Dial, Goodman comments only. "It was just one of those things; it didn't work out with FSG.") Kamil, Goodman says, "must have read this manuscript five, six, maybe seven times. She wrote on every single page all over in pencil—and she did that twice. She cared so deeply for this book and the characters in it. She would talk about them as if they were real people, which is how I feel about it—but you don't expect other people to feel the same way."

From the outset, Goodman's voice was astonishingly confident, mature and witty—and as it turned out, she had in that first published story. "Variant Text," already staked out her own fictional terrain: several characters from the story reappear in later work. In her three books to date, Goodman has created a little universe of family members and neighbors linked by affection, guilt, obligation and necessity. Having gotten to know the Jewish matriarch Rose Markowitz from the point of view of an exasperated anthropology grad student interviewing her for an oral history project in "Oral History," for example, a reader can turn to "Fannie Mae" (both in *The Family Markowitz*) for a story immersed in Rose's own perspective. In the tradition of authors from Balzac to Faulkner, Goodman creates the effect of a fully developed alternate world, in which her characters move from story to story like familiar acquaintances.

In *Kaaterskill Falls,* Goodman turns the Catskills, circa 1977, into a place of beauty, conflict and moral complexity. To the Hawaiian-raised Goodman, upstate New York seemed a kind of enchanted fairy land, alluringly strange: "My mother's family had a summer house in the Catskills, and when I was a kid I used to spend summers there. It's very vivid in my mind, because it was so exotic to me as a kid! If your context is Hawaii, to come to this mountainous place with huge trees, dark forests, cold mornings in summer, the chill in the evening, was amazing. All of that made a tremendous impression on me. Since there were no Jewish schools or anything in Honolulu, Jewish life on the mainland, and in New York in particular, fascinated me. I was looking at it carefully from this other place."

The stories in *Total Immersion* and *The Family Markowitz,* while not lacking in melancholy, are also hilariously funny, largely because of Goodman's ear for the pitch and rhythm of domestic conversation. She comments, "I think my work does well when it's read aloud. For me, writing has always been a kind of performance. It's almost like you do these improvisations; sometimes I say the words out loud, try to hear it in my head and almost act it out, move my hands and try to figure out what the appropriate gesture would be. Writing is a solitary process, but when it's going well you don't feel like you're alone, because it becomes real enough for you that all the characters surround you and you hear their voices."

In *Kaaterskill Falls,* those voices—despite the novel's location in a summer vacation spot—speak in more autumnal, sadder tones than those of most of her previous fiction. For example, while the glib, cosmopolitan Shaw scholar from "Variant Text," Cecil Birnbaum, appears in the novel, he soon gives way to characters like Elizabeth Shulman, a loyal member of a devout orthodox congregation in New York City that travels with the Rav Elijah Kirshner every summer to Kaaterskill Falls. "I loved writing Elizabeth's character," Goodman comments, "because she loves literature and art, but she doesn't respond to them as an academic would. She feels it in her heart. The novel has books and learning in it, but it's not a bookish book. These people really take things to heart—and morally, those are the interesting people to write about."

While the stories of *The Family Markowitz* can be read as a novel, one could never mistake *Kaaterskill Falls* for a collection of stories. Indeed, it finds in the relatively insular, self-contained Kirshner community a kind of modern re-creation of the "three or four families in a country village" that Jane Austen famously defined as "the very thing to work on." When Goodman describes the unforgivable moral offense of a family member's late arrival to a Friday evening Shabbat dinner, or the Rav's decision to withdraw permission that had been granted to Elizabeth to sell kosher food to the community, one feels plunged into a lost world of tightly knit community, binding ethical strictures and, most of all, of individualism firmly constrained by allegiance to authority and tradition.

To a contemporary reader, Elizabeth's obedience to what may seem a rigid, arbitrary limit to her self-expression can be painful to read. "I'm interested in the complexity of Elizabeth's situation," Goodman says, "in the way she takes to heart the restrictions on her life. She can't stand outside of her situation in the way that we might, and judge it that way. These rituals are not rituals to her, they're instincts. So she's not going to run away or do something wild. She's going to try to figure out how to express herself within that framework."

Goodman pauses. "If you're drawing this little world, there have to be edges to the world. I saw Elizabeth's perspective, and I felt her hit an edge." Could this have anything to do with the dissertation she was completing—comparing the aesthetic ideas of Samuel Johnson and John Keats—as she revised *Kaaterskill Falls*? Goodman cites Keats's famous phrase: "I guess this is where 'the negative capability' would come in. I'm one of those people who thinks art should be philosophical. For me, it wasn't a matter of judging the situation, it was a matter of creating this moment that would make the reader think, and feel troubled." And leaning forward on the couch to emphasize her point, her face lights up with what might be best described as a philosophical smile.

IVAN KREILKAMP
July 27, 1998

MARY GORDON

IN A 1988 ESSAY, Mary Gordon describes attending the funeral of a beloved uncle. One by one, members of her large Irish-Catholic extended family approach her. "I just want to tell you I can't stand your books. None of us can," one uncle says. Her cousin the nun confesses, "I just feel I need to tell you that I think your books are dreadful. They're just too worldly for me." Even the deceased, "the most nearly silent man I've ever known and perhaps the kindest," Gordon writes, couldn't read them. "Oh, he was proud of you," her favorite aunt recalls. "But he thought your books were very dirty."

It's hard to imagine what this cast of real-life characters—cousins in spirit to the American Catholics that Gordon has portrayed so sympathetically yet unsparingly in her two-decade, eight-book career—would make of Gordon's latest novel. *Spending* (Scribner) tells the story of Monica Szabo, a semi-struggling 50-year-old painter whose life and work are transformed when a tossed-off question at one of her gallery lectures—"Where are all the male muses?"—gets a startling answer from a man in the audience: "Right here." "B," a millionaire commodities broker who has been following her career, offers her everything she needs to do her best work: space, time, complete financial support, great sex when she wants it (and never when she doesn't), even himself as a model. It all comes with no strings attached—though Monica can't help tying herself in knots over the complicated sexual politics of the situation.

As their raunchy sex segues into painting sessions, Monica begins Spent Men, a series of canvases inspired by the Italian Renaissance Masters, in which a Christ-like figure is relaxed not in death but in the *petit mort* of postorgasmic bliss (an idea Gordon borrowed from Leo Steinberg's classic 1983 study, *The Sexuality of Christ in Renaissance Art and Modern Oblivion*). For Monica, Spent Men is no attention-getting gimmick, but a union of matter and spirit, "the coming together of art and faith in the hands of a woman whose life was no longer shaped by belief."

Reconciling flesh and spirit has long been a central theme in Gordon's own art. "With *Spending,* I wanted to write a book about pleasure in its various forms," she told a journalist on a recent wintry afternoon, settling into the overstuffed sofa in her pleasantly professorial apartment near Barnard College, where she has taught for the past decade. "I feel like pleasure makes people really crazy. We're just not comfortable with it. And a concept of God that would have to include pleasure and ambiguity—that's not something most people can handle." Gordon, a small dark-haired woman of 49, lowers her voice a bit. "A Catholic writing about sex—now that's going to make a lot of Catholics nervous."

The Church makes an appearance in *Spending,* in the form of the protesters—led by an ex-nun who turns out to be Monica's nemesis from her Catholic school days—who picket the gallery showing the Spent Men paintings. As an outspoken advocate of abortion rights and supporter of ordaining women as priests, Gordon has had her own run-ins with the religious right, ranging from the not-so-funny (she says she has received death threats while serving on the board of Catholics for Free Choice) to the downright absurd. She recalls with delight the time she trumped an opponent in the picket lines by bringing up her 1960 Knights of Columbus Medal for superior knowledge of Christian doctrine—an episode that crops up in the book in slightly altered form. "I put that stuff about the protesters in there for fun, really. Anything erotic brings all kinds of worms out of the woodwork, and I wanted to look at those worms in a way that put them in their place. Maybe they really *are* just creeps from your high school."

"For fun" is a phrase Gordon uses often in discussing the book. The subtitle, *A Utopian Divertimento,* signals straight off that this isn't quite like Gordon's previous fiction—lyrical, often grave, focused on claustrophobic family entanglements and the special traps and consolations they hold for women. In *Spending,* the mordant wit and maverick feminist sensibility that have often flashed from beneath the surface of her work rise to the top, giving the book a lighter, faster, almost effervescent feeling, without undercutting the seriousness of the questions it raises about art, money, morality and, as Monica puts it, "this thing of being a man and a woman." Monica tells the story in a sharp, salty first-person voice, as though whispering in the reader's ear a running commentary on the improbable movie of her own life. "I took money from a man," Monica admits to herself. "But at least it had nothing to do with cooking."

Gordon lets her husband, Arthur Cash, an English professor at SUNY-New Paltz with whom she has two teenage children, serve the pre-interview tea. While just as much a longtime feminist stalwart as Monica, Gordon describes herself as "more of a good girl," and far more "guilt-ridden." And she admits to worrying about how readers will react to the novel's window-steaming middle-aged sex. "I loved writing it. But I'm a little bit concerned that people will think, 'Why did she do this? This isn't who she is,' or that they'll think I did it just to be different, to be more popular. A lot of people would be glad if I wrote *Final Payments, Part 13*"—an allusion to her first novel, published in 1978—"but I've always been interested in doing new things. I'd never done comedy."

Spending began as something of a lark. In 1995, Gordon's longtime British publisher, Liz Calder of Bloomsbury, suggested she write a serious erotic novella like Mary Flanagan's *Adèle* or Madeleine Bourdouxhe's *Marie*, both published by Bloomsbury last year. "It was like a cartoon lightbulb went off over my head," Gordon recalls. "Immediately, I said I'd like to write about the male muse. It started as a novella and just got longer and longer. For a long time, I'd been obsessed with how many women die in fiction. As a really radical act, I wanted to do a book about a woman who has sex and nobody dies."

Not only does Monica not die, but, after a few twists and turns of the plot, she lives happily—rich, famous, supremely sexually satisfied—if not necessarily ever after. "And why not?" Gordon says. "It's not like I have them riding off into the sunset. But I did want things to turn out well for her. I speak to a lot of women who are very superstitious about having personal happiness and having happiness in their work. I don't think men are even afraid of asking for both. But for women, it's almost like one of Virginia Woolf's ghosts that has to be put down."

On the surface, Gordon herself seems to have had something of a charmed literary life—wide acclaim and financial success at age 29 with *Final Payments*, seven other well-received books, the teaching job at Barnard, 22 years with the same agent (Peter Matson at Sterling Lord). But she hasn't been without her own ghosts to lay to rest. Gordon's previous book. *The Shadow Man* (her last with Viking before her editor, Nan Graham, went to Scribner) was an unblinking meditation on the troubling double life of her adored father, David Gordon, who died when she was seven. In Gordon's memory, her father was the brilliant, passionate, larger-than life figure who set her on the path to becoming a writer—teaching her to read at age three, making her memorize the Latin mass at five, inscribing translations from Virgil in the margins of books he bought for her to read when she was older. But in her near-forensic investigation, she forces herself to fully confront some of the other things he was: a Jewish convert who became an archconservative Catholic and outspoken anti-Semite; a published writer of devotional poetry who had spent his young adulthood not knocking around Harvard and Paris, as he claimed, but editing a girlie magazine called *Hot Dog;* an immigrant high-school dropout whose own Mid-western family seemed to have disappeared virtually without a trace.

It was a deliberately extreme book, written with a near-operatic blend of passion and horror that shades off into a kind of pitch-black humor in her concluding account of quite literally exhuming and reburying her father. It was also, Gordon emphasizes, a tremendous technical gamble. "Emotionally, it was very difficult. I didn't have the screens that fiction gives you to protect yourself, so I was very vulnerable to the material. And because I was dealing with so much factual material, it was a huge challenge to organize it in a way that was artful."

While she views *Spending* as something of a stepping back from the intensity of her last book ("If there were a mathematical equation for it," she says, "*Spending* would be *The Shadow Man* minus X"), she still feels she's put herself on the line. "To write this I had to give up my sense of being the good girl, the kind of person where everyone says, 'Oh, she's the serious literary person, the real moral center.' And I realized I really was very afraid of not being taken seriously, which is always the risk of not being a good girl."

For all its fairy-tale trappings, *Spending* is a richly nuanced portrait of the feminist artist at 50—classically minded on aesthetic questions but determined to give the old forms subversive contemporary twists. Monica's political and artistic concerns—along with her tastes in painting—are clearly Gordon's own. "Feminism is very dear to my heart," she says, and the relationship of the female artist to the male masters, whatever the medium, is something she's been thinking about for a long time. "Most of the great public work has been done by men, and you can't pretend it hasn't been. But as a woman your experience is different. How do you take from them what you have in common—love of form, beauty, artifice, truth—without being oppressed by their distortions? In a way, that's what you do with parents. At a certain point as an adult you say, what did they give me? And you can't do this unless as a younger person you had some kind of rebellion."

For Gordon, who grew up just outside New York City in a predominantly Catholic working-class town, one form of revolt came during her student days at Barnard in the late 1960s. "It was wild," she recalls. "The Columbia riots were my freshman year, the Cambodia invasion happened my junior year, Kate Millet was in the English department. It was a time of great promise, but very crazy. I was very excited by it all—we really thought we could change the world. I was a working-class person, so I couldn't take the risk of actually getting arrested—I really came too close to not being able to go to college in the first place." She pauses. "Plus I didn't have the courage. But I was certainly very involved in the marches."

Gordon will return to that period with her next novel, about a mother who was a hippie activist in the 1960s and her relationship with her daughter. Like all her other books, this one is being written with the old-fashioned notebook and fountain pen to which Gordon admits being "fetishistically" attached. "To me, the true porn shops are stationery stores. I go in and my heart starts to race!"

While Gordon has kept faith with the political idealism of her college years, she harbors no illusion that art itself can change the world. "Unfortunately, there is only one morality in art," she says, "and that is not to fulfill the form in a way that is unworthy of the form, not to write sloppily, not to give up until what you need to write is saturated with your attention and effort. And then you just have to say to yourself, 'I'm a person who's moved by the beautiful rather than the good.' I may not love that about myself, but that's the way I am."

JENNIFER SCHUESSLER
March 9, 1998

SUE GRAFTON

In *The Maltese Falcon,* Sam Spade, the original hard-boiled detective, tells the story of a real estate agent named Flitcraft who passes a construction site one day and is nearly killed by a falling beam. Overwhelmed by the random violence of everyday life, Flitcraft abandons his wife, his children, his job—his whole orderly, prefab identity—and never looks back.

The Flitcraft principle—that no one, not even a flinty private-eye like Spade, can impose order on a universe governed by blind chance—has preoccupied crime writers ever since, not least of them Sue Grafton, whose own hard-boiled female sleuth, Kinsey Millhone, could pass for Spade's brainy, irreverent step-daughter. "All of us run the risk of dropping dead at any moment of the day," Grafton tells a journalist one recent afternoon in the writing studio of her sprawling Spanish revival home in Montecito, Calif. "How do we know that lightning won't strike or the mudslide won't come down the hill or the truck crash into us on the highway? A plane could crash through this roof and kill us as we speak."

Lest a visitor worry that a conversation with Grafton is all existentialist *Sturm und Drang,* a pixieish smile plays across her face as she ponders the macabre possibilities. She needn't look far. Within arm's reach are volumes on fingerprinting and gunshot wounds, and a complete set of her own blockbuster alphabetical mystery series, from the latest installment, *N Is for Noose* (Holt) to the first, *A Is for Alibi,* which Holt published in 1982.

That landmark novel channeled all the inchoate rage of Grafton's custody battles with a second husband and her stagnant career writing Hollywood teleplays into the travails of a sassy, twice-divorced P.I. cruising the mean streets of Santa Teresa, Calif., in a battered VW Bug. In *Alibi's* final scene—as cold-blooded a metaphor for female empowerment as anyone might wish—Millhone emerges from a garbage can and blows away a treacherous paramour. "I had read the books in which the *femme fatale* turns out to be the wicked one and gets drawn and quartered," Grafton says, with a Louisville twang. "I was taking a very traditional male fantasy and flipping it."

Grafton has been mowing down *noir* stereotypes of women ever since. In subsequent books, alongside Marcia Muller and Sarah Paretsky, Grafton helped reinvent the hard-boiled mystery for a mass audience of female readers—an audience bored by the homilies of romantic suspense that constituted perhaps the largest, book-buying segment of American consumer society.

And Grafton has been rewarded lavishly for her efforts, as becomes clear when the author ushers us across her four-and-a-half-acre estate. Still glistening from an afternoon shower are a croquet court, putting green and a garden bursting with so many artichokes, persimmons, and California poppies that Grafton herself doesn't quite seem to know what to do with it all. Last month, the kiwi trees yielded close to 1000 kiwis which she gave to the yardsmen. "I don't even eat kiwis," she says.

If Grafton occasionally leaves the impression that she has tumbled down a rabbit hole only to find reality turned upside-down (on the hard drive of her computer is a Sue Grafton dossier compiled by Millhone; and Grafton admits that the fictional town of Santa Teresa, based on neighboring Santa Barbara, "has a vividness to me that the real town sometimes fails to exhibit"), the vast popularity of her books nevertheless owes a good deal to the indelible realism of her straight-talking and straight-shooting heroine. The author often receives letters announcing the birth of babies named Kinsey, and Holt recently published *G is for Grafton,* a guide to the fictional universe of Kinsey Millhone as obsessive as any volume of Sherlock Holmesiana. "I resent the fact that she has a biographer," says Grafton. "Nobody's come along to write the story of my life."

Given her unusual road to success, a biographer may well be waiting by the phone. Grafton projects a cool professionalism in discussing the business of writing—clearly the by-product of decades spent honing her craft in the shadows of commercial obscurity. "She's covered all the bases," says Holt publisher Michael Naumann. "She's not just a creative writer but someone who could run a publishing house herself."

The granddaughter of Presbyterian missionaries, and the daughter of a Louisville municipal bond attorney, C.W. Grafton, who wrote detective novels in his spare time, Grafton was left largely to her own devices as a child by parents whom she describes as "alcoholics of a very genteel sort." Encouraged, nevertheless, to read widely, she obtained a B.A. from the University of Louisville in 1961, laying claim to voracious, if sometimes indiscriminate, reading habits. Regency romance novels and detective fiction helped sustain her through her first two marriages, before a fiction contest led to a contract with Macmillan to publish her first novel, *Kezia Dane*, in 1967. A second novel, *The Lolly-Madonna War*, appeared in England from Peter Owen in 1969.

Neither book was crime fiction, and the money wasn't good, but things soon began to break Grafton's way. Even as her second marriage unraveled, her second novel was optioned by Metro-Goldwyn-Mayer. "I left the marriage, took the cat and the three kids and went to Hollywood and lived with a film producer for three years," she recalls. Thus began a tumultuous stint in Tinseltown, as Grafton accepted virtually every screenwriting job that came her way, scripting an episode of *Rhoda*, a slew of movies for network TV and a series of Agatha Christie adaptations co-written with her present husband, Steve Humphries, who holds a Ph.D. in physics.

"I loved the education of it," Grafton says of her screenwriting stint. "There's nothing like a film script to teach you structure, which is what the mystery is about. What I hated about Hollywood was doing business. I hated the democratic process where everybody got a vote. I am not a team player. I was not a good sport. I spent a lot of that time trying to suppress a natural rage that came billowing out when people tried to tell me how to do my work." Grafton has adamantly refused to sell her books to Hollywood, and it's clear that her experience there still rankles. "Kinsey Millhone was my tiny pickax whereby I got out of prison," she says. "And I would be a fool to sell her back to them."

By 1977, in the midst of a custody battle, Grafton found herself at a personal and professional crossroads. Then suddenly, as if brushed back by a falling beam, she began plotting her escape. "I finally said to myself, 'Darling, nobody's holding a gun to your head,'" she recalls.

Borrowing a plot device from Edward Gorey's *Gashleycrumb Tinies* ("A is for Amy who fell down the stairs . . ."), and a fictional setting—Santa Teresa—invented by Ross MacDonald, Grafton set out to create a mystery series in the gritty tradition of Chandler, Hammet and Spillane, centered on a private-eye with whom she could truly identify. "I think certainly the whole issue of homicide was an easy way to funnel a lot of rage and a lot of frustration. At that point I didn't know how to fight. I thought it was enough to be a nice girl. Now I know how to fight and now I have the money to fight if anybody wants to take me on. In those days I was ill-equipped and so fantasy was the great equalizer." That Grafton would change the face—or at least the gender—of crime fiction in the process couldn't have seemed more remote. "I didn't know anything about private investigators, police procedure or forensics. I was learning everything as fast as I could. So I thought, I'm going to make her female because at least that's my area of expertise.

"Later, to hear people refer to me as a pioneer just sounds so silly. I think pioneers are people who know the Indians are out there and they're crossing the mountains anyway. I didn't know the Indians were out there. I didn't know there weren't cities on the other side of the mountains. To back into something out of ignorance hardly makes someone a pioneer."

Still, it's hard not to be reminded of Grafton's contribution to the genre, pioneering or not, when reading *N Is for Noose*. In that novel, Millhone is hired by the distraught widow of a police detective and is asked to find out what was troubling him before he died. To do so, Millhone must infiltrate the old boy's club that is the local sheriff's department. Along the way, she unearths family secrets her employer would much rather have left buried. "I was interested in a marriage in which there was a failure to communicate so that his widow is left wondering who this man is," explains Grafton. "I like the irony of the fact that because she pushed, because she couldn't trust her husband's affections for her, she in fact opened Pandora's box."

The 1 million-copy first printing Holt has announced for the book—the largest in the company's history—may prove a different sort of Pandora's box. Grafton's last three novels, *M Is for Malice, L Is for Lawless* and *K Is for Killer,* sold in the 500,000-copy range in hardcover, up from roughly 300,000 hardcover sales for *J Is for Judgment*. There are close to 10 million copies of her books in print, and she's been translated into 26 languages, outselling even such titans of crime writing as Dick Francis and Robert Parker. But has she reached a ceiling of hardcover sales that a house like Holt, which will publish just 301 titles in 1998 (as compared to the 4000-odd annual titles of the newly incorporated Random, Inc.), doesn't have the power to shatter? Marlon Wood, who has been Grafton's editor since acquiring *A Is for Alibi* based on a 65-page manuscript, doesn't believe so. "I do think we can push her further," says Wood, who sees Grafton's hardcover performance, not the mass market business from Fawcett, as the force that drives the Grafton franchise. "The tail isn't wagging the dog any more," says Wood. "You are no longer expecting to go out small with a hard-cover assuming that the paperback will bring the market to you. The hardcover has to establish the writer now and the paperback reaps the rewards."

Without question, the hothouse flowers on Holt's generally up-market list couldn't flourish without the perennial support of a staple like Grafton. "It certainly is a major source of our company's income," Naumann says of the series. "But that is always true, whether it's Sue Grafton or Koonts or Grisham. Without big books, we couldn't publish smaller books. The truth is, when Sue Grafton started out, there were other big books that supported her."

As Grafton plots out Millhone's 15th adventure, it's clear that the rage that propelled her first mystery novels has softened. She now has two grandchildren (one named Kinsey), and keeps to a routine as idyllic and quirky as any writer could hope for, rising promptly, she says, at 5:58 a.m. to walk on the beach for three miles before repairing to her office at 9 o'clock to begin the day's writing. "I don't wear pantyhose and heels, but I treat this as a job and I wear makeup. I don't work in my pajamas."

Grafton receives piles of letters from zealous readers and is attentive to their concerns, within limits. "I get chided a lot for coarse language. But I have met some scuzz bags in this world who cuss like sailors. I actually tone it down, but they still come after me for that, I say 'Fuck 'em.' "

Millhone, who has aged one year every two-and-a-half books, has been slow to catch up with the changes in her creator's life. At the present rate, Millhone will be 40 years old when Grafton reaches what she says will be *Z Is for Zero* sometime around 2015. This has created a wholly unintentional gulf between their worlds that Grafton may erase by fast-forwarding 10 years without aging her characters. "But I will have to announce it because my readers, like most mystery readers, are very detail-oriented," Grafton says with a roll of the eyes," and they get very upset if I make a mistake."

JONATHAN BING
April 20, 1998

DONALD HALL

Eagle pond farm is familiar to even the casual reader of Donald Hall. The weather-beaten spread, hard by Route 4 at the foot of Ragged Mountain in Wilmot, N.H., has been home to Hall's maternal clan since 1865. It is the subject or setting of many of his poems and essays, providing a consistent reference point for more than 40 years of work. It is the place where Hall spent summers growing up, returning for good in 1975 after remarrying and giving up tenure at the University of Michigan to write full-time. And it is the house where his wife, the poet Jane Kenyon, died in 1995.

In *Without* (Houghton Mifflin) Hall records the unbearable facts of a present he and Kenyon were powerless to alter. A slow-motion portrait of Kenyon's descent into the horrors of aggressive treatment following her leukemia diagnosis in 1994 at the age of 46, the collection continues without recoil through to her last days, spent choosing the poems for Kenyon's *Otherwise: New & Selected Poems* (Graywolf), and her final minutes. A second section addresses Kenyon directly, after her death. With their deliberate cadences, the poems seem written from a place beyond solace or anguish, a contracted world that leaves Hall bereft, with no relief, but still insisting on trying to say what has happened.

Readers will of course be tempted to draw parallels between Hall's book and Ted Hughes's bestselling *Birthday Letters*, whose publication made front-page news: both men were married to poets whose work was often highly personal and who were beset by depression and mania, and both collections address the poet's departed spouse in verse. While the real-life likenesses end there, *Without* is already generating the kind of attention unthinkable for many books of poetry. The book has a first printing of 10,000 copies (perhaps five times the usual); Hall has recently been profiled in *Mirabella* and for National Public Radio; more media attention is sure to follow. While some of the reception is obviously due to a master poet who has written a culminating work, it raises questions about what it takes for a book of poems to penetrate the national consciousness.

In *Without*, Hall is forced to fight it out with a career's worth of demons: death, family, sex and how to proceed in a life that offers no guarantee of value or redemption. The struggle is made still more poignant by the fact that no one expected Hall to be alive to tell of it. Hall had written about his own illness a few short years before in books like the *Museum of Clear Ideas* (HM) and *Life Work* (Beacon), both published in 1993, speaking plainly of his colon cancer and the metastasis that took more than half of his liver. An Emmy Award-winning Bill Moyers special, *A Life Together,* found Hall and Kenyon resolved to make the most of their time together at Eagle Pond, as the threat of recurrence loomed. But with Kenyon's diagnosis, *The Old Life,* as Hall called the book of poems he published the year of her death, was over.

That Hall has remained at Eagle Pond Farm, where Kenyon "led the way back" after their marriage, seems fitting at the very least. On a gray February morning, *PW* is met at the kitchen door by Hall, and by Gus, the long-haired "dear mongrel" who makes appearances in Kenyon's poems and, more frequently now, in Hall's. Almost immediately, Hall ushers us into his study, closing the door to reveal the wall of photos of Kenyon he writes of as "The Gallery" in *Without*.

"That's the woman I married," Hall says of a young, slightly awkward Kenyon hidden behind thick framed glasses. "And that's the beauty she became," he says, gesturing to Kenyon "foxy/ and beautiful at 45," with tresses of dark hair offset with silver framing her strong features and even gaze.

Hall's own appearance has changed dramatically from the man of the Moyers special, reading tours and book jackets. Wisps of thinned red hair reach his shoulders, and a nearly gray beard spreads densely across much of his face. Hall is also rather tall; the net effect is authoritative, if not imposing. As he moves to sit in a chair by a window facing the road, waving us to a couch across the room, it's difficult not to feel a little daunted. But Hall quickly makes one feel at ease, talking with what one recognizes as characteristic frankness about his prolific and esteemed career.

That career now includes 13 books of poems and what Hall calls the work that "supports my poetry habit": essay collections, textbooks, profiles of poets and artists, children's books and short stories.

Hall's 1955 poetic debut at age 27, *Exiles and Marriages* (having himself married three years earlier), was such a success that he had trouble living it down. Part formalist send-up of bourgeois dalliance and divorce and part grave T.S. Eliot-influenced metaphysical inquiry, the book captured the literary zeitgeist of the period Robert Lowell called "the tranquilized fifties" perhaps too well. A glowing *Time* magazine review—rare even then for poetry—ran along with a photo of Hall as a serious young Harvard graduate (his colleagues on the *Advocate* included John Ashbery, Kenneth Koch and Robert Bly, who remains his best friend), one who would go on to win the Lamont poetry prize for his first outing. Hall, now 69, chuckles over his younger self's precocity. "I remember the man who wrote those poems, and in the immortal words of Richard Nixon, 'I peaked too soon.' I began to do better work later on," such as *A Roof of Tiger Lilies* (1964), "that wasn't noticed."

If that initial burst of fame tapered off after a while, it was enough to fuel a transition to a successful academic career. Having picked up a second bachelor's at Oxford and spent time as one of Harvard's Society of Fellows, Hall settled at the University of Michigan at Ann Arbor in 1957. He had two children with his first wife, and went on to publish and edit widely during the ensuing two decades. The marriage ended in 1969, and Hall entered what he has called "a bad patch of mid-life." When he met Kenyon in Ann Arbor, she was 22 and he 42; they married two years later. The impetus to move to Eagle Pond, inhabited by the family ghosts that populate Hall's work, came from Kenyon. The two were to devote themselves to writing, with Hall embarking on a freelance career that continues to this day. Hall's textbook, *Writing Well* (now in its ninth edition, with Addison Wesley Longman), was selling briskly, which "made it possible to think about coming here" in 1975.

Kicking the Leaves vaulted Hall back into prominence in 1978, going on to sell nearly 100,000 copies over the years. Many of its poems reappeared in *Old & New Poems* (Ticknor & Fields, 1990). "The standard sentence in the reviews of that book," Hall quips, "is that Hall has been around a long time and published a lot of books, but it wasn't until he quit teaching and moved to the New Hampshire house with his second wife, the poet Jane Kenyon, that he began to get good." Hall begs to differ somewhat but allows the pundits a measure of truth. "I felt a little aggrieved for some of my old poems, but if my work got better while I was here, I think it was partly because I was watching Janie, with tremendous stubbornness and hard work, get better and better."

Kenyon had just published her third book (exclusive of her translations of Anna Akhmatova), *Let Evening Come*, to warm reviews, and the two began to read together more frequently. Hall had already found further critical success with *The Happy Man* (1986) and *The One Day* (1988). The latter, a long poem in four parts that was 17 years in the making, won the NBCC Award for poetry and was a Pulitzer nominee. The book also, along with a collection of naturalist essays called *Seasons at Eagle Pond*, inaugurated Hall's long relationship with Houghton Mifflin, its (now defunct) imprint Ticknor & Fields and editor Peter Davison.

Hall remembers these times as some of the couple's happiest. "Jane's reputation had finally caught up with her poetry. And we went out and read together, and we lived in this house, and got up early, and worked. We had to make boundaries in order to live together and do the same thing, but we did, and it was just magnificent." Kenyon's *Constance* came out in 1993, along with Hall's *Museum of Clear Ideas* and *Life Work*. After Hall's illness, the couple went out on a joint book tour and also traveled to India for a second time.

They did their last reading together in January 1994, at Bennington. "We came back here, and she began to have flu symptoms. And I flew down to Charleston to do a reading and a lecture, two nights gone." After missing a connection on the way back, "I called and asked how she was doing. She told me about this terrible nose bleed, and how she had gone to the hospital to have it stopped, and that they were doing blood work. She was more upset, though, about the car's not starting and having to get it towed. This is hard to believe," Hall says, visibly agitated and upset, "but as I stood there, I thought 'Jane has leukemia.'" He pauses again, apologetically: "I can't stop telling this story."

Hall began drafting *Without* during Kenyon's treatment. "I nursed Jane here and at the hospitals, but there was a lot of other time to fill, and the most absorbing thing I could do was write. She often couldn't, but she was glad somebody could." As they had done during Hall's illness, the couple resolved to take things exactly as they came. "Jane and I were not deniers, we were proclaimers. We were not cheerful with one another. Writing about this is what I would have expected from us, and Jane did, too."

After Kenyon's death, Hall stayed at Eagle Pond, drafting and re-drafting—often up to 200 times—the poems that would become *Without*. Slowly, he began to send them to friends and to read them in public. "People came up to me and spoke as if I had been brave to read these poems aloud. I don't feel brave. Talking of grief, talking of suffering, is something I seem to need to do. For some people, that's not their way. But to bring it to someone else, I think, relieves me," Seeing *Otherwise* through to press was also a comfort.

Asked if he thinks that the circumstances of Kenyon's death have anything to do with her increased posthumous fame, Hall concurs; "Her fame is infinitely greater since her death, but she was aware that people were talking about her more and more, and reading her more, before she even got sick, so I don't feel too badly about that. She knew that people were beginning to find her." If *Without* gets more people to discover Kenyon's work, Hall will be all the more pleased. "She'd kick my ass if she thought I was promoting her at all before."

The idea of a glimpse into the raw stuff of a writing life shared—and, in different ways, cut tragically short—between two accomplished poets may be the main attraction for readers of both Hughes's *Birthday Letters* and Hall's *Without*. In the latter's case, the book will almost certainly be taken up, as Hall notes, "as a companion to the grief of others." But, he continues, "Art is what gets it from here to there." Just as any work must put up or shut up, it is the poems themselves that will hold readers to *Without*. "I may have failed in what I attempted to do, but a poem is not a poem unless it is a work of art. It may begin with a scream of pain, but you make that into a work of art or you have utterly failed."

Since completing *Without*, Hall has not sent out any new poems to magazines, although he has been writing, and is "not ready to think about" his next collection. He will do a stint "teaching literature to poets" at New York University after a 10-city reading tour, where he will read Kenyon's work as well as his own. "Before, she wouldn't let me, but I'm reading her because I want to be with her. And I think that everything I write for the rest of my life will be affected by Jane, by the loss of her and her poetry. I'm surrounded by her. She's here."

MICHAEL SCHARF
March 23, 1998

JANE HAMILTON

A YOUNG MAN COMING of age in suburban Illinois in the 1970s, obsessed with ballet, literature and classical music, aware that he's gay but determined to remain closeted. The protagonist of a novel by David Leavitt, Alan Gurganus or Dale Peck? Not this time. While these gay male writers would seem to own the territory, it's a female novelist praised for her depiction of women who has dared to trespass in an area generally reserved for men who have lived the experience.

A Short History of a Prince, Jane Hamilton's third novel (Random House) isn't the first time this author, who claims apologetically to have had "a very ordinary life," has so effectively imagined herself into the mind of a character thrown to its fringes. Interviewed during a recent visit from her Wisconsin home to her publisher's Manhattan offices, Hamilton declares a spiritual kinship with the troubled central characters of her three novels: Ruth, the emotionally abused but brave and resilient protagonist of *The Book of Ruth* (1988), whose dreams of domesticity vanish in an eruption of violence; Alice, the restless, self-destructive heroine of *A Map of the World* (1994), who is responsible for the death of a child and spends time in jail falsely accused of sexual abuse; and, now, dreamy, aesthetic Walter, whose lonely, unfulfilled life is defined by the secret he dares not share. "I spent my entire youth being in love with gay men because they were the most interesting and compassionate people I knew," Hamilton says. "For me, writing Walter didn't feel like a stretch."

In *The Short History of a Prince,* teenager Walter McCloud's passion for ballet is not sanctified by talent. Despite his artistic aspirations and his absorption in classical technique, he is awkward and ungainly. His desire to dance the role of Prince Siegfried in a production of *The Nutcracker* is granted in an ironic manner that shames him, and this dark fulfillment is followed by the crucifying

94

experience of his life, when he's discovered wearing a ballerina's tutu and is sadistically humiliated by the ballet master and mocked by the young man he loves.

Though Hamilton herself was never publicly embarrassed, she keenly remembers her own adolescent despair at failing to become a graceful dancer. "My legs were big; my derriere was big; I had no turnout; my feet were flat—but still I really loved it," she recalls. "What I bring to the character of Walter is my experience of dancing and of being the worst in the class. Probably most people feel that way some of the time, but I internalized the feeling. I felt I was out of the mainstream."

Inspiration came from another source as well. The character of Walter McCloud is also based on her dearest friend in high school, to whom the book is dedicated. The inscription reads: "For JMW—for Boonkie." According to Hamilton, Boonkie is "the spiritual twin" to Walter. "In some ways, Walter is the marriage of this friend and myself. I wanted the word 'prince' in the title because Walter is a prince in every way." She thinks that the characters in her previous books were "only warm-ups" for Walter, that his quiet suffering and endurance is faithful to the longings and insecurities of outsiders in society who take refuge in the spiritual solace of literature, dance and music.

Hamilton herself projects nothing but prairie wholesomeness to jaded New York eyes. She is sturdily unpretentious, with none of the professional glamour that bestselling authors generally radiate. It's not just her well-scrubbed, makeup-free complexion, her hair yanked back and anchored with an elastic band, or her comfortable outfit of baggy sweater and tights. She has a strong jaw, a clear and level gaze and a modest and candid way of talking about her problems with the creative process.

Moving in 1982 to the small rural community of Rochester, Wisc., population 1000, was a crystallizing experience of social alienation for Hamilton, "I felt I was an anthropologist in a foreign country," she says. Born in 1957, she had been raised in suburban Oak Park, Ill., the youngest of five siblings in a close-knit home where reading was a cherished pastime and writing a given. Her mother composed poetry; a verse in Jane's honor called "A Song for a Fifth Child" was published in the *Ladies' Home Journal.* Her grandmother wrote for a feminist newspaper and tried her hand at novels. "I just assumed that if you were a girl-child you were supposed to grow up and write," she says.

Whatever her ambitions, they went underground when she graduated from Carleton College in Minnesota in 1979, and impulsively stopped off on the way to New York (and the vague offer of a job in publishing) to visit a friend who was working on a farm for the summer. "They needed help; it was picking season. So I stayed a week, then I stayed two weeks, a month. I fell in love with my friend's cousin, Bob Willard, and I married him. It took me about 10 years to think I could belong there. And maybe another four years to think I wanted to belong there." Having children, a boy and a girl now 13 and 10, contributed to her acceptance in the tight-knit community. The crucial factor was her service as president of the board of the public library, a labor of love she calls "a lifesaver."

Looking back, Hamilton says she's grateful for the detour. Her applications to graduate schools had been rejected; "I felt bad about that, but I knew that I wasn't ready for a high-powered graduate program. Ultimately, it was good for me to be in this tiny town where the book review didn't come. I was in my own little fog trying to figure out the forms for myself. I wrote, but I didn't know what I had to say yet. So it was serendipitous that I ended up in the middle of nowhere."

Except for the four months of intense activity during apple-picking season, Hamilton had a lot of free time in which to try her hand at short fiction. "I spent basically three years writing one story," she says with a rueful laugh. Eventually she sold it to *Harper's*. She won "a few" Wisconsin Art Board grants and an NEA grant. But she was still searching for her subject.

The inspiration came from an event that rocked Wisconsin's rural communities: in a nearby town, a man murdered his mother-in-law. Hamilton recalls feeling immediate empathy for the murderer's wife. She herself was living in a very small house with her husband and his aged aunt. "Even though I loved these new relations of mine, I could understand how a situation could get out of hand. I was young, I was frustrated. I needed my own territory and I didn't know how I was going to get it. And so I took my frustrations and plugged them into someone entirely different from me. I wanted to see if I could slip into someone else's skin."

What she found was a strange emotional bond with her inadequately educated, culturally deprived and miserably poor heroine. "*The Book of Ruth* is fueled by Ruth's voice because I felt possessed by Ruth," Hamilton says. It was not easy to sell such a downbeat slice of life. The agent Hamilton had used for her short stories was not interested in the novel. When a friend gave her a list of agents, Hamilton dutifully worked through the alphabet, sending out the manuscript and receiving rejection letters in return. "Finally I was at the end of the alphabet. The last name was Amanda Urban." With no idea of Urban's clout in the industry, Hamilton made her "last stab. She called me within a week and said, 'Who are you?' She sold it in another week," Hamilton reports.

Katrina Kenison at Ticknor & Fields bought *The Book of Ruth.* Reviews were good, and Hamilton didn't care that sales were modest. Before *Ruth* won the PEN/Hemingway Foundation Award in 1989, Martha Levin at Doubleday/Anchor bought the paperback rights for a "really small sum, maybe $2000," Hamilton says with no discernible regret.

The favorable critical reception and the prestigious prize, in fact, threw Hamilton into the proverbial second book slump. She was "paralyzed," she says, by the thought that she'd now have to produce a book every two years. But as the self-imposed deadline came and went, she was relieved to find that she was again "writing a book just for myself." She began what became *A Map of the World* after a child in her son's day-care center drowned in his family's swimming pool. The initial chapters, which express the almost palpable anguish of the heroine, who is responsible for the death of her best friend's daughter, were surprisingly easy to write. Problems arose when she couldn't figure out how the story would proceed after that crucial scene. Feeling adrift, she wrote three versions of the novel, each with a different middle and ending. "Those books were terrible, just terrible!" she groans.

Meanwhile, Hamilton had been impressed by a documentary about a couple who were falsely convicted of sexually molesting children in a day-care center. A short time later, she herself was angrily confronted by her best friend for letting their two small daughters take off their clothes on a hot summer day. Accused of unnatural behavior for something she considered perfectly normal, Hamilton was undone. "I didn't want to write another trendy novel about sexual molestation," she says, but the subject seemed inescapable.

Placing the book was not a sure thing. Kenison had left Ticknor & Fields, and the imprint was soon to fold. According to Hamilton, Binky Urban again found the editor with the appropriate sensibility—Deb Futter at Doubleday. (Hamilton followed Futter, whom she calls her "soul mate," when she later went to Random House.)

Even before Futter saw *A Map of the World,* however, Hamilton had the help of another kind of editor: Steven Shahan, a lawyer in upstate New York who is married to Elizabeth Weinstein, Hamilton's college roommate, and still the first reader of her work. (*A Map of the World* is dedicated to both of them.) Shahan led Hamilton through the legal process of a trial. He was "absolutely indispensable," she says.

Critics remarked on the stunningly accurate portrayal of Alice's cell mates, most of them black and victimized by life. Though quite different in their histories, the women share an admiration of Oprah Winfrey. Hamilton had never seen the show when, in 1988, one of the producers called and invited her to lunch as a surprise for Oprah, who had loved *The Book of Ruth.* At that time, Oprah was not yet established as a messianic force in the publishing world, and Hamilton was amazed that Oprah quoted lines from the book from memory.

Several years later, when Oprah announced the formation of her TV book club, *The Book of Ruth* was her third choice. Immediately, sales of the paperback edition, which had been selling well (to the tune of 75,000 copies), soared; the current net figure is well over a million. Given the often finicky market for midlist fiction, Hamilton says, "Oprah does what God couldn't do."

The reference to the deity is only half jocular. Like all of her protagonists, who search for meaning in a world seemingly devoid of solace, Hamilton has only a marginal adherence to conventional Christian faith. "I've always broken out in hives when I go into any organized religious situation," she says. All three of her protagonists find that biblical injunctions mock the truth of their lives, and yet each of them arrives at a moment of understanding. Transcendence comes to Walter just when he is about to lose his family's three-generational homestead, the one element that's "essential to his having any faith at all in life," Hamilton says.

"I think of my characters being extremely Christian in the way they lead their lives," she adds. "Maybe my books have a lot of religious grappling because I'm still trying to figure it out for myself."

Having experienced the disapproval of some of Rochester's

churchgoing ladies over *The Book of Ruth,* she is bracing herself for another negative reaction, this time for placing a gay hero in a town very much like Rochester. Yet she feels she is a writer with a mission: "I want to express something important here. I really love Walter and I want other people to love him, too. He has a special place in my heart."

SYBIL STEINBERG
February 2, 1998

ROBERT HUGHES

"Television is very educational," Groucho Marx once quipped. "Every time someone switches it on, I go into another room and read a book." For Robert Hughes, *Time* magazine's famously pugnacious longtime art critic and a man with no mean gift for the one-liner himself, the relationship between the box and the book, between low culture and high, cannot be so neatly expressed.

As a writer with a professional interest in the state of the visual world, he has often railed against "our moronic national babysitter," the "teat of electronic kitsch" that has replaced literature and the visual arts as our primary source of information. But Hughes is more than your average anti-television moralist. He's spent a good deal of time in the belly of the beast, making numerous documentaries about art for television stations in America, Britain and his native Australia. *The Shock of the New,* his eight-hour blockbuster about modernism that aired in 1980, was a runaway success. The book version, published by Knopf the following year, sold nearly 54,000 copies in its original cloth edition: the 1992 paperback edition included Hughes's scathing postmortem on the art of the 1980s.

Now with *American Visions* (Knopf), the straight-shooting, streetwise critic who got his art education not dozing at slide lectures but touring Italy by motorcycle in the mid-'60s has set out to discover America. The television version, to be aired on PBS, is something of a road movie, documenting Hughes's travels (this time by convertible) to all corners of the republic to investigate, like some media-savvy de Tocqueville, a question as broad as Interstate 40: "What can we say about Americans from the things and images they have made?"

The lavishly illustrated volume that accompanies and greatly expands upon the TV series is neither a coffee-table trophy nor a dumbed-down account intended to flatter its subject or its audience. As usual, Hughes's adopted country (he retains his Australian citizenship) and some of its most beloved artists come in for some hard knocks.

"I'm quite sure I wouldn't have been able to broach this question of American visual culture without being a little outside it," Hughes tells an interviewer over lunch in a small French restaurant in New York's Soho district, a few blocks from the comfortable loft on one of the neighborhood's busiest corners where he lives with his wife of 16 years, Victoria. "There are certain American ideals I share," he says. "But I'm not an American, and I don't feel American. We Australians never had this idea of being a light unto the world, a beacon unto the nations. We were jailbirds, moral failures, put at the end of the earth for a reason."

Hughes, a hearty 58-year-old with an air of cultivated raffishness, seems to relish the statement. But he is not so much an outsider as an insider's outsider—a critic who lives in the heart of the art world but remains aloof from its cozy business practices and self-congratulatory politics, an establishment contrarian who is utterly at home in the sacred precincts of high culture but who can usually be counted on to say something a bit profane.

"I certainly don't think of myself as adopting the missionary position every time I go on TV," Hughes says between bites of pasta washed down with *rouge*. "Doing a project like this is not about providing some kind of ultimate scholarly experience. It's about providing decent and respectable and disinterested intellectual entertainment. Americans tend to think of it in terms of teaching, but there *is* such a thing as intellectual entertainment."

For Hughes, the didactic strain of American art and culture is a meandering but unbroken line going right back to the nation's earliest European settlers. "Even though the Puritans didn't produce much that was remarkable in the way of visual art, the very fact of their iconophobia had the most profound possible effect on the way Americans thought about images afterwards. They brought to America the idea of the radical new as a cultural value. They didn't believe in the avant-garde, but they did believe they'd make a new heaven and a new earth."

Born in Sydney in 1938, into a prominent family of lawyers and politicians, Hughes spent his childhood hunting, fishing and, especially, reading. He was educated by strapwielding Jesuits whose intellectual discipline Hughes—now a lapsed Catholic—relishes in retrospect. His was a "monocultural, classically colonial" upbringing, as he later wrote, which held that all beauty and wisdom emanated from Western Europe, and from England in particular.

Art in the Hughes household amounted to little more than family portraits: "a few patches of color on the walls," Hughes says he understands well the sort of "hunger in the eye" experienced by such 18th-century American painters as John Singleton Copley and Benjamin West, who had no access to formal instruction or even to decent art to look at. Things in Australia, however, weren't quite so dire. "There were pretty okay museums in Sydney, mostly of Australian art," Hughes recalls. "The museum of New South Wales had a decent collection of Pre-Raphaelites, which of course at the time I thought were absolute shit."

In his senior year of high school, a group of students was encouraged to see a special exhibition of modern European painting. "I remember going in there and laughing my head off at all this abstract crap, and being particularly amused by a painting of Joan Miró's, which would later belong to a friend of mine in New York. It was a square of burlap with the black numeral 49 on it, and then there was a wiggly, starlike thing like a daddy longlegs, and a couple of red blotches. I remember staring at it and thinking, 'This is ridiculous; this is preposterous; this is not art.' But then I asked myself, 'Well, then, what is art?' I think it all started there, to strip it down a lot."

Hughes entered Sydney University in 1956 and proceeded to flunk an art course that "even a moderately diligent amoeba could've passed. I wanted to run off to Paris and wear a beret and smoke Gauloises and paint pictures of naked women," he says, but his family persuaded him to accept the compromise of architecture school. Hughes, however, was more interested in painting (he had the first of his several shows in 1960) and journalism; he was soon contributing articles to Australian newspapers, eventually drifting toward art criticism. "Australia was the only place in the world where I could've gotten away with it," he says. "Everybody else was as ignorant as me."

When Allen Lane, the founder of Penguin Books, gave him "a fabulous advance of 300 pounds" to write a history of Australian art, Hughes dropped out of school, never to return. *The Art of Australia,* published in 1966, remains in print. He left for London in 1964 and after a brief stint there headed to Italy for a few self-imposed semesters of Madonna-hunting by motorcycle. He eventually returned to London, where he wrote for a number of papers, did his first art documentaries for the BBC and both enjoyed and suffered through the general craziness of the period. He also married an Australian (the couple eventually divorced) and produced a son, Danton.

In 1970, *Time* editor-in-chief Henry Grunwald hired Hughes as the magazine's art critic, a perch he has occupied ever since. Grunwald, who in his recent memoir described Hughes as "too elemental a force to tie down," gave him ample time off for outside projects. Perhaps the oddest twist in Hughes's career came in 1978, when he was chosen—along with former *Esquire* editor Howard Hayes—to anchor ABC's fledging newsmagazine *20/20*. The pair were fired after the disastrous first episode. But Hughes had already been paid for a year's services, and his "brief career as the news equivalent of the blonde with the envelope," as he once put it, gave him the means to concentrate on *The Shock of the New*.

It was in the decade following that volume's publication that Hughes hit his stride as the brilliantly destructive critic the times demanded, penning brutally funny assaults on the likes of Julian Schnabel, Jean-Michel Basquiat and Andy Warhol, as well as on the generally corrupting influence of the money flowing into the art market and museums from Wall Street's newly minted, would-be Medicis. (Most of Hughes's essays from *Time*, the *New Republic*, and the *New York Review*, were collected in *Nothing If Not Critical* in 1992.)

As the decade wore on, Hughes turned his attention to history proper. *The Fatal Shore*, a spellbinding account of the founding of Australia's origins as a penal colony, appeared in 1987. Nearly 10 years in the making, "Kangaroots," as he dubbed the book, showcased Hughes's considerable narrative gifts and became a bestseller. *Barcelona*, published in 1992, began as a study of his favorite city's art and architecture but grew into a study of Catalan nationalism. *The Fatal Shore*, like *The Shock of the New*, was edited by the London-based Charles Elliot for Knopf. Susan Ralston in New York joined Elliot as co-editor of *American Visions*. Lynn Nesbit is Hughes's agent.

The polemical Hughes returned in full force in 1993 with *The Culture of Complaint* (Oxford), a sharp one-two against the twin villains of political correctness on the left and "patriotic correctness" on the right. No less a bastion of fashionable artworld opinion than *Artforum* called it "a wonderful handheld-camera view of the dumb zones of American life"; most critics seemed to enjoy the tour more than they thought they should.

The delicious sound bites got the lion's share of the attention, but the book was just as much a defense of true cross-cultural encounters as a blast against the blinkered separatism that Hughes saw passing for multiculturalism in America. The book also contains the germ of a memoir of a Catholic boyhood in a then sleepy corner of the British empire; Hughes says he's thinking of writing the real thing when he gets a chance.

"Australia is a more properly functioning multicultural society than America," Hughes says. "On the whole, we're pretty damn tolerant. But then, we don't have a history of slavery to deal with. And we don't have that same fondness for really crazy apocalyptic religious notions."

Running through *American Visions* is a palpable impatience with the broad current of hazy spiritualism in American art, whether represented by the thunderously sublime landscapes of Albert Bierstadt or Barnett Newman's "utterly vacuous" minimalist canvases intended to evoke the stations of the cross. Hughes conveys a far greater sympathy for the equally broad tradition of artists who found, to borrow William Carlos William's phrase, "no ideas but in things": Audubon shooting hundreds of birds the better to observe their minutest features, or the sculptor David Smith wrestling new expressive possibilities from that most industrial of metals, steel.

Hughes—a self-confessed weekend "wood butcher" and an ardent fisherman (he frequently trolls the waters near his Long Island home with buddies Alexander Cockburn and Peter Matthiessen)—owns up to this, with qualifications. "I *do* like the romantic and spiritual side of art," he says, "just so long as excessive claims are not made for it. Barney Newman famously said that if people read his work properly, it would mean 'the end of all state capitalism and totalitarianism.' You've got to be a nitwit or a paranoid to believe that kind of stuff. Art is not to be judged by how much it changes manifest political action in the present, and it's not there to make us feel better about a bad world."

So what is it there for? As usual, Hughes doesn't miss a beat. "It's there to endow whatever falls under the artist's attention with a meaning that can be handed on to people looking at it. It's not an act of evangelism. It's an act of transmission and—oh, God, I hate this word—of *sharing*."

For all his continuing irritation at the political and artistic cant of our own time, Hughes today seems almost mellow, as though confident that art is long, and the careers of hucksters, phonies and even well intentioned mediocrities are short. "You've got to allow yourself the luxury once in a while of baring the old yellow fangs and digging them into some suitably pretentious antelope," he says with a cock-eyed grin. "But basically I'd rather write about my superiors."

JENNIFER SCHUESSLER
April 14, 1997

GARY INDIANA

THE CULTURAL FAULT lines of Los Angeles and the sensational legal battles that have transpired there—*California* v. *Simpson* being the latest—have spawned a glut of mostly nonfiction books about victims and defendants, lawyers, corrupt celebrities and the often tedious proceedings of the L.A. court system. *Resentment*, Gary Indiana's poisonously funny novel from Doubleday, the story of the media circus surrounding the Menendez-like trial of Carlos and Felix Martinez, two brothers who gunned down their parents in their Beverly Hills mansion, gives the theme of a city spellbound by a criminal trial a surprising new twist. In *Resentment*, the city itself is tried, convicted and sentenced to death.

Indiana's L.A. is a sun-bleached, traffic-congested panorama of casual mayhem and sleaze. Orbiting the Martinez trial are Seth, a freelance writer of middling talent who drunkenly runs down a pedestrian and flees the scene; Seth's erstwhile boyfriend Jack, a cab driver afflicted with AIDS; J.D., the host of an offbeat radio talk show; and a large cast of players and poseurs. Just when the glittering miasma of scandal and millennial malaise promises to give way to a courtroom verdict, Indiana levels the city with a massive earthquake.

"My tendency as a writer is to amplify the negative," says Indiana, tracing a horizontal paint stroke through the air with one of the Parliament cigarettes he chain smokes. "I wanted to show the kind of poison that would spread all through that society, the way something gets into the ground water and gets disseminated everywhere. The trial seemed like a perfect thing to me as a kind of toxin that everybody's attention would be focused on, probably at the expense of more important things. I wanted to show that there is a world outside of this microcosmic keyhole to which everybody's eye is pasted."

Slouched in a chair in the kitchen of a friend's apartment in lower Manhattan, Indiana leaves the impression that interviews are an activity he'd do anything to avoid. He clearly enjoys mapping out the archly cynical view of modern life that governs *Resentment*—"we're a dysfunctional society in the way the Menendez brothers were a dysfunctional family, where conflict resolution is just the immediate inductive leap to homicide," he opines.

But questions about the elusive personal history of this author known only by a pseudonym he concocted three decades ago are often met with a waggish epigram, spoken between slugs of Brooklyn Lager. Asked what he means when he calls a prominent editor "the best kind of asshole," Indiana replies: "To me the world is divided into creeps and assholes. And give me an asshole any day."

The seamy underside of public life has often captivated him. "Writing Dangerously," the title of an essay on Mary McCarthy from Indiana's 1996 essay collection *Let It Bleed* (Serpent's Tail), is a phrase that might also describe his own maverick career. An icon of the avant-garde, Indiana is as comfortable cruising the urban infernos of New York and Los Angeles, the two cities in which he now lives, as he is in an art gallery, on a film set or academic symposium. He has traveled, often by himself, in treacherous areas of South America, Asia and Africa. *Let It Bleed* features exposés of Euro Disney and the American porn industry; the trials of Jack Kevorkian and the LAPD officers accused of beating Rodney King; as well as essays on art, books and the AIDS crisis, many of which first appeared in the *Village Voice*, where Indiana was senior art critic from 1985 to 1988.

Indiana's publishing track record is unconventional, too. Indiana's agent Emma Sweeney shopped *Resentment* around town before selling it to Betsy Lerner at Doubleday. ("Now they want you to go and sit with editors and pitch them just like in Hollywood. I met these people who seemed to me absolutely monstrous. Betsy was the only editor I liked.") But each of his four novels has been published in hardcover by a different house, a trend he ascribes to the politics of the business and to the stigma that he is a "downtown" writer, a tag he contends has allowed critics to relegate his books to the cultural margins. "I don't like the way the hierarchy is structured in the literary world," he says. "I can't place myself in it, and I can't place myself outside it. I feel much closer to artists and theater people than I do to other writers. I find the literary world to be dead; stultifying; emotionally, intellectually and in every other way constipated.

"All those kids in the '80s who were taken up by the literati, they were the bad chroniclers of downtown," he comments. "I have not been in a nightclub in 15 years. I really live a very disciplined life. I don't know where that unsavory reputation comes from."

Certainly his fiction has something to do with it. His first novel, *Horse Crazy* (Grove, 1988) chronicles a Manhattan writer's obsessive love affair with a recovering heroin addict. (An author photo by Robert Mapplethorpe shows Indiana as a dour choirboy in a turtleneck and blazer—a startling contrast to the grunge attire and impish look he sports today.)

In 1993, Pantheon's Errol Morris published his second novel. *Gone Tomorrow,* a young actor's confused account of a debauched film production in South America in the early years of the AIDS epidemic. *Rent Boy* (Serpent's Tale, 1994) depicts a male hustler who is embroiled in the kidnapping plot of a sinister organ-transplant surgeon. "They say that sharks never go to sleep," explains Indiana, referring to his protagonist's accelerated trajectory through the Manhattan underworld. "I wasn't thinking so much about male prostitution, but about somebody who's relentlessly moving in order not to have to think about things, which is I think the condition of most people in New York."

Although these books hint at elements of the author's own experiences, Indiana is guarded about his private life and grows evasive when pressed to describe the "mildly dysfunctional" Catholic family from Derry, N.H., in which he grew up. He suggests that *Resentment*'s twin themes of parricide and long-simmering rancor stem, in part, from the resentment he harbored for years toward his older brother (the pilot of Air Force II for 15 years and a father of four), and a brief fantasy he entertained during "the occasional terror we experienced when my father was drunk," as he writes in the publicity copy that accompanies the novel. "My brother and I now have a great relationship and I attribute that to having written this book," he says.

In the late 1960s, he fled to Berkeley and assumed the name Gary Indiana. "I wanted to make myself up. And be the person I invented rather than being a slave to genetics or a slave to my family," he recalls. Dropping out after two years, Indiana moved to Boston and drifted between clerical jobs at a mental hospital and a plastic-surgery clinic then became a paralegal for a legal-aid lawyer, whom he accompanied to Los Angeles. His interest in the arts, theater and books blossomed, but it took a near-fatal car accident on the Ventura freeway in 1974 to direct his attention from the political front lines to the artistic grass roots.

"I think the accident made me realize that what I was doing with my life was trying to expiate the sins of the world rather than do something worthwhile with myself. I had all these pieties about how you should devote your life to the betterment of your fellow male. The accident brought all of that into focus, somehow, that I should just be a writer. That would be my contribution to the world, rather than investigating slum apartments in Watts."

Indiana moved to New York and was soon immersed in the artistic ferment of the East Village, directing plays in an unnamed theater on East Third St. "I didn't think of it as an underground, or downtown or any such thing," he recalls. "What existed at the time was a situation where you could be somebody that made themselves up out of nothing and be welcomed into a very large community of artists. The situation I found when I came to New York was that you didn't have to have gone to the right schools with the sons and daughters of Conde Nast and all these Ivy League shits who run the literary world. You could be somebody from a poor family who didn't finish college. And if you did interesting work then people encouraged you."

While many of his peers became either famous or chemically dependent, Indiana entered a period of "hyperproductivity," writing for *Art Forum, Art in America* and other magazines and traveling to Europe, acting in low-budget films, even performing in a scene with Rainer Fassbinder. In 1985, at the zenith of the 1980s art-market boom, the *Village Voice* made Indiana its art critic—a job that catapulted this already controversy-prone writer into a collision course with the art establishment.

"I'm a very unbuttoned person and that was a period when there was so much money of arrivistes being thrown at the art world because they didn't know what else to do with all the billions they were making in the Reagan years. And this kind of insanity set in. You'd just sprinkle a little fairy dust on somebody and they were a millionaire the next week."

At the *Voice*, Indiana came into his own as a trenchant critic of the image world, exhibiting a stylish vitriol and a penchant for needling newly minted celebrities (his "dissenting opinion" on Richard Serra's controversial public monument, *Tilted Arc*, likened fashionable artists to debutantes and Serra himself to Albert Speer). These elements would soon figure into his fiction, which is often appreciated by the cognoscenti for its vituperative caricatures of well-known writers. Despite the Author's Note—a preemptive legal device—insisting that *Resentment* is not a "novel with a key," this book may well become the *succès de scandale* of the summer for its hilarious treatment of such figures as Ingrid Sischy, Dominick Dunne, Hilton Als and Jamaica Kincaid. Asked if he expects to be taken to task for this, Indiana reflects: "If people want to read it that way, then I can't stop them. About certain characters. I would say that payback is a very bad motive for writing a novel but it is one of the perks." Payback for what exactly? "The ridiculousness of people. If you're obliged to swallow somebody's absurdity for decades at a time, you're certainly entitled at some point to just say, 'oh, you're so full of shit,' " he drawls.

"I'm basically somebody who sees the world as a comedy. We live in a world of rampant hypocrisy where people never say what they think, they never say what their real opinion is in public. They never divulge just how much they resent other people, how much they envy, how much they despise."

Those who don't read beyond the smoke screen of gossipy invective in *Resentment* miss the point, he says. "People now believe that telling the truth is the biggest sin that you can commit," he comments. "I do think people should be able to laugh at themselves and other people and laugh at the great joke that we're living in.

"I mean, we're all going to the same place. And I don't care if you're rich or you're poor or what you are, we're all going to end up in the same place, either in an urn or under a marker. So why take it so seriously?"

Indiana pauses to caress a cat that has just jumped onto the table in front of him. As he babbles lovingly into its coat, his features contort into those of a mournful clown. He is a cat owner, that much is clear, but few details about his domestic circumstances are forthcoming. "I'm very agitated about one thing or another most of the time," he says. "I'm not an operator. I get up between six and seven every morning and I start working. I usually go swimming for an hour. And then I usually either work or go to the movies.

"I'm not somebody who writes happily," he adds. "I will do anything to avoid writing. So I generally foment a tremendous amount of anxiety no matter what I'm doing. When I'm actually doing it, it seems to go fairly well. But I'm going to come back as Fran Leibowitz. Because if I didn't have to make a living, I would be the most perpetually blocked writer in the world."

JONATHAN BING
July 7, 1997

RONA JAFFE

Rona Jaffe sits curled in an armchair in her apartment on the Upper East Side of Manhattan, surrounded by treasures from her travels and flanked by a wall of floor-to-ceiling bookcases that include her 15 novels and six bestsellers in a rainbow of languages. Lithe from the gym, dressed in blue jeans, blazer and pearl stud earrings, Jaffe looks clean-cut yet subtly hip. At 65, she seems the embodiment of the independent and powerful career woman she has long inspired readers to believe they can be, starting with her first bestseller, *The Best of Everything*, published by Simon & Schuster in 1958. Now, however, Jaffe is adding an interesting detail to that image. She is leavening her success as a commercial novelist with a measure of altruism and social awareness.

"I thought, what a nice thing to do, to give women the gift of time," says Jaffe, describing the impetus that led her to create The Rona Jaffe Foundation Writer's Awards two years ago. The only literary prize in the country given exclusively to women, the awards have given female writers at the beginning of their careers up to $7500 to use on child care and other basics. According to Jaffe, many of the nominees, who have ranged in age from their 20s to their mid 50s, have children and have been squeaking by on $10,000 or less.

"I do identify with these women," says Jaffe. "There was a time when I didn't have any money." She talks in a multilayered Manhattan voice with a trace of cultured Radcliffe drawl over the chatty middle-class Brooklynese of her childhood.

Jaffe says that the awards grew out of the Rona Jaffe Prizes at Radcliffe College, which she has given annually to two undergraduates since 1987. "I had a lot of encouragement when I was at Radcliffe," she explains. "I grew up feeling that many people had helped me become a writer, and I wanted to give that back."

Set in New York City, as are most of her novels, Jaffe's latest, *Five Women*, out from Donald I. Fine, follows five women through five

decac ... :ome traumatic
child! ... rly hopes. Typical of ... vomen who live
comp ... scope from her
previ ... various parts of
the c(... n Irish Catholic
Bostc ... iarrative is also
uniqt ... each character
achie ... Readers learn in
Five ... even privileged
lives ... tive sentence.
   Al(... : about the personal ... n and her desire
to help other women. She appears not so much to conceal as to con-
serve her deeper thoughts and feelings. Still, asked what motivates
her when she sits down to work each day, she answers without a second's hesitation: "Fear of failure."

This trait is what motivated Jaffe to write *The Best of Everything*
while working as an associate editor at Fawcett Publishing. Released
when Jaffe was 26, the book shocked people with its clear-eyed portrait of what Jaffe describes as girls "brought up to fulfill the image of
what boys wanted." The novel both held up a mirror to and challenged "the '50s rat race to the altar." It was a major bestseller.

This brave message proved to be a governing force in Jaffe's career. Through the decades, her work and her own life have evolved
from the notion that a woman can choose to put a career, a life,
above marriage and family. Unlike most other girls of the '50s,
Jaffe grew up searching for an identity that didn't depend on her
connection to a man. Jaffe's father, a high school principal, and her
housewife mother moved with their only child from Brooklyn to
Manhattan when Rona was 11 so she could attend the Dalton
School.

"My mother told me that I dictated my first poem to her when I
was two and a half," Jaffe remembers. When she was nine, Jaffe
started sending pieces to the *New Yorker.* "They probably thought I
was an adult who didn't write very well," she laughs.

Jaffe didn't just want to write, she says; she wanted to be a writer,
a witty observer like Dorothy Parker. She wanted to jump out of the
confines of her own middle-class childhood and become an adult, a
citizen of a bigger, more glamorous world. She sent juvenile novels to

publishing houses; they were rejected too. Jaffe recalls being "practically suicidal at 14 because I wasn't getting published.

"As soon as I knew that writing was something you could do as an occupation, I wanted to do it—that or become a movie star, and my parents dissuaded me from pursuing that." Later, while establishing herself as a writer, Jaffe studied acting at Lee Strasberg's Actor's Studio. All her adult life she has known and felt an affinity with actors, even the maniacally willful and narcissistic actor among the five women in her latest novel.

"If people really want to write and they have that fear of failure," Jaffe continues, "they don't talk about how wonderful it would be if they had the time to write—they make the time, they teach themselves, they learn."

Jaffe's voice was there from the start. By the time she entered Radcliffe, she was already practicing the kind of social description that would appear in her fiction and nonfiction. After graduating, she toiled on a novella that didn't sell. "It took my boyfriend in the mail room at William Morris to tell me that what it needed was a plot," she laughs. That first attempt did help persuade Jack Goodwin at S&S to offer a contract for *The Best of Everything*. When Goodwin died before its publication, Robert Gottlieb became her editor. And when the book appeared, she became a celebrated novelist and adjusted to the role as if she had been preparing for it all her life.

The novel sold to 20th Century Fox, and Jaffe was sent on a publicity tour to sell books. Far from being overwhelmed by the sudden media attention, Jaffe coolly critiqued tapes of her TV appearances. "I would say to myself, I should do this, I should do that; I should stop giggling," remembers Jaffe. "Which is my good side? Is that a good color? I did it all very objectively."

During the '60s, Jaffe wrote four more novels for S&S, including a children's book and *Mr. Right Is Dead,* a novella and five short stories. Not surprisingly, Helen Gurley Brown hired Jaffe to write cultural pieces for *Cosmopolitan* with a *Sex and the Single Girl* slant. For one such assignment, Jaffe followed Ava Gardner around the globe, never meeting her but interviewing everyone Gardner knew. She interviewed Streisand and Paul Newman and spent a week with the Supremes in Puerto Rico ("They called me the Fourth Supreme," she remembers). The most memorable article she wrote, however, was about single social life behind the iron curtain in Hungary.

"I even had my own spy," says Jaffe with a wide smile, recalling a man who "followed me around in Budapest. I gave a party and invited all these young kids, and this man was beside me the whole time. I went out to buy scotch and he came with me."

Jaffe points out that her first novel, her 1985 Delacorte bestseller *Class Reunion* and her newest novel address changes in the ways women have perceived their identities and self-worth. "I recently realized that approximately every 20 years, I look at life again and see where we are." *Five Women* shows friends from different social and ethnic backgrounds struggling to find enduring truths in the midst of loss. Of the five protagonists, Gara Whiteman seems closest to Jaffe herself. Unlike the other characters, Gara is a native New Yorker and an only child. A psychotherapist, Gara is Jaffe's designated witness, a grown-up version of the kid who wanted to watch closely and figure things out. Gara struggles through a difficult relationship with her mother, the end of her 22-year marriage and breast cancer. Yet she is able to observe the sometimes devastating changes taking place in her life and the lives of her friends with the assiduous attention of a lifelong overachiever. Gara seems to hope that if any process is followed closely enough, it may yield the previously hidden clues she needs to help her get through.

Jaffe's detailed, unsentimental description of Gara's illness makes up the most powerful chapters in the book. A cut above the entertainment Jaffe dependably dishes out in the rest of the novel, these resonant chapters spell out the specifics of surgery and chemotherapy. Readers will inevitably conclude that they are based on real experience.

"Fine; let them," says Jaffe firmly. "My darling agent, Anne Sibbald, said this is the best description of breast cancer she's ever read in fiction." That, Jaffe implies, is the important thing.

Gara learns to tolerate solitude, to face mortality. She has a romance in the end, but she has been disabused of the romantic dream that a man is the answer to the riddle of her existence. True independence turns out to be a goal that demands sacrifices the girls in *The Best of Everything* couldn't imagine. True freedom, Gara learns, means recognizing that each of us is fundamentally alone.

Jaffe spends up to a year planning a book. Once the writing begins, she works eight hours a day until the book is done—*Five Women* took about a year. She puts "every single thing I know that moment in time into a book." When it's finished, she goes "back into life and learns other things," and the long process starts over again.

Publishing, she admits, definitely feels like a tougher business than when she was writing *The Best of Everything*—when "I used to read pages over the phone," a luxury which few editors have time for today. Although Jaffe's last several novels have not been bestsellers, she has a reported 23 million books in print. In addition to S&S, Jaffe published one novel at Random House and one at Morrow before setting in at Delacorte for *Class Reunion* (1979), *Mazes and Monsters* (1981), which became a TV movie with Tom Hanks, *After the Reunion* (1985) and *An American Love Story*. Her novel, *The Cousins*, was published by Don Fine.

Agented by Sibbald at Janklow & Nesbit, with her work in print for almost four decades, Jaffe would seem to have little in common with the often long-deprived women who receive her foundation's awards. Jaffe takes a mock grumpy pleasure in being recognized as a benefactor. She stresses that the awards are determined by an anonymous selection committee. They cannot be applied for, and she is not a judge. "People know this by now, but they still come up to me and say, 'I know you can't apply, but can I nominate my friend?'" She sighs and smiles.

Jaffe has no desire to write a memoir. "You have to tell people your secrets, and I could never do that," she says. "Also, I think memoirs are fiction in their own way, too. We really don't know how things happened. We see it a certain way."

Her reference to "the monsters of the id" in the prologue to her current release may be as wide a window as Jaffe is willing to open on her personal life. But the creation of The Rona Jaffe Foundation Writer's Awards has allowed her to rechannel that creative energy. In this new act of compassion and generosity, she has tapped the memory of that spirited little kid from Brooklyn who was determined to be a writer. She has imagined her moving a step further, growing beyond her famous role as a proudly self-sufficient trailblazer to become a mentor.

TRACY COCHRAN
June 16, 1997

116

JAN KARON

WHEN PW MEETS novelist Jan Karon for lunch in Blowing Rock, N.C., we're not surprised to find her saying grace over a side of liver-mush in Sonny's restaurant. Readers who subscribe to Karon's free newsletter already know that livermush is a western Carolinas specialty made of liver, spices and cornmeal formed into one-pound bricks, sliced up and fried to order. Sonny's, which resembles the Main Street Grill in the fictional town of Mitford, N.C., the setting of Karon's four novels, is part of a tour she provides us of Blowing Rock landmarks which were springboards for the Mitford town map.

Karon's series has been growing in popularity since her first novel, *At Home in Mitford,* was released by Lion in 1994. Since then she has published *A Light in the Window* and *These High Green Hills* with both Lion and Viking and, most recently, *Out to Canaan,* exclusively with Viking. All the books center around an Episcopal priest and his down-home friends in Mitford. Real-life problems touch the community but never devastate its citizens; *Out to Canaan* concerns a mayoral race that divides the town; between the tireless love of God and the tireless work of Father Tim, Karon invariably gets things patched up within 400 pages. The scripture in the novels is always King James, and biblical references are passed back and forth between characters the way most friends share private jokes or words of encouragement.

But Karon's books differ from most Christian fiction, much of which is genre fiction and agenda-driven rather than character- and plot-driven. As a writer, she is interested not only in the conversion to Christianity—numerous characters in her books have prayed what she calls "the sinner's prayer" and accepted Christ—but in the everyday nature of Christian life. "I do love and am interested in the life of the church," says Karon. "But more than the life of the larger church, which Susan Howatch is compelled by, I'm compelled by the minutiae, the church suppers, the cake sales, the rummage sales."

It's rare for a writer to cross over from the Christian market to the mainstream, but Karon has done so with aplomb; *Out to Canaan* climbed the lists of national bestsellers and is the recipient of an ABBY honor. The novels' popularity stems in part from their feel-good tone and spirit; they're well-written but not overly crafted, and full of Karon's easy humor. Their success also reflects Karon's devoted contact with her readers, her appearances at libraries, churches, book clubs and festivals. Also, she prays a lot. It's hard to hold a conversation with her without God creeping in somehow—and Karon invokes Him as intimately as she would a mutual third cousin with whom she's just had a long visit.

Karon is a poised Southern lady of 60 with blonde curls, a petite but curvy figure and what in the South is known as "good skin"—it frequently glows. She's quick to make a joke and quicker to laugh at one. She gets weepy when she talks about things that are important to her. She wears a cross whose chain is decorated with dogwood blossoms of yellow, white and rosy gold. To look at her, you might think she volunteers at a hospital or organizes garden tours. But, as Father Tim so often finds, all is not as it seems.

Karon received only eight years of formal schooling; she's a straight-A high-school dropout. Her life has not been a Mitford stereotype, and although she's unwilling to give many details of her experiences before she moved to Blowing Rock in the late '80s, the signs are there: photographs of a daughter whom she mostly raised alone, awards for her advertising writing, photos of her beloved grandmother, who lived to be 100.

"I did marry very, very young," Karon admits. "It sounds like one of those Southern shotgun weddings; it actually wasn't." A native of Lenoir, N.C., she began her working life at 18, when she was already a mother, as a receptionist at a Charlotte advertising agency.

"I kept sticking ads on my boss's desk," she explains. "I'd write an ad or a campaign for everything that was going on in the shop. That's how I became an advertising writer." At firms in San Francisco and New York in the decade that followed, Karon wrote advertising copy for travel and tourism accounts before ultimately returning to Charlotte.

Yet Karon found her advertising work unfulfilling, and when her marriage ended in divorce after three and a half years, it was a struggle to raise her daughter by herself. At 42, Karon reached what she felt was an impasse in her career and her life—what she now calls a dark night of the soul. It was at this juncture that Karon underwent an experience she describes as "being saved" and became a born-again Episcopalian. "There were no visions at the foot of my bed. There were no bolts of lightning," she explains. "As time went on I began to see very clearly that something great had happened that was far too mysterious for me to understand."

While Karon had been brought up in the Methodist church and recalls that her two career dreams as a child were preaching and writing books, she hadn't done much about either in the intervening years. "I began to pray about stepping out, away from advertising, and doing what I felt it really had been my calling to do, and that was to write books," she recounts.

She moved to Blowing Rock in 1988 because she wanted to be back in the mountains—Blowing Rock is more of a perch than a town—and her brother and his family had a summer home there. After finding a cottage and settling in, she began a novel whose characters she describes as paper dolls. "And then one night, I was lying in bed," she says. "I had this mental image of a priest walking down a village street. I had no idea what it could mean, but I began to sort of follow him in my mind, and it began to become the whole Mitford thing."

Karon laughs about the first Mitford book's content compared to many contemporary works of fiction. "No cussing, no drinking, no drug smuggling, there's nothing going on in this book," she laughs. She approached the editor of the local paper, the *Blowing Rocket,* with two chapters, and he agreed to run a serial. Her compensation for the stories was free copies of each issue, which at that time cost a dime apiece. "After running that thing every week for two years, we had 170,000 words," she says, and she decided to try to get it published. "I sent it to Houghton Mifflin," she recalls. "I said, 'You've been publishing Miss Read all these years, and I really do think you might like this book.' Well, they didn't."

The novel was finally accepted by Lion, an evangelical Christian house, where it was edited by Bob Klausmeier, who is now at Augsburg Press, a Lutheran publisher. She was still doing freelance advertising, and upon receiving her $7500 first advance from Lion, she decided to boost the marketing a bit. "I began to make friends of booksellers," she recalls. "I was in there like a rep, on the road, pushing my books." It was a Raleigh bookseller, Nancy Olson of Quail Ridge Books, who in 1996 introduced her to agent Liz Darhansoff.

By that time, Karon had sold a third book to Lion, but she didn't have a new manuscript. Darhansoff showed the books to Carolyn Carlson of Penguin, and a relationship was born.

Lion, however, was unwilling to sell publishing rights to Viking outright. Eventually the two companies struck a copublishing deal: Lion would distribute the books to Christian bookstores, and Penguin would handle the mainstream market. *Out to Canaan* is available exclusively from Viking.

"I can't afford to lose the Christian market," Karon says. "But I want to write for everybody—I do not write just for Christians. I write for readers, period, and let the chips fall where they may."

Asked to describe her typical reader, Karon at first demurs ("I hate to do this . . ."). She says her readers range in age from 10 to 98 and are predominantly female. "[My typical reader] is in a long-term marriage, never divorced, 52, 53, 54. Has worked, would really rather stay home. Has had some health problems, loves her husband; they like to read aloud to each other. They travel together. They probably have an RV. She has a sense of humor. Goes to church, or used to go to church. My guess is about a third of the audience is male and a number of them are clergy."

Although Karon's advertising background has undoubtedly helped make her a savvy promoter of her own books, she maintains that if she had looked at market trends, she might have been led in the opposite direction of Mitford. "If I'd written some real *Sling Blade,* hard-hitting stuff, that might be more expected. I come out of advertising, which is a tough business, and I write what could be called gentle novels," she says, acknowledging the irony.

"I think people have been beaten up by contemporary fiction," she continues. "A lot of it makes you sad and makes you agonize. I have found that people are willing to sort of go on sabbatical with me to Mitford, because it just feels good. Maybe another reason is, they don't have to work very hard in Mitford. There are no great intellectual obstacle courses for them to run."

While Karon doesn't feel much alliance with Southern fiction past or present, her characters are unmistakably Southern, both in action and in speech. "People ask, 'Where do you get your characters?' " Karon says, "and I have to say, 'My characters get me.' That is the truth. God gives us free will, and I extend the same courtesy to my characters. I don't have a clue what they're going to do.

"I just start, and it's a joyride, which also is very frightening. It's like flying with the windshield iced over. I feel that if I can keep the element of surprise, if, as the writer, *I* can be surprised, perhaps my readers will sense some of that surprise. If I can weep and laugh with my characters, perhaps my readers can also."

Karon's life, in a small resort-town cottage decorated fervently in what one might call wild Victorian with cabbage roses, is not the idyll one might expect. "There's a certain sort of *Entertainment Tonight* quality about being an author," she says. "Your readers want you out there in their face, your publisher wants you out there on the road; and of course it does sell books."

Karon now has an assistant to help with paperwork and scheduling—she still personally answers all her readers' letters—and is actively at work on five books, with ideas for more. She has signed a contract for a fifth Mitford novel in addition to two novellas, one concerning Father Tim and Cynthia's wedding, which invisibly fell between *A Light in the Window* and *These High Green Hills,* the other about Christmas in Mitford; and, eventually, a Mitford cookbook. Her first children's book, called *Miss Fanny's Hats,* will be out next February from Augsburg where she is again working with Bob Klausmeier. She intends to write two more novels, one about the building of a home in 18th-century Virginia and one about a couple in their 60s who tour the country in a recreational vehicle. At press time, she is in the midst of a nationwide tour for *Out to Canaan,* with time out for meetings to discuss film rights to Mitford. It's easy to feel that she'll need to live as long as her grandmother to finish all her projects.

Yet the surprising twists of Karon's own career and the immense satisfaction she finds in writing fiction have instilled in her a circumspection about the vocations we choose. "It's my instinct to say, 'Follow your heart,'" Karon reflects. "But following your heart can be very misleading. I've followed my heart and gone down some real dead ends, you know? I think really the hard part for most people is knowing what they want to do. It's not doing it; it's knowing what it is."

RENÉE CRIST
May 26, 1997

ALFRED KAZIN

Few writers in the annals of American letters have lived so public a private life as Alfred Kazin. In his classic 1951 memoir, *Walker in the City*, Kazin drew an unforgettably vivid portrait of the literary critic as a young man in the working-class Jewish enclave of Browns-ville, Brooklyn, walking and reading his way back to the old America of the 19th century, "that fork in the road where all American lives cross," even as he catalogued the sights, smells and sounds of an immigrant world that was itself soon to vanish.

Two subsequent volumes of autobiography, *Starting Out in the Thirties* (1962) and *New York Jew* (1978), followed the native son out into the larger world. There was Kazin's immersion in the radical literary politics of the Depression years; the brilliant success of his first book, *On Native Grounds,* in 1942; World War II and the Holocaust; an unusually peripatetic teaching career; three marriages, two children, love affairs; and over the years at least a passing acquaintance with just about every major figure on the scene. Most importantly, there was the steady stream of essays, reviews and books that have kept Kazin in the forefront of American literary criticism for nearly 60 years now.

In his memoirs, as in his criticism, Kazin's writing has been marked by a persistent introversion, a focus on the sovereign self against the backdrop of political and social drama. "I've always felt myself to be not lonely, but on some kind of strange personal journey," Kazin tells a journalist on a sunny afternoon, hours before the start of the Jewish New Year. "As a kid, I felt I was not easily associated with other people."

The publication by Knopf of his ninth book of criticism, *God and the American Writer*, marks the latest stage in the journey. With this book, Kazin heads back once again to the 19th-century American crossroads, examining the shards of faith manifest in the work of 12 classic American writers, ranging from Lincoln's scripture-tinged speeches on the sacredness of Union to Emily Dickinson's thoroughly private expeditions into immortality.

What Kazin delivers, however, is anything but a dry sermon on the old religion. Some six decades out of Brownsville, Kazin still sounds like the same ecstatic reader who propped books open on his bureau while getting dressed in the morning, who sat on the fire escape devouring everything from boys' adventure stories to Whitman and the forbidden New Testament as if reading for his life.

"Like all my books," Kazin says, "this one came out of a deep, personal obsession. I've been working on it in one way or another for 20 years." Since his agent, Lynn Nesbit, placed the book with Knopf's Robert Gottlieb in the mid-1980s (Harry Ford took over the project after Gottlieb's departure in 1987), Kazin has bided his time in finishing this elegant summation of his "crazy enthusiasms," as he puts it. "On the whole, I have to say that I'm a kind of freak in the sense that I don't know many people who have my interest in the subject. Today there are very few people who are interested in religion in the way the 19th century was." The book stops with Frost and Faulkner, Kazin explains, because most postwar writers, including the Jewish novelists he has often championed, "in a sense deal with religion as something that's dead."

Sitting on the couch in the modest apartment on New York's Upper West Side that he shares with his fourth wife, Judith Dunford, Kazin, wearing a rumpled grey sweatsuit and running shoes, seems less the tweedy eminence of recent author photos than an engagingly expansive great uncle, happy to pass the afternoon talking about his favorite books and just reminiscing. Prostate cancer and the ordinary bedevilments of old age have slowed the famous walker considerably, but the writer in Kazin still seems to be sprinting full-speed. How many authors, after all, can boast of publishing five books in their retirement alone, as Kazin has since taking mandatory leave of the City University of New York in 1985, at age 70?

Not that Kazin, now 82, seems much impressed by his own feats. Asked about the nods to "our greatest living man of letters" that so often crop up in even the most critical reviews of his work, Kazin responds, in a voice still bearing traces of Brownsville, "I don't believe a word of it! It's all baloney. I'm not a great man of letters at all. I'm lucky, very lucky, to have been able to write about what I could write about, to discover I had a certain gift. When I was starting out and I got to write 150 words about some schmutty novel, I was pleased and proud to get the assignment. To me it was all writing. I've never thought I was second-rate, but I never thought I was important."

Talk inevitably turns to his own religious commitments, to what he calls "the agony of being an eccentric believer." While he confesses to being "emotionally drawn to everything Jewish," Kazin describes his own belief in terms recalling his book's 12 Protestants, almost churches unto themselves in the fierce separateness of their imagination.

"The reason I'm not in a synagogue is that I'm a very personal believer. William Blake, who's been a big influence on me, once said, 'Organized religion: an impossibility.' I understand that. To believe is to believe individually. I suppose in many ways my belief, such as it is, is also mixed with an urgent, almost desperate belief in spiritual freedom. My favorite Jew is Spinoza—the 17th-century philosopher who was excommunicated from the Amsterdam Jewish community and whose works were banned by the Church—and always has been."

"I don't defend or justify or even try to explain the strange lonely feeling I have about these things," he continues. "A great deal of the time it makes me sick, because I realize it doesn't give me the kind of satisfaction a believer finds getting down on his knees and saying 'Yes, I believe in heaven.' I'm not sure entirely what I believe, but I do know I have that feeling, which comes from some ancient Jewish tradition, which has nothing to do with contemporary middle-class American Jewish life."

Kazin considers himself a product of the socialist solidarity of the Jewish working class, which he sees as itself a remnant of the 19th century. "I've always been very anti-bourgeois in every sense. The people I grew up with were penniless Jewish workers. One thing I always identify as a signature of my early life was my mother organizing packs of women during the evictions that took place every day during the Depression. They'd move the furniture back inside, go get the city marshals, all that." One of the few times he recalls seeing his father break down was when Sacco and Vanzetti were executed in 1927.

What Kazin now calls the "naïve idealism" of Brownsville carried him into the Leftist intellectual world of the Depression years. After graduating from City College in 1935, Kazin cobbled together a living writing book reviews. His real break came in 1937 when Carl Van Doren, a onetime Columbia professor then working as a publisher's scout, urged him to undertake a history of modern American writing. Kazin famously set up office in the main reading room of the New York Public Library and, five years later, emerged with *On Native Grounds.*

The book was "a big hit and all that," as Kazin puts it. It was instantly hailed by such critics as Lionel Trilling as much for its tone of moral urgency, its Whitmanesque insistence that the emergence of the modern American spirit was itself the greatest possible literary subject, as for its thoroughness and brash originality. As Kazin would later write, the book was undertaken in the midst of the Depression and completed during a world war by an angry young man who was "very critical of the system but still crazy about America."

Just how young he was did not pass unnoticed. "My father used to keep a copy on my sister's piano," Kazin recalls. "Of course, my parents couldn't read it—they wouldn't have understood it anyway. But whenever I'd bring a friend by, he'd pick it up and say, 'It's by my son! He wrote it when he was six months old!' "

With the extraordinary success of the book, a brilliant new critic seemed to have sprung full-grown from the collective brow of the radical literary scene. Kazin got a job traveling the country as a correspondent for *Fortune* and, in 1944, won a Rockefeller Grant to report from England.

But it wasn't until after the war, when Kazin turned not to America's roots but to his own, that he was truly born as a writer. Returning home, he realized just how much the war had fundamentally changed the face of America—and just how radically the emerging details of the death camps had changed him. "After the war, I lost the social feeling that had infused *On Native Grounds*," he says. "I no longer believed in the ideal society. After the Holocaust, I felt human nature was impossible to trust."

His first marriage had also collapsed. "I was looking for something to hold on to, and I suddenly realized that I didn't just come from some shabby immigrant quarter, that my past was something I could write about."

The book that became *Walker in the City* began in the late 1940s as an elaborate celebration of all of New York. After the failure of a brief second marriage, Kazin found himself living in the back of a painter's studio on Pineapple Street in Brooklyn Heights, still struggling with the book. "One day I had the courage to look at the whole thing honestly and realize that the only decent part was the part about the old neighborhood," Kazin recalls. "I was living my memory of sense perceptions, of smells, voices, echoes. Brownsville was a ghetto in one sense, but it was also a sounding board. And to my surprise, the book I wrote out of the most compelling personal need became a book cherished by a lot of Jews." And clearly by a much larger readership as well. It was published in 1951 by Harcourt Brace and has been in print ever since.

Over the years, Kazin has taught everywhere from Harvard and Notre Dame to Black Mountain College in North Carolina, as well as abroad. While he eventually got a tenured position at State University of New York at Stony Brook, and later at City University of New York, academic life never much suited him. "I hated being a professor, hated the academic world. I thought it was terribly small, very narrow. I didn't have a Ph.D. I was always the odd man out. But I always loved teaching. Again and again, I would get so excited about something being discussed in class that I'd rush back to my notebooks and put it down."

Kazin's notebooks have been an essential part of his literary life since boyhood, the private wellspring of much of his public output. In 1996, Harper-Collins published a selection ranging from 1938 to the present as *A Lifetime Burning in Every Moment.*

The notebook Kazin says he keeps "now more than ever" will also form the backbone of his current work-in-progress, *Jews: The Marriage of Heaven and Hell.* While he's cagey about the exact contents, he does say the book will contain reflections on the state of Jewish life in America and in Israel, as well as more variations of the bottomless theme of his immigrant origins. "Every bone in my body was brought up Jewish," Kazin says. "But I also tend to be very critical, a bit heretical. Every once in a while I stick my nose out of the den and show that I'm taking a chance."

"I look at my own children," Kazin continues (his son, Michael, is a labor historian at American University; his daughter, Cathrael, a former federal lawyer, now lives in Israel), "and their lives are so different from mine. I often wonder what my grandchildren will make of *Walker in the City* if they ever pick it up. It will seem prehistoric, like the discovery of America."

Which, in its own way, is exactly what it is.

JENNIFER SCHUESSLER
October 27, 1997

FAYE KELLERMAN

As we arrive for an interview, Faye Kellerman is outside the front
door of her house in Beverly Hills wearing baggy white exercise
clothes, carrying a bottle of water and peering across the driveway, through the bushes and down the street. Apparently there is a
suspicious-looking van in the vicinity. "Down side of the job," we
think smugly, feeling sorry for crime fiction writers and also slightly
vindicated, given the sheer terror and random paranoia readers may
experience in Kellerman's 11th book, *Serpent's Tooth* (Morrow). This
lasts about 20 seconds, the time it would take any visitor to realize
that, in fact, Kellerman is very happy, very relaxed and very successful.

Inside the front door we are greeted, or rather mown down, by
Kellerman's 12-year-old daughter, Ilana, and a friend. They are looking for some towels before going out to the pool. We recognize an
L.A. kid when we see one, and the Kellermans have four. Inside their
8000-square-foot house, one senses the presence of kids and dogs
and at least the potential for general hilarity and pandemonium, tem-
pered by bright cleanliness and carefully framed art on the walls.
Someone is in charge here. Our guess would be the fine-boned
woman with the curly hair gesturing and leading us into her library,
to a seat by the fireplace where she motions for us to pull up a step-
stool. This is Kellerman's office, where she writes her books.

More than three million copies of her books are currently in print,
having generated more than $2 million in royalties; her husband,
crime-fiction writer Jonathan Kellerman, has written 14 novels that
have made more than $22 million. Between them, 15 of their books
have been bestsellers. Each writes a book a year; Jonathan's are published in the winter, Faye's in the summer. Each keeps an office in
the house where they work for several hours each day. The two offices are joined by an intercom.

"I write books about how good people manage to retain their

127

goodness, about the tensions of faith," Kellerman says, leaning across a table decorated with silver-framed family photographs. "Novels are about passion and drive and addiction, and in all of my books passion wins out," she says. Indeed, Kellerman is a sucker for the kind of slow-burning, long-lasting love story that defines her series characters, LAPD Lieutenant Peter Decker and his wife, Rina Lazarus.

In *Serpent's Tooth,* Kellerman pits Decker against a new set of character tests and temptations. "I like characters to be challenged in a nefarious plot," she says, "but I never use sex or violence gratuitously. My characters are not low-lifes."

In a blood-spattered, thrillerish opening scene, a killer opens fire in the trendy L.A. restaurant Estelle's, killing a dozen people and leaving another couple of dozen wounded. Decker eventually breaks the case by exercising compassion and pure persistence, and enlisting the help of people who love and admire him—namely his loyal co-workers and his good children (much to Decker's chagrin, his eldest daughter has decided to follow in his footsteps and become a cop). "It's an almost female set of skills he brings to bear," says Kellerman, and it's a very frustrating case for him. In mid-case, he is accused of sexual harassment by the evil blonde bombshell, a key witness and the ultimate 1940s-style seductress, to whom Dexter is uncontrollably attracted. His marriage to Rina, the model of wifely patience, fortitude, sensuality and faith, is in a fallow period, in which, for the first time in the series, she gently complains of a lack of attention.

"All characters are some part of their author," says Kellerman, in the predictable author disclaimer. But Rina, it has been said, is very much like her creator. She puts family first, is practical and virtuous (though hardly naïve) and is an orthodox Jew. "My husband describes me as Betty Crocker with a 'tude," says Kellerman with a grin, repeating a phrase that very accurately describes Rina Lazarus.

Faye, 45, and Jonathan, 48, have been married for 25 years. Both of their families moved to L.A. (his from New York City; hers from St. Louis) in the 1950s. The couple met at a Jewish community center in 1970 and were married two years later. Theirs is an orthodox, kosher home. Their son, Jesse, 19, is at Harvard. Rachel is 16, Ilana is 12 and Aliza is 5.

When Jonathan and Faye met, he was finishing his Ph.D. in psychology at the University of Southern California, and she was earning a doctorate in dentistry at UCLA. "A writer has to be flexible, able to change directions creatively," Kellerman says, and it is clear that the two limbered up during the first two decades of their marriage, a period in which Jonathan left his psychology practice after winning an Edgar for his first novel, *When the Bough Breaks* (1987), and Faye, just out of dental school in 1978, and seven months pregnant, decided that she, too, wanted to write.

"This was no great loss for the American Dental Association," she says. "I am a much better writer than I would have been a dentist. Besides, my son was more interesting. As an undergraduate in math, and in dentistry school, I learned a lot about organization—you can't grope for your tools mid-procedure—and a writer needs, above all, to be organized.

"People make mistakes," she says of this period. "The good news is: You don't have to live with them!"

Ritual Bath, her first book (both authors lived through years of rejections), was published by Arbor House in 1986. "Barney Karpfinger was my agent," she says, "but Ann Harris [then editor-in-chief of Arbor House] was the one who really took a chance on me." After Arbor House became an imprint of Morrow in 1987, Kellerman "was inherited by Liza Dawson, who stayed with me until her recent move from Morrow to Putnam. We got along famously, and I still consider her a great editor and friend." Avon's Carrie Feron edited *Serpent's Tooth.*

Ritual Bath was followed by *Sacred and Profane* (Arbor House, 1987) and *Quality of Mercy* (Morrow, 1989), a historical novel. Why the brief experiment with historical fiction? "My first two books used the harsh language of detective novels. As a new writer, I wanted to experiment with language—I wanted to be poetic and be more descriptive. I enjoyed it, but it was very difficult and time-consuming and I found that I could say more about contemporary social issues in the crime fiction format."

When asked if she worries that her books might compete with her husband's, Kellerman shrugs. "Halevai," she says, a Yiddish expression meaning, "It should only happen." "Maybe in the future I could sell as well as he does. I have no complaints. We do very well."

"It is exhausting to write," Kellerman admits. "It's like painting, one layer at a time. I spend a lot of time crafting my books, sometimes relying on news clips and the Internet, although I find my imagination far more interesting than real life.

"A writer has to be able to focus," she says, "and men and women think differently in this regard. I can work in very short bursts when I need to, accomplishing a lot in 20 minutes. I think this is a part of being the family's primary caretaker . . . it forces you to sustain interruptions." There is not a trace of bitterness in her voice. "I may be a working girl," Kellerman says, "but I don't consider it nearly as tough as being a mother, and certainly nowhere near as important."

In writing *Serpent's Tooth*, Kellerman spent a lot of time hanging around police stations and getting to know detectives. "I wanted to give a sense of what a detective's life is really like," she says. "Detectives I spoke with, especially here in Los Angeles, told me they are always working against being typecast. Cops here feel that they have to fight against everyone, and they are often very religious people."

These nuances give Kellerman's crime fiction the real-life quality that reviewers often praise. As the circumstances of Kellerman's protagonists have become better established, her reviews have also improved, in part, because she has taken more risks, made her characters more multidimensional and her plots more complex. Of her writing process, Kellerman says: "It's very important in crime fiction to flesh out characters, at the same time cutting out extraneous things and keeping the plot moving." Kellerman starts with an outline (which, she claims, ends up being approximately one-half meaningless), then decides where to hang certain elements of the story. After submitting a manuscript to Liza Dawson, Kellerman says, "I take about 60% to 70% of her advice. But I myself am a merciless editor. Every 50 to 100 pages or so I'll give the manuscript to Jonathan, who will tell me which scenes drag and where I make illogical leaps that don't work." That is as far as their collaboration goes. Although Jonathan and Faye appear to do just about everything else together, they keep their writing as separate as possible, a practice that keeps their books distinct as well.

Kellerman loves the idiosyncrasies of L.A., and her books are obviously informed by the local milieu and mores. "I watched the verdict," she says of the O.J. trial, "but not the Friday night Bronco chase," a fine distinction among L.A. denizens that implies a limit to Kellerman's interest in the commercialism of tragedy, an L.A. commodity. Kellerman runs for an hour each morning accompanied by guard dogs, which leads one to wonder if she is afraid for her children. "Of course they don't listen to you," she says, proudly telling *PW* that when her son first got his driver's license, she was able, through sheer willpower after one too many sleepless nights, to disconnect the alarm in her room that told her when he got home.

"[L.A.] is a bit of a cultural vacuum," she says, "but it's not in-your-face like New York. People come here first to make money."

Kellerman has never courted the film industry. "I'm thought of as an L.A. writer, but Hollywood and I are, frankly, orthogonal. Movies these days are way too high on pyrotechnics, and anyway, I don't see my books cinematically. Sure, they've made offers, but I guess I've refused because they haven't been good enough. I write about real life and I don't like writing by committee." Indeed, the author admits to a Midwest sensibility that extends beyond parlor manners. "I cut to the chase, no nonsense, and I like people who are not pretentious. I love writing and I love reading," she says, surrounded by earthquake-proof bookshelves full of crime and adventure books, mysteries and books on Judaism and religion.

After completing each novel, says Kellerman, "I need a period when I'm creatively bored." She is already immersed in *Moon Music*, her next contribution to the "cottage industry" (as her husband once called their marriage). She will work three to four hours each day until November when she expects it will be finished. It will then be six weeks or two months before she has an inkling of the next book.

As our interview winds to a close, the doorbell rings. These days, one might read about Fuller Brush men, but few people have actually ever seen one. When Kellerman opens the door, there he is, elderly, complete with glasses and Midwestern charm and a suitcase full of what this home-and-family-centered crime fiction-writer claims are, bar none, the finest brushes money can buy. It is absolutely as though she has created him out of thin air. "I'll take four of those ones with the long handles," she says, before leading us to our car, then vanishing, brushes in hand, into her bustling and formidably well-kept domicile.

SUSAN SALTER REYNOLDS
August 18, 1997

STARLING LAWRENCE

STARLING LAWRENCE IS a member of a new and so far rather exclusive club: that of publishing folk who have made a successful transition to writing fiction. One thinks of Jim Landis, formerly of Morrow; John Herman, formerly of Ticknor & Fields; and, most spectacularly and recently, Joe Kanon, formerly of Houghton Mifflin, with his big bestseller *Los Alamos.*

There's one essential difference between Lawrence and the others, however. He is still very much in the trenches, as editor-in-chief at Norton, and has now managed to create two notable books in his spare time.

Lawrence is a tall, good-looking man in his middle years with a manner at once self-deprecating and enthusiastic. With his bow tie and well-cut jacket, he looks every inch the image of the Norton editor—gentlemanly, a little scholarly perhaps, but without a trace of academic pomposity and with a quite swashbuckling sense of a book's commercial possibilities, as well as a sense of pleasure in sheer quality.

Sitting down in a Chelsea restaurant recently, both Lawrence and his interviewer find, as publishing professionals, that it takes a while to get around to discussing his two-year-old short-story collection, *Legacies,* and his new novel, *Montenegro,* both published by Farrar, Straus & Giroux. First there is amusing shop talk about some books that, with great fanfare, proceeded to sink without trace, like an ocean liner heading straight down the launching slipway to the bottom. "That's a sobering introduction to a discussion of literature," says Lawrence, known to nearly everyone as Star. As for his own literary career, he says: "I've been writing for 12 or 15 years, and have only recently begun to try to get published. 'Nothing in haste' is my motto."

So his publishing career to date, monochromatic as to house, but full of dazzling colors in terms of authors, takes up much of the first part of the interview, while designer water is sipped and salad consumed. (It seems typical of Lawrence that, since his interviewer was buying the lunch, he did not think at first to ask for wine but then, once the mutual inclination for it had been understood, went on to consume more than one glass with evident relish).

After graduating from Princeton in 1965, and doing some postgraduate studies at Pembroke College, Cambridge, Lawrence—not untypically for the time—embarked on a spell of do-gooding, place-holding activity: in Lawrence's case, a term in the Peace Corps, teaching English (via old English folk tales) to French-speaking Africans in Cameroon. At one stage, he wrote, for his own pleasure, a story about his landlady in Cambridge and showed it to Brendan Gill, an old family friend, "wondering whether some sort of journalism or magazine writing was what I should be doing." Gill told him, however, that he shouldn't think of it unless he felt he simply had no alternative but to write. "I didn't feel that way, so I decided that being involved with words as a journalist was not what I wanted to do."

On his return from Africa, Lawrence went to see Walter Lord, an author and friend of his wife's family, who put him in touch with Evan Thomas, at Norton, and he was hired as a reader for Thomas and Eric Swenson, another Norton legend. "It seems an old-fashioned idea now, but that was how you began then. I was king of the slush pile for years at Norton, and it was there that I found James Grady's *Six Days of the Condor*, which was hardly a typical Norton book, so perhaps that's why they kept me around." (The story of a renegade agency much like the CIA was a considerable bestseller in the mid-1970s, however, and later a Robert Redford movie.)

Lawrence is at his most self-deprecatingly jocular in describing his Norton career. "I moved up the ladder in obscure and irregular steps. After a time you find you can do what anyone else can do, then it's a matter of proving to the outside world that you can do it, finally you begin to get your hands on things. I would write enthusiastic rejection letters, make a few silk purses out of sows' ears." But perhaps it was Lawrence's aforementioned eye for books that he calls "out of the typical Norton path," that solidified his role. His finds included Martin Katahn (*Rotation Diet*); Michael Lewis (*Liar's Poker*); and the maritime historical novels of Patrick O'Brian. ("There's a host of books much less notable, some verging on the unmentionable, that won't be cited here," adds Lawrence.)

The story of Dr. Katahn's runaway bestseller is one Lawrence clearly enjoys telling, as well he might. "He first came to us with a modest proposal for a diet book that seemed very sound, though we had not been in the habit of publishing this kind of non-academic work; but he'd once been very fat, and had proved how well it worked on himself. That first book sold maybe 6000 copies; his second one did perhaps 10,000 to 15,000; then *Rotation* went to 800,000—a very encouraging sales curve."

O'Brian, who has become a sort of cult author and now enjoys a huge following on both sides of the Atlantic, had done several novels with other U.S. publishers without developing any "critical mass" before coming to Norton. As Lawrence recalls, two friends had recommended O'Brian's work, and he had filed away the thought. Then, on a buying trip in London, he noticed some of his titles on an agent's shelves and took a couple away with him.

After reading a quarter of one on the plane going home, he decided immediately to have him. "I know people think of him as a man's author, but women read him as a kind of Jane Austen, and since she is the writer he reveres most, he'd be very pleased."

Lawrence seems in no particular hurry to talk about his own work, perhaps because it has moved in such mysterious ways. The prologue to *Montenegro* will in fact lead eventually to another novel, and perhaps two, about the character Toma, who is only an element in the present book. A Serbian immigrant, Toma helps invent the long-distance telephone relay (one of the memorable moments in *Montenegro* has him vibrating a knife in the ground, a tremor which can be picked up at a considerable distance, as a harbinger of such a discovery).

"It was a sequence of novels I wanted to write, but I realized I had no idea how to write one," says Lawrence. "So the stories in *Legacies* were like five-finger exercises to teach myself how to write fiction." (By way of illustration, he recalls a friend who, wanting to be a screenwriter, actually retyped James Agee's entire screenplay for *The African Queen* so as to feel, beneath his own fingers, a great screenplay emerging on the page.) The *Legacies* stories are mostly based on life in northwestern Connecticut, where the Lawrence family owns property. The stories are elegantly crafted accounts of loss and change in the lives of mostly affluent, careless people. The book sold, says Lawrence, quite without complaint, "respectably, which means poorly, I guess just a few thousand."

He was pleased with the reviews, however: "I was glad it was taken as well as it was, though bad ones wouldn't have stopped me. Doing it to my own satisfaction was the most important thing—*not* doing it would have been worse than getting bad reviews."

How does someone in a significant position in publishing set about being published? In what he calls "a pleasant happenstance," the agent who took him on was Sarah Chalfant at Andrew Wylie, with whom he lunched one day and found congenial. Wylie was not an agency with whom he had done business previously, so "there were no other irons in the fire," Lawrence says. When it came to finding a publisher, Lawrence gravitated toward FSG as the kind of house that could publish his book with style. This almost in spite of the fact that Jonathan Galassi, editor-in-chief at FSG, is an old friend. "The first rule in my kind of situation is: Don't ask any favors," Lawrence comments. "My son asked if it helped that it was published by a friend. My wife said that probably made it harder, and I think that's probably true."

The book is a fast-moving tale of a young Englishman, Auberon Harwell, who, around the turn of the century, is subsidized by an ambitious and crafty English politician to check out the situation in the rocky fastness of Montenegro, where Austrian, Turkish and Serbian nationalists are in conflict. He will go in the guise of a botanist seeking out alpine plants. Right from the start (when he bribes his way through customs in a tiny Albanian port, sets off up a steep mountain road with a horse and a mule, meets a raffish brigand and soon finds a dead body), Auberon has to prove his mettle. He also has to exorcise some deep-set faults in his nature, displayed in a highly erotic early flashback set in a Mayfair brothel. For Lawrence, the fact that his protagonist has what he calls "feet of clay" makes him more interesting to write about. "I don't want an unsullied saint as a protagonist."

Lawrence goes on: "I don't think human nature changes that much, and if you are writing about a man in very different times and circumstances, it helps if a late-20th-century reader can feel he has impulses comparable to our own." Curiously, although what most impresses the reader about *Montenegro* is the assurance of the spectacular action scenes, including an ambush, an earthquake and a couple of grisly slaughters, it wasn't the adventure story that most attracted the author: "As I was writing it, that was the part I had least confidence in. The characters interested me far more than what they did."

Particularly close to his heart is Lydia, a young English girl teaching languages at a small academy in the provincial capital, who in a sudden flush of passion launches herself at Auberon and later plays a movingly heroic role in the story. "She was a complete surprise to me," confesses Lawrence. "She really came out of nowhere, and when I stopped writing, the hardest thing to get used to was no longer having the characters in the forechamber of my mind, and I missed them. I found out it's really just as Patrick O'Brian says: When you're writing well, everything else in your life is down there."

Yes, Lawrence has visited Montenegro, now one of the two republics (Serbia is the other) that make up what is left of Yugoslavia. He remembered the magnificent, brooding landscapes from his honeymoon in 1985; and for contemporary color, he depended above all on three women writers: Rebecca West, whose *Black Lamb and Grey Falcon* was essential, and two 19th-century travelers who wrote journals, Georgina Muir McKenzie and Edith Durham.

In keeping with Norton's tradition of putting editorial before publicity, Lawrence had no marketing plan in mind for *Montenegro.* "I like writers who write from a commanding impulse. I hope this is a good book, because it has everything in it I knew how to put in." And although the suggestion has been made (by *Publishers Weekly,* among others) that it would make a fine movie, Lawrence insists: "I don't think in those terms. I just write scenes I'd like to see."

His next book, already adumbrated in the prologue to *Montenegro,* will follow Toma through his life as an inventor in the United States; Auberon and Lydia, who seem headed for Serbian domesticity at the end of *Montenegro,* may or may not make a repeat appearance.

Having said all he wants to say about his own book, Lawrence can't resist a few parting words into a journalist's ear about currently cherished works of his own authors. He is, of course, rejoicing in the surprise best-sellerdom of Sebastian Junger's *The Perfect Storm,* ruminating on it with a thought that could well apply to his own novel: "It's amazing and wonderful, in the world of hype around us now, that there are books where word of mouth still carries the day."

JOHN F. BAKER
August 4, 1997

BRAD LEITHAUSER

It's a room straight out of Central Casting, Paris branch. But then, before we even get to his office, Brad Leithauser has already warned this journalist that he is happily living "a very clichéd American writer's life" in Paris.

The scene: a tiny, poorly lit garret, six floors above the famously writer-filled Left Bank. In one corner, beneath the acutely sloping ceiling, is a single bed; opposite that, an ancient shower unit and a miniature stove. Between them, an open window offers a pinched view of the Paris roofscape. Almost all the available space on the battered writing desk is taken by a laptop computer and an open volume of Tennyson. Only one other book is in evidence: a worn paperback copy of *Madame Bovary*, used—without irony or symbolism aforethought, Leithauser insists—to support a broken leg on the room's only chair. The room is too small for other furniture.

All the conventions signifying 'typical writer's garret' are present. But Leithauser, whose latest novel, *The Friends of Freeland*, (Knopf), is anything but a typical writer. In 14 years, he has published four novels, a collection of essays and criticism and three collections of poetry, as well as many thousands of words of journalism, making him one of the very few contemporary American authors comfortable writing and publishing in multiple literary modes.

The way he tells it, the casting of such a wide literary net is a deliberate stance. "I like the old-fashioned idea of being a person of letters," he explains over carafes of Bordeaux at Cafe des Lettres, a low-key writers' hangout only a short stroll from his office and 20 minutes from his home near the Cathedral of Notre Dame. The combination of crisp white shirt opened at the neck, tight-buttoned vest, and slightly disheveled hair and mustache give him the aspect of a vacationing lawyer (he graduated from Harvard Law School in 1980), but over the next two hours, Leithauser's soft-spoken erudition and zeal for all things book-related mark him conclusively as a thoroughly well-rounded literary man.

"It's really only in the last generation or so that fiction writers aren't interested in poetry and don't write it," he continues. "But almost all the American writers of the 19th and early 20th century wrote both, and I feel like I'm trying, in my own limited way, to preserve what seems to me a salubrious tradition."

The tradition seems to extend beyond writing poetry, prose and fiction to Leithauser's expatriate leaning. Since 1980, he has been creating for himself a sort of literary exile, living and working outside the U.S. whenever possible. His current residence in Paris comes after intervals in Japan, Rome, London and Iceland—an unlikely spot for an American writer, perhaps, but one whose past, present and possible future became the major source and inspiration for *The Friends of Freeland*.

He credits his periods abroad to the many scholarships and awards he has won, including a MacArthur Grant as well as to the support of Mount Holyoke College in Massachusetts, where he shares the Emily Dickinson Lectureship in the Humanities with his wife, the poet Mary Jo Salter. But Leithauser gives the impression that, even without such financial and structural aid, he would have made his way to work outside the States anyway.

"If I were sufficiently dedicated and disciplined, I probably could work anywhere," he says. "But be that as it may, I have found that I work better overseas. For one thing, the phone rings less often. There is less daily junk, fewer bills to handle. We don't even have a car to worry about here. It's a real simple, pared down life, and it's very good for work."

Leithauser's hefty new novel seems to confirm the benefits of exile; at 500-plus pages, *The Friends of Freeland* is his most expansive work to date. A political satire set on the fictional north Atlantic island of Freeland, the novel tells of the disastrous re-election bid of the country's 20-year president, Hannibal Hannibalsson. According to the author, parallels with the American political system are deliberate.

"I didn't finish in time, but I was hoping the book would come out in time for the American elections in November, because ultimately I hoped—among other things—that it was a comment on the degradations of thought and integrity in a political system that's completely poll-driven."

Although the campaign dominates the book, the exuberant narrative also has room for an idiosyncratic love story set in 1960s Chicago, a jokey discourse on Mozart's unwritten symphonies, a pointed swipe at American cultural imperialism and the creation of entire geological, meteorological, mythological and cultural systems for Freeland.

"One of the dangers of writing something like this is that you can lose all sense of form," Leithauser says, chopping the air before him in a characteristic burst of hand gestures. "But one of the happiest moments of writing the book came when I realized I could fit in so many observations and themes, from politics to music to the Icelandic Sagas."

Judging by our conversation it would take several works of the scope of *The Friends of Freeland* to contain even a fraction of Leithauser's observations and concerns. In a little over two hours, he touches on the Gettysburg Address, the joys of French and Japanese architecture, John Updike's verse, John le Carré's thrillers, Saul Bellow's imagination, the battle between man and machine for chess supremacy (the subject of a *New Yorker* article collected in Leithauser's 1995 essay collection, *Penchants and Places*) and the insomnia he says has led him to divide the world into people who sleep through the night and people who don't.

As much as anything else, Leithauser is a man both confident in his opinions and comfortable holding them up for discussion.

Born in Detroit in 1953, he was raised in what he calls a literary household. His mother, Gladys, whom he considers his first critic, is a writer of children's and young adult books, and Leithauser already considered himself a poet by the time he entered Harvard College. At Harvard in 1973, he won an Academy of American Poets prize and at the urging of a creative writing teacher, seriously began writing fiction. Despite the subsequent decision to enter law school, which he calls the equivalent for his generation of what entering the military was for the previous one, a conventional legal career was never really likely, and in 1980, Leithauser left the U.S. to edit legal articles in Japan.

There he completed his first poetry collection, *Hundreds of Fireflies* (1982) and began work on *Equal Distance* (1985), a comedy about expatriate Americans in the East. The book was well received in the U.S. and was followed a year later by a second collection of poems, *Cats of the Temple* (1986). A second novel, *Hence* (1989), grew out of extensive research on computer chess tournaments, and a third collection of poetry, *The Mail from Anywhere,* appeared in 1990. Leithauser's last novel, *Seaward* (1993), was something of a departure in that it forsook the lightness of tone of the first two novels in favor of a more somber approach befitting the story of a man visited by his wife's ghost. All Leithauser's books have been published by Knopf, which also publishes Mary Jo Salter. His agent is Lois Wallace.

Leithauser's close relationship with Knopf began even before publication of his first book. "When I was in college," he remembers, "I received a letter from Ann Close, who was then a new editor at Knopf. She had heard from somebody that I was a good writer and asked that I keep in touch as I continued writing. Her approach was different, and I harbored the hope that we were both in it for the long run."

After 21 years, Close remains his editor, and Leithauser says he prizes a relationship that gives him the freedom to write books he fears have a relatively small market. Indeed, despite his acknowledgment that "even very, very good poets don't sell particularly well," poetry remains Leithauser's primary interest.

"I spend more time writing prose, but if I could only write one thing I would write poems," he says. "It seems to me the highest and most noble and satisfying calling. On the other hand, one of the things I like about writing fiction and prose is that there's lots of 'busy work'—research and mindless secretarial tasks. With poetry, if you're stuck, you're stuck, but with fiction and prose, there's always junk to do.

"The other thing with poetry is that I find I can work on it in little tiny snatches. I'll get 15 minutes between classes and I'll pull out one of my poems to look at. My wife jokes about how I often have a poem I'm working on beside me in the car and I'll look at it at a red light—I don't do that with fiction. That's more like sitting down for three or four hours at a stretch. It seems in the little interstices of your day it's much easier to fit in the poetry. It comes out slowly, about 10 pages a year, but I think it's fair to say that that's because I have an obsession with rhyme and meter."

Leithauser uses the word 'obsession' frequently, but not carelessly. He acknowledges a whole range of writerly fixations, from supernatural fiction and ghosts (he edited the 1994 *Norton Anthology of Ghost Stories*) to the physical appearance of his publications (a self-confessed art director's nightmare, he involves himself in jacket design and regularly appears uninvited at printshops to supervise the production of his books). But his most ardent obsession—and one central to the genesis of his new novel—is for Iceland.

Typically extensive research on all things Icelandic for a 1987 *Atlantic Monthly* article left him a serious Icelandophile. Two years later, courtesy of a Fulbright Award, Leithauser moved to Reykjavik for a six-month teaching stint at the national university. Fascinated by the country's "improbable, eccentric quality, and the feeling that, unlike the rest of the world, it's not going to be eventually split between Ted Turner and Walt Disney," he stayed 12 months and shaped his take on the culture into a model for the fictional Freeland.

Leithauser's Icelandophilia also embraces the country's literature, and he seizes the opportunity, like a born-again Christian offered a chance to talk about faith, to extol *Independent People,* the best known novel of Icelandic writer Haldor Laxness, who won the Nobel Prize in 1955.

"In the case of Laxness and *Independent People,* " he admits, "obsession is too weak a word for it. I think it's the greatest book ever written by a living author and I'm absolutely fanatical about it. I honestly do, in some mystical, vaporous way, feel that when Laxness was writing *Independent People,* he had me in mind as the ideal reader.

"And I think it's the hope you have as a writer—that somewhere you're going to reach some reader, preferably removed from your own experience, that feels married to your book. This may be the apologia of a poet who knows he's not going to have as many readers as he'd like, so that you want quality rather than quantity, but I feel one has to proceed under the assumption that there is some reader out there who's going to say, 'this is the Book of My Life.' You're writing for that ideal reader, and as soon as you abandon that, the road gets very slippery."

Although he was still tinkering with *The Friends of Freeland* up to the end of last summer, Leithauser has already completed the third draft of *A Few Corrections,* a new novel he describes as a psychological detective story that, chapter by chapter, corrects the obituary of a respectable Midwestern businessman. He is also working on a novella in verse, which he considers his most ambitious work yet, and is preparing a long novel about a paleontologist. Taken together, it's enough work to keep him at his desk, he says, to his 50th birthday in 2003.

Leithauser, ever the man of letters, seems intent on keeping his ideal reader busy.

COLIN LACEY
January 27, 1997

JOHN LEONARD

SPINNING NIMBLE SOUND bites on books and movies as resident CBS media critic, John Leonard provides a refreshing contrast to the ponderous pontificators of Sunday morning TV. Leonard has long been a trenchant theoretician of both the highbrow and the lowbrow aspects of our culture, broadcasting his maverick reviews on NPR, in the *New York Times, Life, Newsweek* and a half-dozen other magazines—including the *Nation,* where he is currently co-literary editor.

Leonard's eighth book, *Smoke and Mirrors: Violence, Television and Other American Cultures,* out from the New Press, isn't likely to ruffle his CBS sponsors. A sprawling history of the medium, it delivers a weighty riposte to all who consider the tube to be the enemy of civility and high art. TV is neither an opiate nor a Pandora's box, contends Leonard, but a medium of intermittent gravity and grace, capable of great feats of empathy and postmodern élan, refracting, but rarely reinforcing, the disorder of contemporary life.

Leonard's life has had its own disorders. After 16 years on the staff of the *New York Times,* including a brief but incendiary tour of duty at the helm of *Book Review,* Leonard's career seemed to crash and burn. He battled alcoholism and narrowed his focus, reviewing television for *New York* magazine, but little else. In a candid conversation, Leonard acknowledged the toll his years as a critic and gadfly of the culture industry have exacted upon him, both personally and professionally. But his enthusiasm hasn't dampened for needling the powers-that-be or for celebrating what he deems great art, be it in print or on the screen.

"Institutions are very peculiar places," Leonard says coolly, legs crossed in a wicker chair in his spartan *Nation* office. "They can, up to a point, encompass contradictions. They can congratulate themselves for having a house-pet dissenter. Because they're buying style, and living with the peculiarities that come with it. I had a long leash at the *Times* for a number of years, and I've had an equally long leash at CBS, but at any point they could pull the plug and you will have to find another place to do what you do."

Leonard discovered the allure of intellectual dissent as a lower-middle-class latchkey child in Southern California in the 1950s (Leonard and his younger brother lived with their mother, a secretary, and rarely saw their alcoholic father, who lived in Washington, D.C.) "You invent yourself when you're a teenager," he says. "I had an underground newspaper as a high school sophomore, I subscribed to the Congressional Record. I was the president of Longbeach Young Democrats my senior year. There's a picture of me with Adlai Stevenson in 1956. He's exhausted, he knows he's going to lose the election. I look like a teenage Robespierre who's going to put all his enemies against the wall and kill them." At 58, with a tweed jacket and an unruly beard, Leonard looks less revolutionary than professorial.

A scholarship student, Leonard dropped out of Harvard in 1958 and was hired by William F. Buckley to write for the *National Review*, before getting married and moving to Berkeley to finish his B.A. As a program director at Pacifica Radio, he began reviewing books in weekly 15-minute installments. "It was a great period in literature. It seemed like everything I picked up was just terrific: *Catch-22*, *The Crying of Lot 49* and *The Golden Notebook* and *The Tin Drum*." Delacorte published Leonard's own first novel, *The Naked Martini* (he calls it "a college and New York young man novel"), when he was 25.

In 1964, the author moved to the East Coast and into a new phase of his life, settling in rural New Hampshire to write and raise a family, then in Boston, where he pledged himself to the War on Poverty. "I taught with Jonathan Kozol in a church in Roxbury until we got kicked out by black power people in '67. Then I was in the anti-war movement," he says.

In 1967 a reader's job opened at the *Times Book Review* and Leonard, already estranged from the political front lines, jumped at the chance. "I had two kids. I came cheap," he recalls with a laugh. A year and a half later, he was promoted to staff reviewer. Within two years, Francis Brown, who for 27 years had been editor of the *Book Review*, stepped down. Dan Schwarz, then the Sunday editor of the *Times*, took a gamble and appointed Leonard editor. He was 31.

It's impossible to imagine the cautious bureaucrats who run today's *Times* placing such authority in the hands of a brash, inexperienced young editor. "I was a wholesome young man at a time when institutions were run by older men looking for surrogate sons," Leonard muses. Emboldened by his rapid ascent, Leonard soon proceeded to transform the *Book Review.* He hired Victor Navasky to inveigh against publishing hypocrisies in a column called "In Cold Print," and devoted an entire issue to books opposing the war in Vietnam. "I thought it was a tenured professorship. I went out and bought a house in Manhattan because I assumed this was it."

What Leonard did not anticipate, however, was feeling entombed by the administrative bureaucracy of the job. "I was an office desk jockey. And I wasn't writing, which had always been my normal respiration of intelligence." As Leonard is quick to assert, it's difficult to win a popularity contest as editor of the *Book Review.* But the mounting criticism from the newspaper staff and its readers proved too burdensome. "It took me four years out of the five years I was there to realize the *Book Review* is always the subject of paranoid complaint. I made it more political, more literary, less middle-brow, and everybody complained. But it wouldn't have mattered what I'd done. They always complain."

In 1975, Leonard stepped down to become chief cultural critic at the *Times,* he began writing book reviews twice a week and launched his "Private Lives" column, a sage chronicle of domestic life on the Upper East Side. The column was immensely popular, and was anthologized in a 1979 collection from Knopf titled *Private Lives in the Imperial City.*

Leonard's own private life, in the meantime, was slowly unraveling. He stopped writing fiction, after four novels, in 1973. He was divorced in 1976, but later married his present wife, Sue, who is a history teacher at the Brearley School and co-literary editor with Leonard at the *Nation.* As Leonard's political skirmishes, particularly with *Times* editor A.M. Rosenthal, grew intense, his career as a book critic, which once had a breakneck momentum of its own, seemed to stall.

A world-weary candor, the hallmark of a veteran 12-Stepper, enters Leonard's voice as he reflects on the slow disintegration of his career at the *Times* and the corrosive politics that finally drove him to leave the newspaper. "What changed at the *Times*—and you can't pin it down to say that it's cause and effect—is that about the time of the election of Ronald Reagan, the newsroom changed. I became a suspicious character. They didn't want me reviewing Henry Kissinger's memoirs. It wasn't as though my politics had never been there before, but suddenly they were saying 'this is editorial, this isn't a book review.'

"Well, book reviews *are* acts of criticism. They're editorial. So suddenly it seemed to me I was fighting a battle every day over what I could say and couldn't say. At one point I panned Betty Friedan's *The Second Stage.* I didn't know she was a friend of Rosenthal's, and he was just furious. Suddenly they took the daily job away from me, for a while, as punishment.

"I got angrier and angrier. I looked around and realized: I'm extremely unhappy. I'm drinking myself into a stupor. If I don't leave the *Times* now I'll never leave the goddamn paper."

But quitting the *Times* was not the panacea he envisioned. In 1983, Leonard took a writing job at the newly revamped *Vanity Fair,* reviewed books for NPR and New York *Newsday,* and TV for Ed Kosner at *New York* magazine, but years of turmoil at the *Times* had taken their toll and in 1986 he was hospitalized for alcoholism.

"I felt that I'd made a number of huge errors. Since I never before thought about a career, I just bounced from one thing to the next. I loved going to work for the *New York Times.* I was still of that generation that when they called, you went. You never gave it a second thought."

Leonard is exacting in his judgment of the changes the book section has undergone since his tenure. "I find it appalling that the front page of the *Book Review* isn't used every week to celebrate a book occasion. That there's no copy. There ought to be one review that you put on the cover and say, 'this is the event this week in the world of books.' "

A leadoff illustration, Leonard says, "is a cop-out. This is your front page. So what's your important story? [The *Book Review*] is not doing what I always wanted it to do—which is to surprise you. To make you pay attention. To shake you by the lapels, to say this is important, these are the ideas that are unleashed in the culture today. Go out and buy it. Change your life."

But Leonard's gripe with the *Book Review* echoes what he considers a deeper and troubling trend in book culture at large. "What I find in too much book reviewing, generally speaking, is that everybody is being so careful. So grudging and Olympian in their criticism, as though some genuine warmth and enthusiasm for a book would cost you your own personal body heat. I don't understand it. There are so many good books out there."

When Leonard's personal enthusiasm is operating at full-tilt, as it often does in *Smoke and Mirrors,* his prose is an inimitable blend of aphorism, satire and gonzo wordplay, a style indebted to critics like Pauline Kael, Leslie Fiedler and the *Partisan Review* crowd, who helped Leonard find his own voice in the early '60s. "They had that mandarin taste, which I still have. It's the standard by which you measure things. But they also had that weird love of movies, that weird love of baseball."

Smoke and Mirrors is a rambling polemic, freighted with streams of unfiltered statistics, TV trivia, synopsis and literary allusion. But in his own defense, Leonard might say that his goal was to replicate the experience of actually watching TV. The idea, he explains, was "to recapitulate the rush of all of these things happening and give you the sense of speed and multiplicity and bombardment that comes from one angle or another—to indulge in the prose precisely those kinds of things that happened in my head while I was watching.

"It's very funny to write a book about TV for a publishing house like the New Press," Leonard adds, "where they can correct your Heidegger, they can correct your German and French, but if I omitted a genre of TV they might not notice because [the editors there] don't do a lot of TV watching."

Yet in many respects, the New Press is a comfortable home for Leonard. Three years earlier, the house published *The Last Innocent White Man in America,* an essay collection that serves as a John Leonard primer. He envisions a third volume from the New Press, a counterpart to *Smoke and Mirrors,* that will do for the high culture of literature by non-white writers what *Smoke and Mirrors* does for television.

Regardless of the subject matter or rostrum he chooses, Leonard consistently serves not just as an arbiter of the high and low, a literary provocateur or a freelance talking head, but as a defender of the true values of culture against the shoddy and mundane.

"The high point of my professional life," he says, "was in 1993 when Toni Morrison won the Nobel Prize and she called me up and said would you come to Stockholm. I did and I found I was surrounded by people whose books I've reviewed. The inferiority that we feel in the presence of genius gets dissipated to an extent when you look around and realize that you were useful as a citizen, you were useful as an early warning signal system."

JONATHAN BING
March 17, 1997

JONATHAN LETHEM

Ever since a wise-cracking, motorscooter-riding kangaroo named Joey Castle pistol-whipped Conrad Metcalf in the parking lot of the Bayview Adult Motor Inn in *Gun, with Occasional Music,* Jonathan Lethem has had the world of mainstream literary fiction looking nervously over its shoulder. When that novel, Lethem's first, was published without fanfare by Harcourt Brace in 1994, most reviews labeled it a mystery novel, "a very strange one," the 34-year-old author recalls. But in fact, Lethem never saw himself as a mystery writer at all. Even as he was writing *Gun* he had another, wholly different project on the back burner: *Amnesia Moon,* a post-apocalyptic American desert road novel. Then came an eclectic science fiction story collection: *The Wall of the Sky, the Wall of the Eye,* and last year's *As She Climbed Across the Table,* a love story and academic satire with a Lethem twist: it turns out that one of the competitors for particle physicist Alice Coomb's affections is a highly charismatic black hole known as Lack.

It is difficult to connect the author of these outrageous fictional scenarios with Lethem's restrained, rather ascetic appearance. He discusses his books earnestly and intently. With his stylishly spartan wire-rimmed glasses, dark V-neck sweater and close-cropped hair, Lethem has nothing of the mad genius about him. It's as if he had harnessed every bit of inner ferment and rebellion—against social and literary expectation—and turned them toward the writing of his books.

As case in point, take his latest novel, *Girl in Landscape* (Doubleday), a beautiful but grim work that exists somewhere in the previously uncharted interstices between science fiction, western and coming-of-age novels. Most of the characters who run amok through its pages are ordinary children—which is to say, rebellious, sexually curious and violent—who experiment with all sorts of forbidden fruits, including a visionary out-of-body state that is reached, perversely enough, by *not* taking drugs. A maverick John Wayne–type character looms in the background for most of the tale, his figure starkly silhouetted against the backdrop of an alien sky, but he meets his match in the precocious adolescent protagonist, Pella. "Where did I find the confidence to write from the point of view of a 13-year-old girl?" Lethem asks. "She comes out of impulses and emotions in me. The fact of her being a girl is secondary." Lethem's confessed external sources for the story were Carson McCullers and Shirley Jackson, for that "tomboy-coming-of-age-sexual awakening vibe," and his obsession with the John Ford film *The Searchers*, in which the John Wayne character tries to rescue a young girl who has been abducted by Indians. "It's an obsessive quest, and he's an anti-heroic, racist, angry figure. I wanted to explore what it was like to have your sexual coming-of-age watched over by this bullying man," Lethem says. Although it takes place on another planet, Lethem argues that *Girl* is less about science fiction than any of his other novels. "I'm very proud of *Girl in Landscape*," he says. "I know it's a weird one, but I think it's the most novelistic of any book I've written."

For an author whose first book came out in 1994, the phrase "any book I've written" sounds almost glib, but when asked about his prolific output—five books in as many years—Lethem demurs. "It's a real sleight-of-hand that's about to be exposed." It turns out he hasn't really been writing a book a year. It's just that he ended up finishing 10 years worth of work in a five-year period, and now he's more or less caught up with himself. Of course, that still adds up to a book every other year—a pretty good clip by most standards.

Lethem grew up in Brooklyn, N.Y., the son of an "unfamous painter" dedicated to his art but always forced to work another job. Growing up, Lethem looked forward to a similar career. He studied painting at the High School of Music and Art, in Harlem, and spent the long subway rides to and from Manhattan engrossed in novels that were not on his high school syllabus, whether because they were a little too weird, a little too low-brow or a little too avant-garde. The list of his early influences is eclectic—including Philip K. Dick, Charles Willeford, Jim Thompson, Thomas Pynchon and Kurt Vonnegut—and it provides a key to Lethem's sensibility, his scorn for what he calls "the obsolescence of bankrupt categories," his exuberant, intellectually sophisticated emulsion of high and low. From the age of 15 until the year *Gun* came out, Lethem worked in a series of small, out-of-the-way secondhand bookshops in New York City and California. In the 1980s, he was reading books that had come out 10 years before, "because that's what the used bookstores are loaded with"—a habit he still maintains, although he cites Jeffrey Eugenides, David Bowman and Ian McEwan as contemporaries whose work he follows with particular interest. Although Lethem attended Bennington College (for just three semesters) during the period when Donna Tartt and Bret Easton Ellis were there, he was a studio art major, not part of the writing crowd, and kept his own attempts at fiction under the table. He finished a first novel, which was never published, about the time he would have graduated, but says he knew as soon as it was finished that it wasn't any good. "It was just the X number of bad pages I had to write," he says. He started writing stories after that and moved to Berkeley, where he again eked out a meager existence on used-bookshop wages and wrote whenever he wasn't at work. Although he was never affiliated with the university, Lethem was briefly married to a graduate student there, Shelley Jackson, and his experiences with her were part of the inspiration for *As She Climbed Across the Table*. The book is dedicated to her, though they were divorced by the time he finished it. "If you asked me then, I would have said I'd be working at bookstores until I was 45," he says. "You have to understand—all my heroes were dark horses. They all had embattled careers because of genre prejudice, something I've had the good fortune to be spared. It's like I'm standing on their shoulders. I sort of feel Philip K. Dick died for my sins."

Indeed, recognition of Lethem's writing did come relatively quickly. The hard part was finding an agent, which took about a year and entailed some frustrating rejections. Lethem says he would have taken pretty much anyone who would have him, when he finally stumbled into a happy association with Richard Parks (who remains his agent today). A year and a half later Parks placed *Gun* with Michael Kandel at Harcourt Brace. Then, in March of 1994, just when *Gun* was being released, Kandel was fired. The book might have been orphaned had it not been so cheap to publish. The advance was only $6000, and there was no publicity campaign to cancel. Lethem's greatest concern was the loss of a sympathetic line-editor, especially since they had just signed a contract for *Amnesia Moon*.

That was when things suddenly began to turn around for Lethem. A reviewer at *Newsweek* noticed *Gun* in the vast pile of unheralded review copies. Characterizing it as an "audaciously assured first novel," *Newsweek*'s write-up catapulted the previously obscure book to the public's attention. "There are certain nodes of centralized cultural power," Lethem muses. "It's scary, but it's nice to have one of them working on your side when it happens."

The big change occurred when Alan Pakula optioned the movie rights, enabling Lethem to quit his day job at the bookstore. Since he never expected his subsequent books to do so well, Lethem tried to stretch the money from *Gun* as far as possible, living what he calls a "bohemian garret existence." Harcourt Brace eventually rehired Kandel, who oversaw the publication of *Amnesia Moon* and acquired *The Wall of the Sky*. Paperback rights for the first three books sold to St. Martin's, and foreign sales have been strong. Lethem's next three books, *As She Climbed Across the Table*, *Girl in Landscape* and the novel, as yet untitled, that he's working on now, were all bought by Bill Thomas at Doubleday. David Lynch and a partner recently optioned *Amnesia Moon*. Lethem seems particularly pleased as he pulls from his shelf the new Vintage Contemporaries edition of *As She Climbed Across the Table*. Vintage has also bought paperback rights to *Girl in Landscape*. "It's really flattering to be in Vintage Contemporaries because I read that line with so much enthusiasm in my 20s. I discovered Richard Ford that way, Frederick Exley, so many writers," Lethem observes.

As a result of this commercial success Lethem is now able to write full time, but the most important thing, he says, is that his books are widely read. "I'm completely in print, which is amazing. I don't know how long it will last, but it's exciting to me to know that my work is out there in the cultural fray." He goes to his desk for a newspaper clip showing Holly Hunter and several other actors after a staged reading of a story from *The Wall of the Sky, the Wall of the Eye*. "It's thrilling because that reading had nothing to do with New York literary hype. It came from someone's excitement at reading my work."

After 10 years in California, Lethem returned to his hometown of Brooklyn a year and a half ago because, he says, he wanted to live in the city that will be the setting for his next two novels (which are not otherwise linked). He lives and writes in a tar-papered building in the largely Polish neighborhood of Greenpoint, far from the nearest Manhattan-bound subway station. The area of the apartment dedicated to living space is simple, spare, yet comfortable, bed tucked into a hallway alcove, tiny living room furnished with a 1950s armchair and a sleek vinyl-covered couch. One wall is lined from floor to ceiling with narrow-gauge bookshelves perfectly suited to Lethem's collections of pulp paperbacks. The office is by far the largest room in the apartment—one that a less single-minded person might have used as the bedroom or living room. Lethem says he gets up in the morning and goes straight to work, often not leaving the house until lunchtime, when he ambles to a local Thai restaurant for a bowl of noodle soup as a way of breaking up the day. There are days when his only outing is a quick visit to the newstand for a paper.

Brooklyn makes a cameo appearance in *Girl in Landscape,* as a ravaged, barely inhabitable eco-nightmare of a city, but the scene quickly shifts to the Planet of the Archbuilders, a frontier reminiscent of the Wild West. "I was putting my toes in the water for coming back home to Brooklyn in *Girl in Landscape,*" Lethem says. He characterizes the Brooklyn book he's working on now as "a sort of a madcap crime novel—not a mystery because there are no murders, clues, solutions, but the characters are rascals." An "Oliver Sacks type" neurological dysfunction is prominently featured in the story, and the voice shares some of the zaniness of *Gun* and *As She Climbed Across the Table.* Whimsy is important in all Lethem's books, even the comparatively dark *Girl in Landscape,* in which the language-obsessed alien characters, enamored of what they consider the poetic possibilities of English, take names like Lonely Dumptruck, Specious Axiomatic and Somber Fluid.

This persistent, playful humor, which tends to support serious thematic concerns, is one of the ways Lethem manages to pull off such improbable narrative stunts. "There are a lot of things in my books that come from a need to keep myself amused during the long, lonely writing day. I try to avoid taking myself too seriously. That would be toxic."

ELIZABETH GAFFNEY
March 30, 1998

Patrick McCabe

O<small>N A</small> W<small>EDNESDAY</small> night so dark and wet it has cleared the Sligo streets of life, *PW* arrives at Patrick McCabe's terraced house in the center of town and immediately feels like an intruder into a scene of everyday domestic turmoil. McCabe, a two-time Booker Prize nominee, is cursing a computer that will not allow his 13-year-old daughter to go on-line in search of information on the *Titanic*. It's for a school assignment, she complains; he tells her to look it up in a book; she tries once more to connect, failing again. More mutterings at the screen are drowned out by the sounds of other householders marching from room to room upstairs. The telephone rings, and a young girl—the author's other daughter, presumably—shouts that it'll be for her. Leading us to the relative calm of the kitchen, McCabe clears away the remains of the family dinner, deposits the dishes in the sink and sets to making a large pot of coffee. Just when we are settled in at the table to begin, McCabe is called to the telephone, to which he lends one ear while with the other he monitors the commotion from above.

It's a scene of such blazing normality that squaring it with McCabe's mischievous fiction, which takes place in a landscape of distracted, collapsing sanity and features characters ranging from the bizarrely dysfunctional to the comically murderous, is a difficult, if not impossible task. Indeed, dressed casually in an old pinstripe jacket, T-shirt and jeans, and surrounded by the detritus of home life, the 43-year-old author, considered a sort of high priest of rural Irish dementia, seems out of place. His world seems, however cluttered, wholly sane. But such incongruity may in fact be the key to understanding the worlds he creates in his fictions.

McCabe's conversation, once we get down to it, is peppered with references to Walter Pater, Graham Greene and European art, but also Bob Dylan, the films of Sam Fuller and a range of 1960s science fiction films. He speaks soberly and seriously of his new novel, the

Booker-nominated *Breakfast on Pluto* (Harper Collins). While pausing to respectfully tip his hat to James Joyce and Carson McCullers, he arrives at the more Technicolor description of the book as "Roy Lichtenstein goes to Leitrim"—evoking both the garish coloring of *Breakfast on Pluto* and the Irish county in which much of the story is set. He goes on to describe a planned collection of short stories as being like "a mondo movie about a small Irish town in the 1960s; Sherwood Anderson's Winesburg, Ohio, after a feed of drugs."

In his fiction, too, gleeful ambiguity is the name of the game. Served up in a chatty, colloquial narrative voice, his darkly satirical burlesques strut the line between comedy and horror, while his characters are equal parts lovable and chilling. In his breakthrough third novel, the Booker-nominated *The Butcher Boy* (Dial, 1993), a disturbed 13-year-old narrator slays his best friend's mother and terrorizes his home town while remaining on the outside a likable young charmer. His next work, *The Dead School* (Dial, 1995) focused on an increasingly psychotic school teacher locked in battle with a drug-addled, love-lorn colleague, both of whom remain sympathetic, after a fashion. McCabe's latest offering, which completes a thematically linked trilogy begun with *The Butcher Boy*, features one Patrick "Pussy" Braden, a transvestite rent boy from small-town Ireland with IRA connections, a beehive haircut and an endearing Dusty Springfield fixation. A grown-up version of Francie Brady, eponymous hero of *The Butcher Boy*, 19-year-old Pussy is perhaps the first gender-bending prostitute ever to appear in a Booker-nominated novel, and is certainly the first character of his kind in Irish literature. But as the domestic normality around the author emphatically underlines, just because he has created Pussy and a clutch of other off-the-wall kooks doesn't mean McCabe is himself anything other than ordinary, the author says.

"A lot of people read the books and believe I must be some sort of freaky-deaky dude," he protests, when asked where his bizarre cast of characters actually comes from. "But that's not the case at all. It's not that difficult to put yourself inside the head of a character, and it's no more difficult to put yourself in the mind of a transvestite prostitute than it is to put yourself in the mind of a boy whose heart is broken and who chops up a woman. Writing is like method acting. You sit down and do the work and just switch off when it's over."

Which is probably just as well, given the exploits of his latest creation. Set largely during an IRA bombing campaign in the early

1970s, the new novel traces Pussy's decline from effeminate youth in an Irish border town to the back streets of a London gripped by fear and hatred and under siege from terrorist explosives. Mixing lyrical prose with a range of narrative voices and chronologies—a departure for McCabe, whose previous novels have had linear structures—the book emerges as an archly ironic comedy of horrors that hurls the reader from laughter to repugnance, often in the space of a single phrase. Despite the lurid subject matter, McCabe insists the book is about bigger things than the central character's sexual preferences. "It's about politics and borders and gender borders," he explains, stroking a tightly-clipped beard and mulling over every word. "It wasn't a deliberate step into political fiction, but I grew up in the 1970s when you couldn't avoid politics, and it would have been remiss of me and ignoble to walk away from something that's crying out to be written about."

The second of five children, McCabe was born in 1955 near the Northern Ireland border in Clones, Co. Monaghan. A late convert to literature, he was obsessed with American music and culture, devouring comics (he still has a collection of favorites from his childhood) and seeing as many as 10 Hollywood movies a week. He trained as a teacher in Dublin and taught in a variety of schools by day, but raced around Ireland's theaters and dance halls by night, playing keyboard with a popular cabaret band who specialized in country-and-western covers. He always considered himself a writer, however, and eventually faced the choice of turning professional musician or devoting his energy to novels.

In 1985 he hung up his amps and moved with his family to London, where he taught for eight years and wrote in his spare time. But that is not to say that he has discarded music. On the contrary, he begins a novel not with a plot but with a mood, usually suggested by a song or lyric. Although it deals in the currency of terrorism and sexuality, *Breakfast on Pluto* itself was inspired by a kitschy 1969 U.K. hit by Don Partridge, and is filled with references to music and songs of the early 1970s.

In 1986, McCabe published his first novel, *Music on Clinton Street* (the title was lifted from the Leonard Cohen song "Famous Blue Raincoat".) His second effort, *Carn* (published here as a Delta trade paperback in 1997) attracted positive reviews, but he seemed destined to remain in relative obscurity until, in 1992, and seemingly out of nowhere, *The Butcher Boy* appeared to near-universal acclaim. The Booker nomination brought further attention, and when director Neil Jordan bought the rights to the book, McCabe was granted the financial where-withal to quit teaching and devote himself full-time to writing. One of his first projects was to collaborate on the screenplay with Jordan, who has also purchased the rights to the new novel. The film was released in 1997 and featured a hilarious cameo by the author himself as town drunk Jimmy the Skite. McCabe remembers his brush with the silver screen fondly: "That wasn't acting," he laughs. "It was just being drunk."

As well as financial independence and a move back to Ireland, the international success of *The Butcher Boy* book and film brought more than a few multi-book offers. But McCabe has never believed in selling something he hasn't yet written, and continues to deal on a one-book-only basis. It frees him from pressure to produce, he says. "Going on these odd journeys is so much a part of my personality that I want to go there alone," he maintains. "I don't want someone coming along with me to ask how the journey is going, and reminding me that they've bought the ticket."

Breakfast on Pluto came out of a particularly arduous two-year journey. Writing entirely in longhand, he produced an uncharacteristically long first draft for a novel he intended to be short and spare, and credits his U.K. editor John Reilly (now at Faber) with helping deliver the final draft. But McCabe faced further difficulties with the book: American publishers wanted nothing to do with it. He still seems genuinely puzzled, and perhaps a little hurt, at the reaction the manuscript received stateside.

"Everybody who read it said it was madcap and funny and camp, but that there wasn't enough story to it," he recalls. "A lot of them prefaced their comments with 'Having adored *The Butcher Boy* I was deeply disappointed . . .' Maybe they just didn't get what the book is about."

McCabe remained convinced the novel had an audience. Exasperated with the progress of American representatives, he gave the novel to Irish agent Marianne Gonne O'Connor, an old school friend he describes as among the most gifted agents in the world, and within a couple of weeks she had placed the book with Paul McCarthy at HarperCollins. "What turned it was that I found an editor who understood the book," McCabe explains matter-of-factly. "McCarthy turned out to be one of the most brilliant editors I've ever worked with. He knew instinctively what I was doing."

The subsequent Booker nomination was a vindication of his and his editor's belief in *Breakfast on Pluto*, McCabe says. "You develop the skill of being stoic in the face of rejection early in your writing life and if people smack you around, you just have to endure it," he says. "Even more than a selling point, the nomination is a vote of favor and confidence in a book people were shaky about."

Next on the author's schedule is a diversion away from literature, and into another apparent incongruity. Along with Irish lounge singer Jack L., the author has recorded a 2-CD set of readings and performances with accompanying music, for release next year. The return to music is unlikely to amount to more than a one-off, however. Although he has no plans for new fiction beyond a collection of short stories scheduled for late 1999, McCabe says he remains tied to the routine of writing and domesticity.

"Writing novels is a bit like being a seamstress," he says. "It's a stitch at a time, and if you're away for three weeks and have to come home to start again, the whole thing is unraveled. All those things that turn your life upside down ultimately interfere with the kind of dull, ordinary monotony that is essential for writing fiction."

And while he is anything but dull and monotonous, McCabe is as far from Pussy Braden and the confused terrain of *Breakfast on Pluto* as it's possible to imagine. Bidding farewell to a journalist at his front door, he already has one eye on the computer that had earlier blocked his daughter's schoolwork. Interview over, he is no longer the chronicler of fractured Irish lives and creator of macabre, cracked characters, but an ordinary father who has to get the kids ready for school the next morning.

COLIN LACEY
November 16, 1998

JAY MCINERNEY

JAY MCINERNEY'S FIRST night back in America begins at Elio's, his neighborhood watering hole, with a negroni straight up, a cigarette and what the narrator of McInerney's first novel (speaking to himself) called "the most shameful of your addictions"—a perusal of the *New York Post*.

Tonight, the story that grabs McInerney isn't about a Coma Baby, Killer Bees or Hero Cops. It's about Jay McInerney, quoted yesterday on his British book tour, confessing old romantic sins to a London reporter.

"I always say more than I should the farther I get from home," the well-tailored, 43-year-old crows, his voice pitched to permanent, cocktail-party expansiveness, his jet lag adding a wrinkle or two to his bluff, still-youthful good looks. "Sometimes I think everything I touch turns into a Page Six item."

The suspicion is forgivable. Since *Bright Lights, Big City* hit the shelves in 1984, McInerney has yet to stray out of reach of the spotlight. His wild nights have become matters of public record, his breakups public bloodbaths, his pronunciamentos public stinks. Often scorned or dismissed by the New York reviewing establishment, McInerney has attracted a small core of literary defenders. In the meantime, he has become a household name, someone famous—as, he has observed, few writers since Norman Mailer have been—simply for being famous. In other words, a celebrity.

Is it worth it? That is the question at the heart of *Model Behavior,* the title novella of McInerney's latest collection from Knopf, a work McInerney calls "my meditation on celebrity journalism and the cult of celebrity, which has obviously become our national religion in the last 10 years."

The novella follows two young men, each in his own way a victim of New York's star system. There's painfully camera-shy, head-turningly handsome Jeremy Green, anxious over the reception of his forthcoming first collection, "a gloss on Thoreau—with a nod to Poe's 'Cask of Amontillado'—in which the island of Manhattan serves as a dystopian mirror for the pond of Walden, a septic ecosystem which drives its inhabitants to despair and suicide."

Then there's Jeremy's best friend: slick, social Connor McKnight. Connor has problems of his own. His girlfriend, a model named Philomena, won't sleep with him. Neither will Pallas, the stripper who haunts his dreams. His sister seems to be descending once again into anorexia. He hates his job, interviewing celebrities for *Ciao-Bella!*, a young women's magazine. And for some reason, his latest subject, Chip Ralston—a boy star from hell who seems to have caught the eye of both Philomena and Pallas—won't return his calls.

It doesn't take Sigmund Freud to see a little of McInerney in his latest fictional creations.

In 1984, McInerney was a 29-year-old lapsed grad student and self-described "literary geek" with one brief, unhappy marriage behind him, a new wife (philosophy student Merry McInerney) and a worshipful friendship with his teacher Raymond Carver. He never expected *Bright Lights*—his now canonical account of cocaine-snorting junior glitterati in Gotham—to make it big when his old friend Gary Fisketjon, then a senior editor of Random House (and a biographical source for the narrator's corrupter, Tad Allagash), decided to issue the book as the first of its Vintage Original paperbacks.

Neither did Jason Epstein, executive editor of Random House at the time and éminence grise of the Vintage line. "He said to me, 'There hasn't been a New York novel since I've been alive and don't be surprised if no one wants to know about it,'" McInerney recalls. "It sounds stupid now, but in 1984 that was the conventional wisdom." Random didn't even spring for a party to launch the book.

Then came the glowing reviews and a call from Amanda Urban (who has agented McInerney's subsequent books). And, surprisingly, brisk sales. (The novel has sold 1,000,000 copies to date, according to Vintage.) Before long, the geek was the man of the hour.

"I would have imagined myself to be someone like Jeremy," McInerney says, "until I got the French kiss of popular acceptance. You never know what you'll do until you're in that embrace."

What McInerney did was party. Between his ostentatious drug use ("I've done my best to become a flat-out drug addict, and I've failed") and his well-publicized erotic imbroglios, McInerney became a favorite target for gossip columnists. His second marriage ended in divorce, public recriminations and a mordant roman à clef by Merry about Jay's failings as a husband. At the same time, his next two novels, *Ransom* and *The Story of My Life*, bombed with the New York literary establishment, which he claims singled him out for shabby treatment. "I got a bad rap," he says.

McInerney chalks up some of his bad press to resentment. "I think a lot of the people who write about me think that if they had to write fewer interviews then they would transcribe their life-story and it would be a big success. Or should be."

Could all the bad reviews and snide profiles be products of jealousy?

"No, it's something else too. I collaborated in the creation of my own image as a generational spokesman. It was very easy to read me as the protagonist of my own book, as the symbol of the very thing I claimed to be criticizing. For a long time, it seemed like, 'One more interview, one more photo, how can it be a bad thing?' "

McInerney is quick to distinguish his willingness to please reporters from the self-promotion of Tama Janowitz, a writer often described in the 1980s as a member of McInerney's "Brat Pack," who drew criticism for appearing in paid advertisements after the success of her first story collection, *Slaves of New York*.

"I still think the idea of a writer doing an ad is appalling. I was offered a Dewars profile and a Gap ad, and I didn't do things like that because the day you take money to be an actor, then you're a whore. Tama was embracing this celebrity culture in ways that pointed at the dangers of it all." Indeed, McInerney is still bitter at having been associated with a "pack" of other writers at the height of his popularity. "I was really mad when this school started being created, because I had less to gain than anybody. I was the one who'd been there first."

In 1990, McInerney struck back. In an essay that put him on the cover of *Esquire* (brandishing a samurai sword), he lashed out at the country's most prominent critics, claiming that they were prejudiced against young writers. At the same time, he dismissed the latest work of the two young writers most closely associated with him, Janowitz and Bret Easton Ellis (whom he calls "still one of my closest friends"). And, although nobody knew it at the time, he set to work on the novel that would ultimately regain him wide, if grudging, critical respect.

By the time *Brightness Falls,* his sweeping, Dawn Powellish satire of the publishing world, appeared in 1992, McInerney seemed to have silenced many of his enemies and left his rowdy ways behind. He was married again, this time to a woman seven years his senior, jewelry designer Helen Bransford, and the couple had settled near her ancestral home outside Nashville, returning only occasionally to their Upper East Side pied-à-terre. McInerney seemed to be enjoying the role of the Southern gentleman (although he grew up the son of an itinerant paper executive, McInerney says he has "a lot of memories and interest in the South"). Twin children followed in 1994 and, soon after, a fifth novel, *The Last of the Savages,* which drew on McInerney's admiring observations of the Southern aristocracy.

Model Behavior represents a return to the New York scene, one that mirrors McInerney's own renewed interest in the city. About the time he finished *The Last of the Savages,* McInerney says, "suddenly there was this general vitality, which always corresponds, though most of us cultural types don't like to admit it, to an economic boom."

Not coincidentally, perhaps, McInerney found himself back in the newspapers—this time not in the role of an up-and-coming young Jeremy Green but cast, instead, in a role more proleptic of roving-eyed Connor McKnight.

In the turn of events that McInerney calls the autobiographical "backdrop" to *Model Behavior, Harper's Bazaar* hired him to write a profile of movie actress Julia Roberts. Although he refuses to say how intimate he and the starlet became, the tabloids made much of their acquaintance, and McInerney himself felt that he'd stepped over the line between acceptable collaboration with the celebrity industry and collaboration *tout court.*

"I went out for three nights running with Julia till three in the morning and had a great time. But I felt horribly complicit in the end."

The profile had fateful consequences. In *Welcome to Your Facelift: What to Expect Before, During, and After Cosmetic Surgery*—a book based on her own experience—Bransford claims that it was McInerney's infatuation with Roberts that made Bransford decide to go under the knife. The profile also spurred McInerney to undertake a novel from the point of view of a writer who finds himself trapped on the receiving end of a condenser mic—and whose only escape is to join the tinseltown he chronicles. Connor manages this feat, after Jeremy dies in a freak accident, by adapting one of his stories (called "Model Behavior") for the big screen.

This fictional escape, McInerney insists, reflects a real, pernicious social trend. "Hollywood has been gradually stealing the rest of the culture away. That is what this book is about: finally Connor goes Hollywood. Look back at 1984, about the time when Tina Brown invented this mix of hot gossip celebrity stuff, serious bulletins from Rwanda and political and literary coverage. If it was 30% celebrity stuff then and 70% of the other stuff, now it's reversed. Take Michael Eisner and Jeffrey Katzenberg! Who would have given a flying fuck about these people 10 years ago?"

If *Model Behavior* shows McInerney's disdain for what celebrity is doing to our culture, it also shows a more personal fear of what celebrity does to celebrities. Connor sells out, but Jeremy dies— killed off, one senses, before success can spoil him. He seems too good, or too principled, for the world of McInerney's imagination. After naming a couple of possible real-life models for Jeremy, young writers hardly known for their reclusiveness, McInerney admits, "There aren't many shy writers left. But it's a novel. I needed someone antagonistic to the triumphant pop culture of the day, the triumphant Hollywoodization of the world."

And, it seems, to the Hollywoodization of the self. "Anybody who becomes a movie star becomes successful at projecting a certain image to the public," McInerney says. "It's almost silly to say, 'Who are they really?' They're being fawned on and serviced in such a way that the reality of being a movie star becomes more real than any of that."

Is McInerney describing himself?

He chuckles. "I wasn't gonna say that." Clearly, the thought has occurred to him and to the people around him, including fellow author Mailer, whom McInerney calls his "hero" and close friend.

"After *Bright Lights*, it interested Norman to see me become a public figure in a way that hadn't happened in a while. Two months ago I was bitching about all this celebrity stuff to him, in a way that you only can with someone like that, and he said, 'Don't knock it, kid. You have one thing that most writers will never have, and that's persona. You may have to fight it all your life, but don't undervalue the fact that you have it.'

"He also said to me, one day when we were walking out of some big function and getting our pictures taken ad nauseam, 'Be careful. I'm not sure if you know this, but these flashbulbs bleach your soul.'"

LORIN STEIN
September 14, 1998

JAMES ALAN MCPHERSON

WHEN JAMES ALAN McPherson was a dining-car waiter for the Great Northern Railroad in the 1960s, he would ride the trains out of the south to Chattanooga, along the Mason-Dixon line. He tells what would happen when the trains stopped to change engines: "The man would come on serving sandwiches and coffee in the black coach and he'd say, 'y'all can go up front.' Nobody moved. Why would you go against your whole tradition? Suddenly the whole car was white and you're sitting next to a white person for the first time in your life. When I was about 18 I went to St. Paul, about 1962, and went in a restaurant and ordered a hamburger. I sat near a white woman and her child and it was like committing a crime. I was ashamed of that feeling. I wanted to see more of the world."

McPherson has followed through on that promise. Sitting with *PW* in a quiet, comfortably isolated alcove towards the rear of a small Greek restaurant just off Sixth Avenue in Manhattan, he is soft-spoken and immediately engaging. This former janitor and dining-car waiter—who emerged from the segregated South to earn a law degree from Harvard, a "genius" grant from the MacArthur foundation and the 1978 Pulitzer Prize for his short-story collection *Elbow Room*—is discussing his life in Iowa and his new writing projects. While he's at it, he defines several personally meaningful terms from Latin and Japanese, two languages that figure prominently in his memoir, *Crabcakes* (Simon & Schuster). McPherson is visiting New York from Stanford, where he is on a year's fellowship working on what he calls "an experimental novel" and compiling a collection of his essays.

Under a decidedly worn, and clearly cherished, black straw Kangol cap, McPherson's face, a rich burnished bronze, is animated and quick to smile. His speaking voice, a whispery, staccato rasp, is restrained at first, but quickly builds to a flurry of erudite observations delivered with a combination of professorial precision and the inflections and convivial intimacy typical of black Southern speech.

In 1969, Atlantic Monthly Press published *Hue and Cry*, his first collection of stories, which won the National Institute of Arts and Letters Award for Literature. He followed this auspicious debut with *Railroad: Trains and People in American Culture* (co-written with Miller Williams and acquired by Toni Morrison at Random House), which, like all of his books so far, quickly went out of print and is very nearly impossible to find. *Elbow Room* followed in 1977. McPherson taught at the University of California at Santa Cruz and at the University of Virginia before joining the faculty of the Writers Workshop in Iowa (where he received his M.F.A. in 1971). He is divorced, with a daughter about to enter college.

Whether he's writing about the elite black railroad waiters during the golden age of the passenger train (as in the story "A Solo Song: For Doc Craft," from *Hue and Cry*), re-creating the world of a young child growing up in the South (as in "A Matter of Vocabulary," also from *Hue and Cry*) or conjuring up the comic urban mythologies of small-time black hoodlums (in stories like "The Story of a Deadman" or "The Silver Bullet," both from *Elbow Room*), McPherson presents a wonderfully precise social tableau full of vivid characters and dialogue so lively and true it seems taped. And it's all delivered within narratives so universal and directly meaningful that the stories aspire to the mythic realm of folklore and legend. "If that's there," McPherson says of his fiction's folkloric power, "I learned it from writers like Albert Murray and Ralph Ellison." His stories can also be heady experiential parables like "Gold Coast," a poignant tale in *Hue and Cry* about a young black student working as a janitor and the slow disintegration of the elderly, Boston-Irish super he has been hired to replace. The story is crafted with a succession of disparate, affecting events that immerses the reader in an emotional pool of understanding (an approach to writing McPherson likes to call "tap dancing on the synapses").

Although he has written numerous essays, McPherson has not published fiction in nearly 20 years and, for the most part, has been barely visible on the literary horizon. He has a reputation for disliking interviews—and the promotional side of book publishing in general—and cheerfully admits he's submitting to this one at the prompting of his agent, Faith Childs. He's quick to credit Childs (recommended to him by his friend, the recently deceased and

164

highly respected Chicago-born novelist Leon Forrest) with reviving editors' interest in the manuscript for *Crabcakes,* a sometimes difficult but urgently affecting work that inventively explores McPherson's sense of pervasive social dysfunction and a period in his life of deep personal despair.

McPherson was born in Savannah, Ga., in 1943 ("it was segregated but you were aware of its great history," he says). His father was one of the few licensed black electricians with his own business, "but he could not hold on to it." His mother, says McPherson, was "withdrawn. Her father actually managed Sears and Roebucks stores on a plantation in Florida." And although he has written of growing up in extreme poverty, McPherson comes from a rather accomplished family. One sister is a corporate librarian, a younger one lives in Atlanta and his brother is an airplane mechanic. He has an aunt in Congress representing a rural district in North Carolina, and his cousin, Leonard Brisbon, is the copilot of Air Force One. "Not bad," says McPherson. He attended Morris Brown College, an historically black college founded in Georgia by the African Methodist Episcopal church in 1881, working as a janitor as well as a dining-car waiter on the railroads and graduating in 1965. He mentions both his family and time at Morris Brown with a cheerful pride. "People are surprised that I advanced as far as I have coming from a small private black college," he says. "But I got my start there. I had some teachers who loved literature and they passed that on to me."

Inspired by those train rides out of the South and his uneasy introduction into the world of whites, he decided to attend Harvard Law School after graduating from Morris Brown. Much like those train rides, McPherson says, the law seemed to him to represent "access to another world. I had traveled to Chicago, to St. Paul, Seattle, the whole Northwest, and I wanted to see more. The law represented the same kind of exploration."

At Harvard, he continued to work as a janitor while studying the law and also continued to write; and it now seems that all his occupations have had an impact on his later work. Indeed, working as a janitor was a good job for a writer-in-training. "I paid my rent that way, but it was also an opportunity to see how ordinary people lived in Cambridge. You see one point of view going to law school. If you work as a janitor, you see another. I have always been wary of limiting my perspective."

During summers in Cambridge, McPherson took writing

courses—instead of law internships—and began to think of publishing. "I knew the *Atlantic Monthly* was in Cambridge and I knew they would accept submissions over the transom," says McPherson. Much like the young student protagonist of "Gold Coast," he was working as a janitor in Cambridge when he dropped off a manuscript of that story at the offices of the Atlantic Monthly Press in 1968. "Just before New Year's I left the manuscript at the front desk and said it was special delivery from Cambridge. I couldn't bring myself to say it was from me at the time. I looked like a bum, you see."

Of course the house lost his manuscript, but it materialized three months later (it was under the receptionist's desk), and editor-in-chief Edward Weeks immediately called to ask McPherson "if I had any more stories. I said I have many of them. So Ed Weeks and I worked all that summer on the book called *Hue and Cry*." Critical response was swift. Weeks had asked Ralph Ellison to read the manuscript, and Ellison submitted a glowing endorsement for the book's jacket. "After Ellison endorsed *Hue and Cry*, I interviewed him for the *Atlantic Monthly* in 1970. I met Albert Murray around the same time at the American Academy. They both became mentors to me."

Like his fiction, *Crabcakes* "tap dances on the synapses," presenting a procession of seemingly isolated social interactions separated by time and space and finding subtle psychic connections among them. In *Crabcakes*, McPherson examines the dehumanizing, prosaic regularity (and postmodern reinvigoration) of American racism; Western versus Eastern spiritual values and a disabling "standardization" of the language used to describe the most terrible events of our time. He creates a theater of memory, revisiting Baltimore, in 1976 and subsequent years, to examine his past acts. He recalls visits to old neighborhoods and to Baltimore's old Lexington Market, the place to get the best Maryland crabcakes. "What runs through the book is a sense of deep moments," says McPherson, "A sense of time that is circular. That what goes around comes around."

The book episodically charts McPherson's own period of depression and social withdrawal, beginning in the late 1970s, and his slow re-emergence into the world through the humane, lyrically simple precepts of Japanese culture and Buddhism. Despite his successes, it was the beginning of an emotionally trying period.

"In the 1980s I retreated from everything. My sister would say, 'What are you doing out there in Iowa with all of those white people?' But it was a haven for me so that I could get away from things that were giving me hell," McPherson recalls. "For the last 16 years," he says, "I've lived a very fragmented experience." He wasn't trying to write a memoir, he says. "It just came out that way. It strikes me that the forms in which we write, the conventional forms, have lost their vitality. I wanted a sense of wholeness. No matter what I had to do to get it. So I used all kinds of mundane forms—the sound bite, the folk tale, letters. I tried to use them with something meaningful for myself."

The first half of the book is a meditation on a house in Baltimore that McPherson bought in 1976 to prevent the eviction of an elderly black couple—an act he examines and reexamines. The second part of the book details an ongoing dialogue between McPherson and two Japanese friends, Kiyohiro Mirua, a writer and teacher, and Takeo Hammamoto, a scholar of black literature, that attempts to translate his life and American culture into terms that they might understand. It is also an attempt to apologize to his friends for an insulting social indiscretion he committed—an indiscretion later revealed to be an act of humane care and racial transcendence. To explain, he uses the language and rituals of Buddhism. "I was trying to explain, to a man with no understanding of the complexities of the black/white situation, why I had slighted him."

By the end of *Crabcakes*, McPherson does manage to achieve a sense of peace, emotional wholeness and a revived engagement with life. Two delightful, ironically symbolic events serve to evoke his emotional resurrection: a bee sting he received in the physical and emotionally hermetic isolation of his Iowa house, and an act of simple kindness from a Japanese woman, an acquaintance, during a train trip through Japan. He explains these events using the Buddhist term *ninjo,* a genuineness or "natural feeling" that indicates a close, communal association that transcends racial identity. "Christianity might work for some. Buddhist codes might work. I'm searching for codes that might work for black people today. I'm not trying to put down Western civilization," he says, smiling. "But Western civilization could use a little more *ninjo.*"

CALVIN REID
December 15, 1997

THOMAS MALLON

On the landing between the first and second floors of Thomas Mallon's condominium in Westport, Conn., there stands a black telescope the size of a boy. It is directed toward an upper window and the firmament beyond. "I haven't used it much yet," admits Mallon, giving *PW* a tour of the house he shares with designer and longtime partner Bill Bodenschatz, "but I've always been interested in astronomy. With this, I can do what the real enthusiasts do: see through the galaxy."

A slight 5'7" with delicate features, an impish grin and owlish, oversized eyeglasses, Mallon has the look of the eternal student for whom astronomy might be a natural passion. In fact, it is more than that.

"The two things that most influenced my imagination growing up were the Catholic Church and Project Mercury," he says. "And when I wanted to write about my childhood, I knew that those elements—the religious dimension and the space program—had to be there, because they were what made things happen in my mind."

Although prefigured in the very title of his first novel, *Arts and Sciences* (Ticknor & Fields, 1988), Mallon didn't get to his childhood and the confluence of writing, religion and the larger universe until his second, *Aurora 7* (1991), a well-received coming-of-age tale about 11-year-old Gregory Noonan fleeing his suburban school for Grand Central Station on May 24, 1962, the day that astronaut Scott Carpenter endured a near-disastrous splashdown after orbiting earth. The metaphor of a man viewing our planet from on high and suffering difficult reentry proved effective in charting the emotional journey of a sensitive boy dealing with the trauma of a distant, baffled father.

"That kind of governing, central metaphor," says Mallon over a brunch of muffins, chicken curry and strong black coffee, "relates to what I think fiction should be: it should be about something, it should go someplace, not necessarily make an argument, but do more than render a series of moments."

Indeed Mallon has gone places in his fiction. In *Henry and Clara* (Ticknor, 1994) he went to the presidential box at Ford's Theatre on April 14, 1865, when Lincoln was shot, and told the story not only of that night but also of what happened to the young couple, Henry Rathbone and Clara Harris, who shared the evening with the president and first lady. Their lives, although ending in spectacular tragedy 30 years later, were all but lost to history until Mallon saved them, in a sense, through fiction.

And in his latest novel, *Dewey Defeats* (Pantheon), Mallon journeys to a place and time—Owosso, Mich. (Thomas E. Dewey's hometown), in the summer and fall of 1948—when all eyes, certainly in Owosso, were on the presidential race that ended in Truman's famous upset.

In *Dewey*, Mallon tells of the small town's preparations for the seemingly inevitable triumph of its favorite son. But against the backdrop of this civic pride (complete with town council plans for a "Dewey Walk" to attract tourists), Mallon plays out various affairs of the heart: the bookish and beautiful Anne MacMurray's engagement to union organizer (and Truman disciple) Jack Riley; her wooing by the dashing, carpetbagging Republican Peter Cox; the obsessive mourning of Jane Herrick for her son Arnie, lost in WWII; and the silent suffering of Frank Sherwood, a closeted homosexual also mourning for Arnie, with whom he was in love.

"These last three novels," says Mallon, "*Aurora 7, Henry and Clara* and *Dewey,* are really all about bystanders. These are all people who are in some ways connected to the accidents of history. They are going to be acted upon by events, and in some ways I do think that is probably one more very big metaphor for the human condition: we are all bystanders to the plan. I do think there is some graspable divine truth that is out there, and it's what governs us, and it is beyond our control. In that sense, the books may all be about the same thing."

Mallon grew up in Stewart Manor, N.Y., on Long Island. His father was a salesman and his mother kept the home. He was the baby of the family, with one sibling, an older sister. At Brown University, he wrote his senior thesis on Mary McCarthy, whose essays, rather than fiction, made the young Mallon want to be writer.

"Mary McCarthy is my household god of writing," says Mallon, pointing to a small bookcase in his study packed with McCarthy's books. "The sheer intelligence of the writing, so crystal clear and severe. She is a real moralist, and I think to some extent I am too, though I like to think I'm a more forgiving moralist."

But it was the McCarthy style that attracted Mallon more than anything else. He recalls seeing the famous interview she did with Dick Cavett.

"It was the one where she said that every word Lillian Hellman wrote was a lie, including 'and' and 'the.' But Cavett also asked her what style was, and she said it had nothing to do with ornament, decoration, all the things one usually thinks of as style. Instead, she said style was lucidity, perspicuousness, in some ways the absence of what we call style."

And although Mallon is reluctant to say how the McCarthy style shows up in his own writing, it is clear to his readers who see but a surface of fact and detail moving with the insistent, forward beat of history without flourishes, his text not a medium or a reflection of the author's identity but simply the story itself. It is a style that makes Mallon most comfortable, and writing historical fiction is the great enabler.

"I think the main thing that has led me to write historical fiction is that it is such a relief from the self," Mallon says frankly. "It is like getting out of the house: there are times when it is absolutely necessary, and I think I would go mad if I tried to make fiction straight out of my own life. I did it once: *Arts and Sciences* is a very typical first novel, a comedy about graduate school, a comic rendition of myself in my 20s, but I couldn't do it again."

The graduate school experience that Mallon wrote about (telling the story of Artie Dunne in *Arts and Sciences*) was Harvard, where he wrote his dissertation on the little-known English WWI poet Edmund Blunden. He credits the time in Cambridge with allowing him to have the belief that truths are indeed graspable.

"One of the things I loved about Harvard," he says, "and there weren't many, was that we emerged from there absolutely immaculate of critical theory—and anything that would be useful in getting us a job, I might add. And the study we had done was really governed by the spirit of Matthew Arnold and the Arnoldian notion that literature *does* have to do with truth and sweetness and light, and that it does somehow push back the brush so that you can approach the truth. Every vision that we have—whether religious vision or ethical system—is some kind of grand coping mechanism. And to some extent just by thinking about what that ultimate truth might be and positing some kind of reason for something to have happened, it allows you to manufacture a truth that you can take up residence in for a while."

Then, one feels compelled to ask, what is the truth of *Dewey Defeats Truman*, a title taken from the most famously not-true headline in American history?

"It may be that things often turn out better by not turning out the way they are supposed to," says Mallon, after long pondering. "It may be the benign flipside of *Henry and Clara*—which posited the great human truth that we are all in the wrong place at the wrong time, to a certain extent. But in *Dewey*, what seems wrong might be right. Anne, the heroine, goes off with Mr. Wrong, with Peter Cox, in the end, the one she is not supposed to go off with. She is supposed to go off with the earnest working-class hero, Jack. But Cox reaches toward something deeper in her heart, and to some extent that is the truth of the election, too. I think if you ask even most Republicans they probably have a sneaking suspicion that history worked out better by having the underdog win an upset victory, and that Truman was a pretty good president, all things considered."

There is also the matter of Frank Sherwood, the young high-school teacher (of astronomy!) in Owosso, and his evolution throughout the book.

"It is clear in the end," says Mallon, "that Frank is going to go off to New York and be a gay man in a way that is much easier than it would be for him in a small town in the 1940s, and in a way by confessing his love for Jane Herrick's dead son he revitalizes her. At the end of the book where she is dancing across the bridge with her son's ghost, having been given the photo of Frank and Arnie embracing— it is my half-sentence trip into magical realism, and probably as far into it as I will ever go—but she has been filled with life again. When she gets to the other side of the bridge, she will come back to the world."

Despite what Mallon might say about his disdain for the personal in fiction, he seems to be not only writing entertaining and informative novels but also, unwittingly or not, confronting personal issues. In his laudatory review of *Henry and Clara* in the *New Yorker,* John Updike gently chided Mallon for the "winsome autobiographical traces" evident in his early work, while congratulating him for finding a way in later books to remove the traces without abandoning the themes.

"You are going to be present in whatever you write," concedes Mallon, "but I think what Updike was getting at, and I think he was probably right, is that the less directly I have written about myself the more I have gotten into history, the more authentically I've been able to write about myself, or my own feelings. The whole question of sexual identity, for example, is more directly addressed in *Dewey* than in any other book, even though I don't want to much write about my own life, sexual or otherwise. But in some ways, that question is dealt with more interestingly here than in some of the other things I've done."

And Mallon has indeed done some other things. Out on the job market in the late 1970s, he interviewed at Wesleyan. The biographer Phyllis Rose was one of the interviewers, and though he did not get the job, Rose recalled Mallon's talk of the book he was working on, a study of diaries. She mentioned the project to her editor, James Raimes, then at Oxford University Press—"probably the single nicest thing another writer ever did for me," says Mallon—and Raimes, after moving to Ticknor & Fields, published *A Book of One's Own* in 1984, Mallon's first book. It was met with warm praise.

Eventually, Mallon got a post on the English Department faculty at Vassar (coming full circle back to Mary McCarthy's stamping ground) in 1979. Mary Evans, who agented his first novel and has been his agent ever since, subsequently landed nonfiction and novels at Ticknor & Fields, where Mallon stayed through *Stolen Words* (1989), a study of plagiarism, *Rocket and Rodeos* (1993), a collection of essays, and all three novels up through *Henry and Clara*, which came out just as editor John Herman (his last there, after Katrina Kenison and Fran Kiernan) was fired and Houghton Mifflin closed down the venerable Ticknor imprint. Mallon found some time then to assist one of history's more curious bystanders, Dan Quayle, write his book *Standing Firm*, which did a turn on the bestseller list. "I'm not technically a Republican," says Mallon, "though I haven't voted for many Democrats lately."

But the reception of *Henry and Clara* made it clear that Mallon had arrived, "one of the most interesting American novelists at work," as Updike put it. Knopf publishing group president Sonny Mehta offered a two-book contract to Mallon, who had left Vassar after some 12 years to become literary editor at *GQ* magazine, and assigned editor Dan Frank at Pantheon to Mallon. "And Sonny said something that was music to my ears," says Mallon: "give us the novel first." The second book under contract will be a study of letters.

But Mallon is already at work on the research for another novel, tentatively titled *Two Moons.* It is an historical novel, set in Washington, D.C., in the 1870s, and involves an observatory in Foggy Bottom and the discovery of the two moons of Mars amidst intrigue and illness arising from the malarial Potomac. Surely, big plans are in store for the telescope on Mallon's stair landing, and some distant celestial body will soon play in its mirrors, sharp and clear.

MICHAEL COFFEY
January 20, 1997

DANIEL MENAKER

MONDAYS AT 10 A.M., under routine circumstances, Random House editor Daniel Menaker should be tearing through meetings and correspondence in his glass-and-steel office at 201 East 50th Street with all the verve of a former Swarthmore soccer team captain who for 25 years edited fiction and nonfiction at the *New Yorker.* But these days, Menaker's circumstances are not so routine. Knopf has just published his first novel, *The Treatment,* and the veneer Menaker has long projected of the jaunty editor-about-town and literary dynamo, ever ready to run marathons on behalf of the books that he publishes, has begun to fray around the edges like an old pair of running shoes.

"What I miss most is sleep," says Menaker, fixing his interviewer with an owlish gaze. "I was very cavalier about writing *The Treatment.* I thought when it came to actual publication, I would be fine. I've been completely blindsided by how hard it is. It's like a little blotter soaking up the ink of time."

A compactly built man with a plume of gray hair and a Chaplinesque mustache, Menaker is sitting in the living room of the apartment he shares with his two children and his wife, Katherine Bouton, the former deputy editor of the *New York Times Book Review* and now an editor at the *Times Magazine.* With its antiquated hi-fi system, a stand-up piano and a view overlooking the multitiered rooftops of the Upper West Side, the place seems an oasis of calm in an otherwise turbulent day.

Menaker has been on the opposite side of a book contract before (his short story collections, *Friends and Relations,* and *The Old Left,* appeared from Doubleday and Knopf, respectively, in 1976 and 1987). He knows the shuck and jive that job often requires—from book tours and interviews to tactical meetings with his longtime agent, Esther Newberg, and his editor, Sonny Mehta—but his two vocations have never proven quite so hard to juggle. Propping one

174

black-Reeboked foot on his coffee table, he describes, with a dead-pan expression, the mini-identity crisis this book has occasioned. "I have to jump back and forth from one side of the desk to the other," he says. "At one point, I'm avuncular, reassuring, explanatory; the other times, I'm needy, narcissistic, insecure. It's very strange. It's a kind of literary version of Jekyll and Hyde."

How appropriate, therefore, that *The Treatment* is the story of a divided self—Jake Singer, a 32-year-old prep-school teacher in the 1970s belatedly battling the conflicting forces of adulthood and adolescence, irony and commitment and the long-unexamined rami-fications of his mother's death. Jake's own identity crisis is reflected through his extremely vexed relationship with a shrink, Dr. Ernesto Morales. And Dr. Morales isn't just any shrink. He's The Last Freudian. A sardonic, weight-lifting, devoutly Catholic Cuban, whose English is hilariously ham-fisted, Morales takes up residence in Jake's superego like some Star Chamber inquisitor, crusading against repression, de-nial and all of the presently unfashionable bugbears of Freudian psy-choanalysis.

The foibles of such "treatment" may, at first glance, seem a new target for Menaker's satirical arrows. But in fact, his short stories have often explored the workings of the unconscious—jokes, dreams, the mind's ability to accommodate death, loss and random coinci-dence. And, as Menaker quips, "I've certainly had an encounter or two with the couch as other than furniture myself." What began as a sequence of shorter pieces in the *New Yorker* involving Jake and Morales soon evolved into a tale of two families in uptown Man-hattan and the Berkshires—the antipodes of Menaker's fictional world—thrown together by a set of coincidences so uncanny as to shatter Jake's presupposition that life conforms to rational principles.

"If there's any really sustained idea in *The Treatment*," he says, "it's the idea of accidents, the disparity between the way we comprehend and direct our lives and the reality underneath, which is that those beliefs are simply the mind's efforts at constructing a story out of our reality.

"The idea of brute circumstance," Menaker continues, "is very hard for us to deal with. We meet up with people and events in a way that is completely random. These are the great imponderables." Brute circumstances have supervened before in Menaker's life. When he was 26 and a private school teacher, his older brother died from septicemia following routine knee surgery. "Trying to make sense of that event probably did more to make me want to write than anything else," he says.

Making sense of his family, whose history suggests the outline of a tumultuous triple-decker novel, no doubt played its own part. His mother, the descendant of New York WASPs, was an editor at *Fortune* magazine, "a capitalist tool," Menaker says, whose circle in the 1930s and '40s was nevertheless full of socialists—James Agee, John Kenneth Galbraith and Walker Evans among them. Menaker's paternal grandparents were Russian émigrés who named their seven sons after radical social thinkers. Menaker père was Robert Owen Menaker, and there was a William Morris Menaker. Most indelible of all, however, was Frederick Engels Menaker—the lover of gay Olympic decathlete Tom Waddell, the owner of a Berkshires farmhouse later bequeathed to his nephew; and "a central character in my life," says Menaker, "in some ways more than my father and mother."

The loosely connected stories in *The Old Left* (and to a lesser degree, *Friends and Relations*), in which a 30-something teacher/journalist contends with marriage and fatherhood, the memory of a brother's sudden death, and an irascible older uncle, seem lifted largely from these events. "There are huge pieces of fiction in it," he says of *The Old Left*, but "as with most fiction, it consists, as Eliot said, of shoring up one's fragments against disorder."

Menaker's blazing career at the *New Yorker*, which ended when he was poached by Harry Evans at Random House in 1994, was no less tumultuous. Reflecting on the upheaval that's transformed that magazine over the last two decades, Menaker doesn't disguise his ambivalence about William Shawn's stewardship, and while he's careful to credit "the standards and rigor I learned there," he is equally adamant about distancing himself from the cult of Shawn so sharply evoked by the recent memoirs of Ved Mehta and Lillian Ross.

After arriving there as a fact-checker in 1969, Menaker immediately fell out of step with the *New Yorker* old guard and, as he tells it, found it impossible to suppress his unhappiness. "Shawn's *New Yorker* was not a place to be obstreperous," he says. "And I was."

When Shawn printed an article on the Constitution with which Menaker disagreed, he fired off a letter meant for publication attacking the piece. As a copyeditor he was antagonistic toward the work that came his way. He complained about being forced to keep late hours. He told Shawn he found Elizabeth Drew's Watergate diary "much too long and boring." In 1976, there was a union drive at the magazine, and Menaker was the only editor to sign the union card.

Such defiance, he says, was "desperately out of keeping with the atmosphere of the office. There was a slight s&m atmosphere between underlings and overlings that prevailed, and if you spoke up it was considered a sacrilege."

Not long after his arrival at the magazine, Menaker was asked to leave. He was saved, he recalls, only by the intervention of William Maxwell, who began grooming him for a job in the fiction department. During Maxwell's final three months at the *New Yorker* in 1975, Menaker worked in the eminent editor's office, "literally across the table from him." As a fiction editor, the chips began to fall into place for Menaker, not least because, as he puts it, he "calmed down a little. As people began sending me more stuff, my opinions became a little more confident."

Although he won't comment on the magazine's contents these days, the commercialization of the *New Yorker* clearly suited him well. With the succession first of Robert Gottlieb and then of Tina Brown, Menaker's stock continued to rise. "As the *New Yorker* became less its old self and more its new self, I did better and better," he recalls. "First of all, I was older and had more experience, but also I was out from under the weight of the years of the old *New Yorker*. That kind of melted away. Perhaps ultimately to the *New Yorker*'s literary detriment. But to my personal advantage."

He also found his job evolving into something resembling a book editor, his dealings with the world of commerce and hype extending well beyond the hermetic politics of his department. "I had had a tuxedo on once in 25 years before Tina came," he recalls. "The first year Tina was there, I had a tuxedo on five or six times because the *New Yorker* became a functionfest. Working there as an editor suddenly became much more broad. You had to host a party, you had to arrange a photo shoot. And that purity of reading, editing and corresponding was gone. In its place was something much more zesty and open to the world. For better or worse or both."

When Menaker was named Random House senior literary editor in 1994, he was therefore prepared for all but the technical aspects of the job; those skills he learned under Ann Godoff's protective wing. "I don't think I had an hour's conversation with Harry after he hired me," Menaker says. "Ann did everything. In fact, she didn't have to do anything, because I wasn't her hire. She led me step by step through the acquisitions process."

But nothing could have prepared him for the first novel he edited at Random House, *Primary Colors*. Like other surprise bestsellers, the novel landed on his desk with little fanfare. Evans asked him to read it over a weekend, Menaker was hooked and thanks in part to his recommendation, Evans bought it for what was reported to be $200,000. The rest is publishing history. "It just exploded. It was like holding a bomb—a good bomb—in your hand. It just went off," he says. Menaker insists he didn't know the author's identity (all editing was done through the agent, Kathy Robbins) until five minutes before the notorious press conference in July 1996. "I went to Kathy's office," he recalls. "She said to me, 'I want you to meet Anonymous.' She opened a door and there was Joe."

Some might say that Menaker has left one old boy's club for another, given his close affiliations with the Random House-*New Yorker-New York Times Book Review* axis through which so many prominent trade books pass. With the exception of Jonathan Kellerman, whom Menaker now edits, the books on his list are in the midlist range—Deborah Garrison's *A Working Girl Can't Win*, Julie Hecht's *Nothing But You* and George Saunders's *CivilWarLand in Bad Decline*, for example. But all have posted strong sales following stellar reviews and widespread publicity.

Menaker admits he's an efficient pitch man. He has bitter memories of how *The Old Left* was "left sort of dangling slowly in the wind" when his editor, Alice Quinn left Knopf for the *New Yorker,* and he knows all too well that without an editor hustling for such a book, its prospects dwindle. "When I believe in a book do I call everybody in town? Yes. Do they listen? Sometimes.

"Ever since I was 13 and liked to pick which doo-wop song would be number one on the hit parade, I've had a great proselytizing spirit for movies and records that I thought were worthwhile. I want to share them. But I also have the great advantage of really believing in the work I'm doing. I'm trying to sell good books to an audience that I think still exists for good books. So I have a kind of vestigial *New Yorker* idealism about what I think good writing can do for people and how it can create a community and change the way you look at the world."

JONATHAN BING
June 1, 1998

RICK MOODY

RICK MOODY DIGS black: black-leather motorcycle jacket, black jeans, black shirt, black combat boots and black horn-rimmed glasses. The car he's rented to tool around Saratoga Springs, N.Y., during a stint at Yaddu, is white, but that seems beyond his chromatic control. "They're all either white or teal, right?" he says, steering with both hands, as though maybe driving is something he undertakes as infrequently as a haircut. The short ride to Madeline's Espresso Bar takes us by the historic Lincoln Baths, and the 36-year-old author casually recommends that his interviewer go for a soak in the barium-filled water, which he claims, is widely renowned for its curative properties.

Moody ought to know: his latest novel from Little, Brown, *Purple America*, conjoins two fundamental American fears, nuclear power and terminal disease, and does so with such veracity that the author comes off as an expert in both areas. Backed by a $75,000 marketing campaign and a first serial sale to the *New Yorker*, the novel also raises the stakes on the widely praised writer's career. A bridgehead American novel—300 pages of richly textured, lyrical prose that emphatically favors compassion over glib ironies—*Purple America* is a big risk, but one from which Moody refuses to shrink. "It's like being a composer," he suggests, between sips of tea. "First you write the string quartets, then you tackle the symphony, but inevitably, you feel like you gotta try for the opera."

Purple America features three disparate members of a family slouching toward meltdown: Dexter "Hex" Raitliffe, a dithering mid-30-something who's fast outgrowing his slacker affectations; Billie Raitliffe, Hex's mother, suffering from a terminal neurological disorder that has rendered her speechless, immobile and incontinent; and Billie's second husband, Lou, a retiring nuclear-reactor employee who has abandoned Billie. Moody's own encyclopedic authorial presence visits the story in torrents, supplying explanations of everything

179

from the Babcock and Wilcox boiling-water reactor to the history of U.S. Interstate 95. A matrix of discrete accidents, most threateningly a radioactive leak, provides the rudiments of the plot that Moody uses to hurl his characters toward their ultimate confrontation, after each has received the literal and figurative bruises the novel's title implies. For Moody, the novel represents a tremendous leap: "My work has been received as less about emotion than 'literature,' but it's not that way to me at all. I feel that *Purple America* is a book about emotional predicaments, a book about love."

Purple America is Moody's third novel, after 1992's Pushcart Editor's Book Award–winning *Garden State,* 1994's *The Ice Storm* and a 1995 story collection whose titular piece, "The Ring of Brightest Angels Around Heaven," was the first novella to run in its entirety in the *Paris Review* since Philip Roth's "Goodbye, Columbus." This is the book that should finally rid Moody of the WASPish reputation that dogged his first two novels, and that came to a head with *The Ice Storm,* which witnessed the author proclaimed by *Vogue* as his generation's successor to Updike and Cheever—a critical assessment he finds "ridiculous."

Despite his impeccable WASP credentials—an affluent Connecticut upbringing, boarding school at St. Paul's, a B.A. from Brown, a Columbia M.F.A. and a maternal grandfather who once published the New York *Daily News*—Moody has also put in time in the literary-fiction school of hard knocks. Getting *Garden State* into print was a frustrating episode on which he would rather not dwell. The novel's "sole ambition," Moody comments, "was to be finished." A portrait of dead-end New Jersey post-teens struggling for epiphanies in a ruined landscape, "it's clearly the work of a 26-year-old writer, living in Hoboken," he says. (He resides now in Brooklyn Heights, near his best friends, and fellow novelists, Jeff Eugenides and Donald Antrim.)

Moody and his agent at the time, Eric Ashworth, made the rounds with *Garden State,* only to see it languish. Meanwhile, he hung out in the East Village and supported himself by laboring in the belly of the very beast he was trying to conquer, first as an editorial assistant at Simon & Schuster, then as an assistant editor at Farrar, Straus & Giroux. News of the Pushcart Prize surprised the increasingly desperate writer, who had given *Garden State* up for dead and received rejections from every doctoral program he had applied to. "The message came in from Bill Henderson [Pushcart's publisher] on a pink

'While You Were Out' note." Moody remembers, "I was so skeptical about my luck changing that I didn't even call him back at first." His retrospective incredulity at his own good fortune offers a refreshing counterpoint to the bright-young-thing albatross that continues to encumber the author.

Moody was fired from FSG in 1991—a decision he maintains was appropriate, though he declines to explain the circumstances. The unpleasant event, however, signaled a turning point in his life. He had begun his second novel, *The Ice Storm,* during the bleak *Garden State* period. By the time he finished, in late 1992, he had a new agent, Melanie Jackson ("a national treasure") and a book under his belt, two assets that made placing *The Ice Storm* an encouraging prospect. The manuscript was won at auction by editor Julie Grau, at Joni Evans's shortlived Turtle Bay Books.

Turtle Bay went belly-up on the verge of Moody's contract signing, but Michael Pietsch at Little, Brown—who had rejected *Garden State,* and who initially passed on *The Ice Storm*—snared Moody's story about the miserable lives of two families riding out heavy weather in New Canaan, Conn., in 1973. "Michael and I are like John Cale and Lou Reed," says Moody, ever quick to draw analogies between writing and alternative music. "We benefit from friction. He's always been an editor who's unflinching about changing things in my work and giving me, when necessary, a hard time."

The Ice Storm doesn't perfectly mirror the author's adolescence (he lived in New Canaan for only three years, after his parents divorced), but it represents with startling acuity a threshold moment in American life, when the nation's unquestioning trust in the reliability of fathers, from Richard Nixon to the parents of the post-war generation, began to collapse. The Connecticut suburbs—and their '70s flirtation with the sexual counterculture—provided Moody with just the sort of suggestive raw material he required to become, for better or worse, a New York writer who had most definitely arrived.

Pietsch printed 15,000 copies in hardcover, but initial sales were modest. "I think it's hyperbolic to dwell on the positive critical attention that the book received," says Moody, "because the *New York Times Book Review* ignored it, which demoralized me." New Canaan, by contrast, paid attention to the novel's unflinching examination of suburban infidelity. "I was tarred and feathered in the local press," Moody says, with a flicker of iconoclastic glee.

Yet the novel gradually made Moody a minor literary celebrity.

The "Club Vertex" comic, drawn by Steve Dillion, which Moody conceived for *Details* magazine in 1995, was one of the ways he responded to the pressures of fame. "It was too short, but I loved doing it," says Moody, a longtime comics devotee. The story is more explicitly biographical than what Moody's fans are accustomed to expect from a writer who guards his private life. Confronted with a book tour, the author takes a cue from Andy Warhol and hires an actor to impersonate him. The surreal fugue that follows is vintage Moody; by the final panels, it's impossible to determine anymore who the *real* Rick Moody is, so thoroughly has the writer become enmeshed with his mercenary PR persona.

A Warner paperback edition of *The Ice Storm* hit stores in 1994 and will soon be joined by a Little, Brown paperback rerelease of *Garden State*. A film version of *The Ice Storm*, starring Kevin Kline and Sigourney Weaver, will arrive at theaters in September. "I had very little to do with the film," says Moody. "I offered suggestions, a couple of which were seriously entertained, and I met with the actors—Kevin wanted to know stuff like what kinds of ties my father wore—before they started shooting. I was on the set two days, and in the editing room once."

In general, however, Moody finds film to be philosophically antithetical to his literary passions. "Cinema doesn't lend itself to an investigation of interior states," he says, "and those are what most interest me."

This is a huge understatement. Interior states enthrall Moody, in much the way they have the authors who most influenced him: Bellow, Pynchon, Gaddis, his Brown mentors John Hawkes and Angela Carter ("They explained everything to me: what to read, how to live, what to eat") and, above all, Don DeLillo, the writer whose development Moody's most closely resembles. "I see myself as being precisely between the farthest reaches of experimental prose and the most conventionally realistic tradition," Moody says. Mastering the depiction of interior states, however, has involved strenuous labor.

"With *The Ice Storm*, I discovered that I could sustain a longer narrative," Moody reflects. "That's why that book is as user-friendly as it is. The style is restrained—I'm learning about how to work with the novel as a form. I found my real voice about halfway through writing the stories collected in *The Ring of Brightest Angles Around Heaven*, by trying to approach language organically. Instead of superimposing an idea of what style is supposed to be, I allowed voice to emerge without restraints. That style, perhaps unfortunately, is characterized by digression, really long sentences, and an improvisatory tone."

This admission returns Moody to the question of his audience, which has come to anticipate from him either gritty urban picaresques, strewn with grim sex and noxious landscapes; or suburban tableaux, littered with the jetsam of his own '70s youth—Tang, Hush Puppies, adulterous dalliances, government cover-ups—all delivered with a depth of understanding that has earned Moody accolades from a readership that believes him to be hard-wired into their collective cultural anxiety. Will they receive *Purple America* with similar verve?

"The numbers don't mean anything to me," he contends. "What matters is finding people who adore literature. I think the literary audience in America is potentially enormous, and that what sells books is not a degree-zero style and a really manipulative plot. What sells books is telling the truth. I was wrestling with lofty ideas—the American Consciousness—in *Purple America,* and so I'm willing to take a little heat for being difficult."

Moody is a man of careful, some might say prickly, distinctions. When asked if he's obsessive about detail, he replies: "I would say I'm obsessive, *and* I'm interested in detail." *Purple America* is not a postmodern, but a "late modern," novel, not a book about language, but "conversation." In a more pompous writer, such hair-splitting might come across as evasiveness. Not with Moody, who is almost never evasive, but often scaldingly honest, especially when it comes to his appetite for contradiction. This is, after all, an artist who briefly considered attending a seminary, and who freely confesses to being a churchgoer, but who refuses to be tagged as a moralist.

Has Moody at last to begun to relish his success? "I'm so plagued by doubt that I wake nights, afraid that I'm a total fraud," he says. "But I'm beginning to feel that I deserve some of what's happened to me. I want to be an *American* writer. I happen to be a rabid fan of the literature of the century, and I'm going to go where I go."

All the rest of us need to do is keep up.

MATTHEW DEBORD
March 31, 1997

BRIAN MOORE

WHEREVER THERE'S REVOLUTIONARY fire and brimstone, spiritual upheaval and poverty, Brian Moore is sure to go. In his 20 novels, from *The Lonely Passion of Judith Hearne* to *Black Robe* and *No Other Life*, he's transported readers to such locales as his native Ireland, Haiti, France and the Canadian wilderness, a literary trek that's made him an often misunderstood missionary among contemporary writers. Sometimes mistaken for a Catholic novelist whose specialty is religiously and politically charged thrillers, Moore in fact rejects Catholicism—and Christianity in general. Instead of siding with the angels, he clearly sympathizes with the alleged demons and devils— infidels, barbarians, heathens and savages, whose faith is genuine, if sometimes brutally misguided.

Moore's heretic leanings have never been more evident than in his latest novel, *The Magician's Wife* (Dutton). It's a semi-historical work set in France and Algeria during the last half of the 19th Century. His heroine, Emmeline, accompanies her husband on a mission to Algeria after he's recruited by Emperor Napoleon III to deceive Islamic "fanatics" with his magic tricks. But the magician's wife rebels when she realizes that she's become an accomplice in French plans to colonize Algeria.

Despite her moral and political awakening, Emmeline doesn't have the resources to derail the imperialist machinations of church and state, which puts her in the company of numerous other Moore heroines and heroes, whose desperately ordinary lives he chronicles in moments of crisis. Because his characters are so often circumscribed by spiritual and physical squalor in alien pockets of the world, Moore is probably the last writer you'd expect to find living in splendid isolation behind an iron gate in Malibu, his home for more than 30 years, ever since he was lured to Hollywood to write a script for Alfred Hitchcock.

"It was an accident that we found this place, but a happy one," Moore says. Giving *PW* the grand tour, he sounds almost apologetic for the immaculate appearance of the house, with its tile floors and tribal rugs, its mixture of rustic and courtly furnishings, the floor-to-ceiling windows overlooking the coastline. He briefly stops in his L-shaped office, where he has a "bit of a view" of the ocean, a laptop computer, a leather sofa and a pair of nine-foot shelves that hold editions of his books in a dozen languages. Then he steps onto the patio, just in time for a glorious view of the Pacific at sunset.

Moore and his wife, Jean, rented the house when they arrived in California, expecting their stay to be temporary. They later bought—and dramatically expanded—the house when he discovered that the climate was as agreeable to his work as it was to his senses. The novelist exercises mentally as well as physically by listening to books on tape during his morning hikes along the coast. Lately, he's been "rereading" Proust on his cassette player, in both French and English.

The 1966 film that Moore wrote for Hitchcock, *Torn Curtain*, was one of the director's (and author's) most forgettable efforts, but it gave the novelist a seductive taste of Southern California living. The attachment was reinforced not through more film work but by another fortunate accident. Before he could take his Hollywood money and run, Moore accepted a "very easy job" teaching writing in the UCLA English department. "I picked my own students, I was there only one day a week, I never took any work home with me. But when the year was up, UCLA was very keen for me to stay on. I did that for 15 years."

The UCLA library has brought him serendipitous literary benefits. Moore says, allowing him to do much of his research at home rather than trudge off to inhospitable corners of the world, most of which he'd already seen at one time or another. "I found *Black Robe* in the Jesuit diaries there," Moore says of his 1985 historical novel, which vividly recounts the tragically misbegotten efforts of French missionaries to bring Christianity to the Huron, Iroquois and other Indian tribes of Canada. "Rooting around" the stacks, he also found a motherlode of historical documents for *The Magician's Wife*—most notably a book by a Pennsylvania woman, *In the Courts of Memory*, which extensively described Napoleon III's *séries* at Compiègne, where the first section of the novel takes place.

Moore says his initial inspiration for *The Magician's Wife* came from Flaubert, who in a letter to George Sand mentioned Houdin, a famous French magician (whose name was later appropriated by Harry Houdini). "He'd been sent to Algeria to trick the holy men into believing he had greater spiritual powers than they had, and I thought, Christianity has really lost its purity when that can happen. As soon as I read about it, I knew that this was my material."

Born in Belfast 76 years ago, Moore, whose first name is pronounced "Breean," still has a vestigial Irish accent and a healthy Irish complexion. Except for the red-and-blue-checked shirt collar, he looks almost priestly in his navy crewneck sweater and black corduroy pants, straight out of central casting with a manner that's both beatific and curmudgeonly. Haloed by the flaming sunset, he seems positively devilish while talking about his dealings with Hitchcock and UCLA.

Besides the UCLA job, the Los Angeles area appealed to Moore because it wasn't New York, where he'd previously lived. "I was part of the literary scene there for a while," he says, "and I didn't like all the jealousies about who got what advances and this and that. I didn't want to be part of the literary world, or any movement, in any country. There's no less literary place than Malibu."

Like Joyce and many other Irish writers, Moore was just as eager to leave Ireland, or at least Belfast, where his childhood was, if not quite as miserable as the one Frank McCourt recalls in *Angela's Ashes*, almost as oppressive. A doctor's son (who was to write a 1976 novel titled *The Doctor's Wife*), Moore was an early casualty of the Catholic church. "I was brought up in a very religious family. I didn't dare tell my parents this, but from the age of 10, I couldn't believe in Catholicism."

Graduating from St. Malachy's College in 1939, Moore was able to escape Belfast through WWII, serving with the British Ministry of War Transport, which took him to North Africa, Italy and France. He briefly worked on a postwar U.N. mission in Poland, then emigrated to Canada, where he got a job on the *Montreal Gazette* as a proofreader and reporter.

"I enjoyed feature writing," Moore says, "but I was 26, very badly paid, and I said to myself, 'I don't want to be here when I'm 40, with the city editor assigning me to cover a Rotary Club luncheon on a cold winter day.' So I decided to take a chance and write a novel."

Deliberately or not, Moore neglects to mention that he wrote several pulp thrillers (e.g., *The Executioners*) as Michael Bryan, according to one biographical source. The book that he considers his first novel, however, and the one that proved to be his salvation from daily journalism was *Judith Hearne*.

"It was turned down by 12 American publishers as being too depressing," Moore says, before being taken by the Atlantic Monthly Press in 1956, though with temporarily unfortunate consequences. "Orville Prescott praised the book in the *New York Times*, but the publisher had only printed 3500 copies. It took eight weeks to print a second edition, but by then it was dead."

Comatose, as it turned out, but not dead. Amazed that it was later revived and remains in print after 40 years, Moore acknowledges that for an earlier generation of readers, *Judith Hearne* may be his most affectionately remembered novel. It's the emotionally harrowing story of a Belfast spinster, crippled by self-pity, self-delusion and alcoholism, whose pathetic appeals for help are rejected by everyone, including God. *Judith Hearne* may also be Moore's most stylishly written book, with shifting points of view and passages of prototypically Irish lyricism.

As his writing evolved, however, and his novels started appearing with metronomic regularity, every two or three years, Moore says he consciously simplified his prose, heeding Thomas Mann's injunction that "every tale should tell itself." "I'm not interested in authorial flourishes," he insists. "I want the reader to get lost in the book, so he's not conscious of who wrote it and what great similes he uses."

In that regard, his literary model might be Graham Greene, a kindred soul who once called Moore "my favorite living novelist." Though honored by Greene's blessing (which became the most-quoted blurb on Moore's book jackets), the novelist says he'd always hoped to avoid any personal contact with Greene, reasoning, "It's better that he didn't know me." Of the one occasion they did meet, Moore says: "The only thing I remember is that he was a very heavy drinker."

Whether it's due to his unembellished prose or his failure to provide uplifting messages or upbeat resolutions to his plots, Moore says he's never become a brand-name writer, despite three shortlist citations for the Booker Prize and extravagant praise from critics. "I write about different things, different places, different times, in a style that's become simpler over the years."

Moore's elusive ways may help account for what he calls his erratic, "typically American" publishing history. Leaving Atlantic Monthly Press after four novels, he hopscotched from Viking to Holt to Harcourt Brace to FSG, then back to Holt, where he teamed up with William Abrahams on *Cold Heaven* in 1983.

Their alliance lasted through two more novels (and yet another publisher, when Abrahams moved from Holt to Dutton). Then Moore defected to Nan Talese at Doubleday for two novels, *Lies of Silence* (1990) and *No Other Life* (1993), neither of which proved to be a blockbuster. At that point, Moore recalls, "Billy made me a better offer. Nan was an excellent editor, but I felt Doubleday didn't have me at heart, so I went back to Billy for *The Statement*, which did better than any book I'd published in America in years."

The Statement (1996) is perhaps the most representative Brian Moore novel. It's the story of a manhunt in the South of France for a WWII anti-Semite and Nazi collaborator who also happens to be an ardent Catholic.

Moore modeled the novel's main character, Pierre Brossard, on Paul Touvier, a Vichy bureaucrat responsible for the execution of several hundred Jews. Recently reprinted in paperback by Plume, along with three other Moore novels, *The Statement* has even more currency today with the celebrated trial of Maurice Papon, accused of deporting hundreds of French Jews to German death camps.

No wonder that *The Statement* has yet to be published in France. "They don't like foreigners telling them their business," Moore says. So far, French publishers have been no more receptive to *The Magician's Wife*, which has been sold in more than a dozen other countries. While it involves events that occurred two centuries ago, the book is as timely as *The Statement*, the novelist asserts, because it shows how the French "civilizing mission" in Algeria transformed the nation's Muslims into a "warlike and vengeful people . . . and made Algeria a country that's in terrible condition today."

Despite his long residency in the United States, he says, "I've never felt like an American." Nor does he consider himself a Canadian, even though he's officially a citizen of Canada and has a summer home on the coast of Nova Scotia. But that still doesn't make him a novelist without a country, Moore insists, describing an epiphany he had in a cemetery in Ireland, standing over the grave of an IRA patriot. "It hit me that I've lived my life on the other side of the ocean but I'd like to be buried here. It was at that moment I knew I was totally, ineluctably Irish."

JOHN BLADES
January 5, 1998

LORRIE MOORE

Try to be something, anything else," Lorrie Moore urged would-be writers in her debut short-story collection, *Self-Help*, published by Knopf in 1985. For those who stubbornly persist in their "unfortunate habit," Moore had this tip on how to succeed: "Fail miserably. It is best if you fail at an early age—say, 14. Early, critical disillusionment is necessary so that at 15 you can write long haiku sequences about thwarted desire."

Moore's dictum came in the story, "How to Be a Writer," packaged in *Self-Help* with a half-dozen other seriocomic "how-to" pieces. Perversely enough, Moore was a conspicuous failure only when it came to following her own advice—the book, which began as Moore's graduate thesis at Cornell, was an instant success, propelling the young writer into a literary fellowship with Ann Beattie, Raymond Carver, Barry Hannah, Bobbie Ann Mason and other writers who reconstructed the American short story in the 1980s in vastly different ways.

Moore's subsequent books—two novels, *Anagrams* (1986) and *Who Will Run the Frog Hospital?* (1994), plus another collection, *Like Life* (1990)—were welcomed with escalating acclaim, reaching a peak when Caryn James in the *New York Times* nominated her as "the most astute and lasting" writer of her generation.

Those judgments are not likely to be revoked with the publication of *Birds of America*, her third collection from Knopf. Whether documenting the inhuman comedy of home ownership ("Real Estate"), charting the decline of a Hollywood actress ("Willing") or keeping a frightened vigil with parents in a children's cancer ward ("People Like That Are the Only People Here"), these stories are as innovative and emotionally complex as anything Moore has written.

The spiritual and physical transience of her characters helps account for the book's Audubonish title: most of them exhibit some form of avian behavior, however discrete and illusory—looping, migrating, soaring, disappearing on the horizon. "I realized, when I was writing the last couple of stories, that this bird imagery was just running through the book," Moore tells *PW* in an interview on and around the University of Wisconsin campus in Madison, where she's taught creative writing since 1984. "To some extent, unrest and searching always make for a good story." As it turned out, *Birds of America* was also the title of a lesser-known Mary McCarthy novel, "but I decided to go ahead because enough people I talked to had never heard of it."

However grateful for her precocious success as a fiction writer, Moore insists that it's as much the result of hard work as good luck. "I'm not so lucky that I've had any bestsellers or movie sales," she says. "I've had nonstop financial problems my whole adult life. It's always been a constant balance, year to year: Where's the time? Where's the money?"

One might also ask, where's the self-pity? The bitterness? The rage? If Moore suffers from these or any of the other maladies to which midlist writers are occupationally prone, they're nowhere in evidence. On the contrary, as she talks about her hardships, financial and otherwise, she has a distinctly carefree, way-it-is attitude, a mordant cheer. That's a quality she liberally transmits to the characters in her stories—largely populated by materially and spiritually discontented singles, fractious couples, the recently or soon-to-be divorced, many of whose lives are shadowed by misfortune, illness, tragedy.

However profoundly befuddled or bereft, they usually respond by "flipping death the bird" (as Moore puts it in her story, "Dance in America"), with wisecracks, zingers and jokes. That "impulse toward a joke," muses the heroine of "Agnes of Iowa," another story in her new collection, is what "made any given day seem bearable. . . . People need to laugh."

Despite the lyric grace and poetic agility of her prose, Moore's most distinguishing feature has always been her resilient humor, which regularly asserts itself in the most odd and irregular places in her stories. Her prevailing tone is comic despair, suggesting (as she once put it) that "although life is certainly not jokeless, it probably is remediless."

Moore can be hilarious on the page (so hilarious that her one-liners and epigrams could be compiled into a mid-sized "wit-and-wisdom-of" collection). And yet for a few critics, Moore's aggressive comedic impulses tend to sabotage her characters' credibility. Reviewing *Like Life,* Merle Rubin complained in the *Los Angeles Times* that Moore glibly provides "material for all the standup comedians in Los Angeles, but with very little ability to create convincing characters or tell stories that invite us to suspend our disbelief."

Asked about the criticism, Moore explains that she's incapable of harnessing her humorous instincts—not that she'd want to. "The world just comes to me that way. If you record the world honestly, there's no way people can stop being funny. A lot of fiction writing doesn't get that idea, as if to acknowledge it would trivialize the story or trivialize human nature, when in fact human nature is reduced and falsified if the comic aspects are not included."

In person, Moore is no standup—or sitdown—comedian. She answers our questions earnestly and patiently, the Eastern inflection still evident in her voice, even though she's been a Midwesterner for almost 15 years. A confessed "shy person," Moore is friendly and forthcoming enough about her work but cautious about her private life, preferring to meet her interviewer at a coffee house rather than at her home, and adamantly discouraging all autobiographical readings of her fiction. If she's not riotously funny in person, Moore does laugh easily and often. Regally tall, she has longish brown hair with gold highlights and dark, reflective eyes, as animated as "shy stars," to borrow her description of a character's eyes in her story, "You're Ugly, Too."

Born in Glens Falls, N.Y., 41 years ago, Moore was the second of four children whose father was an insurance executive. "Was I a typical second child, fighting for attention by trying to be funny?" she asks, rhetorically anticipating the question. "I was very, very shy, but we all loved to laugh and joke and amuse each other." Moore says that her second novel, *Who Will Run the Frog Hospital?,* which centers on the wistful friendship of two 15-year-old girls, "does draw upon a feeling from my own childhood." But, she insists, "it doesn't correspond in any exact way at all."

In retrospect, Moore's literary career seems almost foreordained. In 1976, at the age of 19, she won *Seventeen* magazine's story contest. Two years later, she graduated from St. Lawrence University, in upstate New York. Taking a job as a paralegal in Manhattan, Moore quickly tired of the drudgery and enrolled in the Cornell M.F.A. program, where she caught the attention of Alison Lurie, another novelist and academic whose guidance and encouragement convinced her she could write for a living.

At Cornell, Moore wrote a series of what she calls "mock-imperative narratives," counseling readers on "How to Be an Other Woman," "How to Talk to Your Mother . . ." and simply, "How." Impressed by Moore's efforts, Lurie recommended her to her agent, Melanie Jackson, who became the first of two long-lasting alliances, rare in contemporary publishing.

Jackson, who had recently left the Candida Donadio Agency and was looking for new writers, sent her stories to Victoria Wilson at Knopf. Wilson not only published *Self-Help* but also brought out her subsequent four books, through *Birds of America*. "She also has Anne Rice," Moore says of her editor. "Which is the reason she can afford to publish people like me. I always think of Anne Rice as the reason I have my house in Madison."

When we suggest that her career has the idiosyncratic, fairy-tale flavor of one of her stories but without all the melancholy comedy and anguish, the author laughs and forcefully suggests otherwise: "I was discouraged all along, by my parents and other people who said, 'You have to be practical.' All but two or three of the stories in *Self-Help* were rejected by magazines. It was a fluke that I got the book published."

Coming to Madison directly from Cornell after she was offered an assistant professorship at the University of Wisconsin, Moore says she was initially oblivious to the city's social and physical attractions. "With all my friends and family living back East, I felt quite isolated and estranged. For the first three or four years, I spent half the year in Madison, half in New York."

The more time she logged in Madison, however, the more it grew—or forced itself—on her. "I had my job, I was dating a guy from Wisconsin who's now my husband, and I thought, What am I doing in New York? I couldn't even afford a decent apartment. I was living in Hell's Kitchen, above a meat market."

Now a full professor of English, Moore not only has a house near campus and a husband, Mark, a "struggling" lawyer, but a four-year-old son, Benjamin. Living in a culturally progressive university town also puts her in close proximity to an informal community of writers, including novelists Kelly Cherry, Jacquelyn Mitchard and Jane Hamilton. "I've settled in," she says. "I'm middle-aged and happy, and I actually like Madison now."

On this agreeably warm, breezy summer afternoon, one can only wonder what's not to like about this energized city, situated on an isthmus between two sparkling, photogenic lakes, with the Wisconsin statehouse at the center. "I have lots of free space," Moore says. "I don't feel like a prisoner of campus, or locked in by teaching creative writing, because I take a lot of leave time."

Judging from what is easily the most atypical and unsettling story in *Birds of America,* however, Moore's life in Madison hasn't been entirely free of grief and pain. "People Like That Are the Only People Here" largely takes place in a hospital's pediatric oncology ward (or "Peedonk"), where a "Mother" and a "Husband" are living a parental nightmare: their "Baby" has been diagnosed with kidney cancer. Almost as funny as it is frightening, "People Like That . . ." recalls the comic rage of Stanley Elkin and Flannery O'Connor, but it's still a one-of-a-kind story, astonishingly balanced between heartbreak and "sick" humor.

No matter how far she distances herself from autobiographical fiction, Moore confirms that the story accurately approximates an ordeal she and her husband experienced with Benjamin. (At one point, the Mother declares: "I write fiction. This isn't fiction.") "We went through something that was very, very difficult with our little boy," Moore says. "It was as if the house had been set on fire, but we'd gotten out the back door. I was stumbling around for a year after that, and the only thing I could think of, the only thing I could possibly write was that story. I felt I was drawing much more explicitly and fearlessly on my actual life, which up until that point had failed to traumatize me. At that point, I was traumatized."

From this story and others in *Birds of America,* it's evident that Moore has accumulated a lot more hard experience and practical know-how than when she was so freely—and satirically—offering advice to aspiring writers in *Self-Help.* That's an apprentice book she'd just as soon forget, Moore says, along with her first novel, *Anagrams.* Even so, she's not ready to disown the book or to retract her discouraging words, stressing the awful truth behind the mockery. "I still think you should become a writer only if you have no choice. Writing has to be an obsession—it's only for those who say, 'I'm not going to do anything else.'" In Moore's case, it's been a serendipitous obsession for her and her readers. With a third novel now under way, it's one that's likely to take flight in even more unexpected directions.

JOHN BLADES
August 24, 1997

STEWART O'NAN

STEWART O'NAN, A writer who relies on his sense of place, is fighting a reluctant battle against real estate. The 37-year-old Pittsburgh native has finally decided to buy a house, moving his family of three out of their ramshackle Avon, Conn., rental to a new house a half mile down the road. When a journalist arrives at his old house, he's taking a break between painting and having carpeting laid in the new place. Thousands of books are packed in salvaged liquor boxes in his living room. He's not exactly happy about this state of flux, but it hasn't kept him from his craft. Atop a desk in a small, tidy corner, his PowerBook hums: he's just finished rattling off an article about the recent Daimler-Benz/Chrysler merger for a German newspaper, for which he's a cultural correspondent. "I got the assignment at 8:30 this morning and was finished by noon," he boasts, the glimmer of a triumphant workaholic in his eye.

O'Nan is not an author who wallows in his down time. Since 1993, when his first book, *Snow Angels,* appeared, he has published four novels and edited a 700-page collection of Vietnam writings that Anchor will publish in October (he has spent $45,000 of his own money on permissions). He was also named by *Granta* in 1996 as one of America's Best Young Novelists. His latest book, the weighty *A World Away* (Holt) follows hot on the heels of *The Speed Queen,* a slight, zippy dose of amphetamine noir that has transformed him into something of a literary celebrity in Europe with sales to match.

Two more divergent novels would be hard to imagine. *The Speed Queen* delivers the death-row recollections of a white-trash Oklahoma spree killer. It's a postmodern epistolary novel, the tape-recorded prison memoirs of a bisexual, widowed, 20-something mother fulfilling her contract with a famous writer who bears a striking resemblance to Stephen King. Nary a sentence passes without some reference to the oversaturated pop-cultural landscape of the

American Southwest, where all roads dead-end at Route 66, cholesterol is embraced and no one drives an import.

By contrast, *A World Away* is, as O'Nan puts it, an "American pastoral" devoid of the swift ironies that make *The Speed Queen* such a raucous thrill. Its prose is stripped of unnecessary ornament and gracefully speckled with antiquated references to the sleepy resort lifestyle of Long Island's Hamptons in the 1940s. *A World Away* describes the often silent struggle of a decomposing family, the Langers, to make sense of its role during WWII, both on the home-front and on the battlefield. It also contains one of the most harrowing accounts of a military invasion in recent memory—of the Aleutians by American amphibious forces in the Pacific Theater. Alternately melancholy and profane, the book represents eight years of work by O'Nan to "polish the novel as much as I could without making it stiff." He's also realistic about how his *Speed Queen* audience will receive the novel: "Most of the people who read *The Speed Queen* read it in one sitting. Many of the people who start *A World Away* aren't going to finish it."

O'Nan has changed more than his artistic tone with *A World Away*—he's also switched professional affiliations. He has a new publisher, a new editor, Tracy Brown, and a new agent, David Gernert. The reasons for these sweeping changes can be traced directly to the dust-up that his original title for *The Speed Queen* caused. That title was "Dear Stephen King." Needless to say the Emperor of American Horror was not happy to learn that his books formed the backdrop to so subversive a work of fiction. "He didn't want his name being used as shorthand for bad writing," O'Nan says, raking his thin blond hair back and cracking open a Diet Pepsi at his battered kitchen table. In fact, O'Nan admires King enormously. "He's the finest writer on the bestseller list by far. He knows what a story is, knows what a novel is, and has a great eye for that concrete domestic American detail." Even as he concedes this, however, one can sense the continuing irritation lurking beneath his genial demeanor. That Doubleday, the publisher of his first two books (*The Names of the Dead* followed *Snow Angels* in 1996), didn't go to bat for his original title clearly continues to rankle him. "Doubleday wrote me off," he contends. " 'If you're not going to stand up for my book,' I said 'then why am I publishing with you?' There was definitely some bad blood between us."

"It was a very painful situation," comments Villard executive editor

Bruce Tracy, who edited O'Nan's first three books at Doubleday. "Once King and his lawyer asked that the title not be used, we didn't have a leg to stand on." Even O'Nan, who now refers to the legal conflicts surrounding the book simply as the "Dear Stephen King fiasco" admits that the prospect of a costly legal battle may have simply proven too daunting for his publishers.

"Technically, they were right," he says. "If they were going to support my title, they would have had to go to court. And they would have had to pay big bucks, ultimately more than the book was worth. But even though *The Speed Queen* is in many ways a better title, that book was, is and always will be 'Dear Stephen King' to me."

For a guy whose Pittsburgh youth was exquisitely normal (including a little drinking and a brief stint with a punk band) and who spent more than five of his pre-novelist years as a structural test engineer tearing airplanes apart at the Grumman Corporation's Long Island facility, O'Nan has reinvented himself as a writer of rare intensity. He has maintained a low-key, domestic life, however, marrying his high-school sweetheart, Trudy (a disaster-services specialist for the Red Cross), in 1984 and raising two kids, Caitlin and Stephen. A 1983 Boston University grad who picked up a Cornell M.F.A. in 1992, O'Nan has mined his interest in technology and warfare to great effect, notably in what is perhaps his most highly regarded novel, *The Names of the Dead,* the story of a Vietnam vet contending with a dreary present and a horrifying past. Vietnam and WWII, O'Nan maintains, are the two central traumas of the American century.

The switch from wrecking planes to examining the wreckage of human lives has been, for the most part, a successful career move. With the possible exception of an unpublished early "philosophical" novel, he has never had trouble finding a publisher: right out of the gate, his stories appeared in prestigious journals and magazines. Apart from the novels, he has published a collection of short stories, *In The Walled City* (Univ. of Pittsburgh, 1993), and edited John Gardner's *On Writers and Writing* (Addison-Wesley, 1994). Then there are the screenplays, not one of which he has tried to sell to Hollywood. "I just do them because I'm interested in the books they're based on," he says. "I just did one of Styron's *Lie Down in Darkness."* He's also adapted Tim O'Brien's *Going After Cacciato* and is considering John Edgar Wideman's *The Lyncher.* "I like the idea of being a working writer," he says, "not of saying that it's going to take me 30 years to write my magnum opus."

O'Nan's advance numbers have climbed considerably from the $10,000 he received for *Snow Angel*—a grim portrait of family collapse that the *New York Times* lauded for establishing a "landscape that is bleak and miserable but utterly believable"—even though he hasn't broken through the $100,000 ceiling yet (*A World Away* sold for $75,000). It is a source of frustration for the writer. Besides Doubleday's failure to promote him aggressively and its cold feet during the Stephen King flap, he wonders aloud why his books haven't brought in more money (though he also deadpans about his ultimately limited readership). To make ends meet, he has turned to the academic circuit, teaching most recently at Trinity College in Hartford and before that at the University of New Mexico and the University of Central Oklahoma—where he vacuumed up much of the local color that enlivens *The Speed Queen*. He has also taken on a few "summer gigs" at Sewanee and Long Island University-Southampton.

It's clear that O'Nan would like nothing better than to latch onto a public that will free him from these workaday distractions. That ambition may soon be realized. He won the Drue Heinz prize in 1993, and his recent successes in Europe have finally allowed him to take a break from teaching and channel all of his energy into writing.

O'Nan's eclecticism has made it hard for readers to get a handle on just what makes him tick. "I get more interested in what I'm doing when I tackle something entirely different," he says of the impetus to move in a completely different—and risky—direction with *A World Away*. "If there is an audience out there for me, I want them to be surprised when the next book comes out."

What makes *A World Away* consistent with his previous books is O'Nan's patience as a writer. The novel entwines four separate stories about a single family. Anne and James Langer—spending the second summer of the war in the Hamptons, caring for Anne's ailing father—have a marriage on the rocks. James, a teacher, has had an affair with a teenage student for which Anne can't forgive him. In response, she begins a dalliance of her own with a soldier stationed nearby. The couple have two sons, Rennie, a medic missing in action in the Pacific, and Jay, a sullen preadolescent "trying to figure out what the hell is going on," as O'Nan puts it, with the war, a vast historical event that dominates the news but seems to have had little tangible effect on his hometown. As if to drive home his central metaphor of loneliness, O'Nan devotes part of the narrative to Rennie's wife, Dorothy, who journeys from San Diego to Long Island with her newborn daughter for the reunion that forms the novel's conclusion.

Throughout, O'Nan relies on pacing that, even during the combat segments, is almost dreamy, seizing on the tiniest detail to animate every emotionally resonant moment. "The people on the homefront could almost pretend the war didn't exist," O'Nan says. "*Almost.* That's a weird way to live, especially if you want to pretend that things aren't happening. The book isn't like stage drama—maximum conflict, all the time—but a collection of quiet moments, full of stillness."

In light of the "Dear Stephen King" debacle, this comment takes on a particular edge, as if O'Nan wished to retreat from his own skirmish with the publishing machine and reclaim some of the territory that sustained him in the past. Indeed, *A World Away* is the most mature and deeply felt novel O'Nan has produced. Always restless, however, O'Nan has kept up his feverish writing pace. Two more manuscripts are ready for Holt, one of which, *Everyday People,* enters the risky zone of African-American characters and dialogue, suggesting that O'Nan is still intent on flexing different fictional muscles. That is, if he doesn't first dive into a nonfiction project, about the Great Hartford Circus Fire of 1944 currently stewing on a back burner.

But O'Nan remains steadfastly cagey about his ambitions, never suggesting that fame is more important than his craft. What's most important, he says, is the reality of his characters. "I want something different. I want you to live and die for my characters even though they have massive faults. Popular culture has brainwashed us into believing that our heroes need to be blameless," O'Nan declares. "And that just drives me nuts."

MATTHEW DEBORD
May 25, 1998

RICHARD NORTH PATTERSON

Let the record reflect that Richard North Patterson does not think of himself as another Scott Turow (though both have written entertaining, character-driven thrillers filled with dramatic courtroom confrontations); he doesn't like being weighed against commercial suspense writers (at least those whose work he views as "all story with no characters or ideas"); and he's definitely *not* James Patterson (the comparison still confounds the 51-year-old lawyer-cum-writer). "I was at a dinner party with some friends once and a woman handed me a copy of *Kiss the Girls* to sign," he says, his sandy-haired good looks giving way to an incredulous smile.

What truly irks Patterson, though, are those who glibly reduce him to a "bumper sticker," who call him "one of the best of a new generation of legal thriller writers." He understands that much of this comes courtesy of his breakout 1993 bestseller, *Degree of Guilt*, which prefigured parts of the O.J. Simpson trial in its panoramic portrait of a scandal-ridden celebrity murder trial. His fifth book and first after an eight-year hiatus, *Degree of Guilt*, like his three subsequent bestsellers, *Eyes of a Child*, *The Final Judgment* and *Silent Witness*, was published by Knopf. All use a trial and the law as flashpoints for ethical and personal skirmishes.

But to hear Patterson tell it, the run-away success of these novels has thrown new hurdles in his path. "What happens is that you write something that's a recognizable subject and there's a tendency to put you in a box," he says. In an effort to break out of that box, he has taken a new direction with his latest book, *No Safe Place* (Knopf). While the novel features an attorney as its protagonist, its backdrop is not a sensational trial but a presidential campaign. The year is 2000, and Democratic presidential candidate Kerry Kilcannon is campaigning against the incumbent Vice-President in California. Kerry's brother, James, was assassinated running for president in the state exactly 12 years earlier. Now Kerry finds himself pursued by his own problems, from a gun-packing anti-abortion extremist to a newsweekly that threatens to run a story about an affair Kerry had with TV reporter Lara Costello.

For Patterson, writing a political thriller was liberating. "It's recognizably me and yet people are going to feel compelled to take a fresh look at me," he says. "I've added some new preoccupations, such as: What's it like running for president in the media age? What constitutes a news story?" His longstanding readers will nevertheless recognize the use of flashbacks, the dramatic plot twists, the social consciousness and the Freudian subtext that here involves Kerry's dysfunctional childhood.

On a recent sunny, windless Monday morning, Patterson met *PW* on the tarmac of the antiquated airport on Martha's Vineyard. Patterson, who lives nine months each year in San Francisco, summers on the Island and promises his family he'll do no work there. The author has adhered to a grinding itinerary for the past three weeks, and his latest book tour hasn't even begun. From his winter home in San Francisco, Patterson traveled to Chicago for BEA, returned to the Bay area for a week of writing and visited Knopf's offices in New York. With his worn topsiders, narrow khakis and sunglasses resting on the placket of his white crew shirt, Patterson blends in among the Island's summer residents. Yet beneath the tanned face, Patterson still evinces a drawn and road-weary expression.

It was, ironically, the punishing routine and frequent travel of a career as a securities lawyer that prompted Patterson to take up writing in the first place. Sitting in the living room of the sparsely decorated cedar-shingle house that sits behind a circular driveway in West Tisbury, as assorted deliverymen and gardeners slip in and out, Patterson talks about his childhood in the Cleveland area and law school at Case Western Reserve, where he took his degree in 1971. "I enjoyed myself more than most law students did, which meant I didn't work as hard." But his efforts were impressive enough to land him a job as an assistant attorney general in Ohio and later a role in the Watergate case as liaison for the Securities and Exchange Commission.

But 21 years ago, an epiphany changed all that. Working in Birmingham, Ala., for a national securities law firm, he was striking out on his third business trip in as many weeks when he saw his one-year-old son, Brooke, waving goodbye through the screen door. Patterson, who now has six children, decided that his life had to change. Then 29, he'd never published anything before, but he mapped out the plot of a suspense novel inspired both by his work on the Watergate securities case and by his obsessive fondness for the mysteries of Ross MacDonald (Patterson had read 17 of his novels). It eventually became his first book, 1979's *The Lasko Tangent*. A novice to the field, he sent an unsolicited manuscript to Norton, where it was accepted by editor-in-chief Starling Lawrence.

Patterson would eventually come to know a number of celebrated editors. As if to punctuate this point, the phone rings, interrupting our conversation. It's Phyllis Grann, president of Penguin Putnam, a personal friend of Patterson's and a fellow Vineyarder—calling to discuss the following week's dinner plans. "What should you bring?" Patterson repeats her question. "Charm, wit and white wine would be great," he says, laughing. He hangs up, returns to the living room and resumes sitting in a white leather chair, crossing one leg over another. "We're old friends," he explains. Patterson's editor is in fact a different publishing mogul—Sonny Mehta—who, Patterson says, believed in him when he was seen as washed-up, if he was seen at all.

Despite his early success (*The Lasko Tangent* won an Edgar in 1979 for best first suspense novel), by the mid-1980s he suspected that his career was floundering. In 1985, Villard published his fourth novel, *Private Screening*, in a print run of only 5000 copies with little promotional support, and Patterson, disheartened by his dwindling hardcover audience, stopped writing altogether. He continued working as a lawyer, moving from San Francisco back to Birmingham. In retrospect, he says, the time helped him as a writer. "What I learned from those eight years is that when you think you're not working you really are." Still, Patterson allows, "part of me is tempted to say I'm really distressed about missing those eight years between 37 and 45. I wish I had them back."

Patterson's eight-year absence made the success of *Degree of Guilt* all the sweeter. That success was due, in part, to good timing (John Grisham's *The Firm* and *A Time To Kill* were still high on the Publishers Weekly mass market paperback list when it came out), Knopf's relentless publicity and the fact that he was a fresh face writing about a sexy topic. "When I re-entered the business it was a more perfect time than I could have managed if I planned this thing," Patterson says.

Of course, Patterson expected none of this when he undertook *Degree* in January 1992. "I was doing it for the pride, to see whether I could still write. The novel came to Mehta from Susan Petersen, then head of Patterson's paperback publisher, Ballantine, who was still publishing Patterson so successfully in mass market that 300,000 copies of *Private Screening* had sold in that format. Mehta signed him up immediately after reading the manuscript for *Degree* on a flight from New York to London. A 250,000-copy first printing followed. Mehta and Knopf then went to extraordinary lengths to promote him. "They re-introduced me to booksellers and to a public who had not read me or forgotten about me," says Patterson.

Despite—or because of—*Degree's* success, Patterson is exceedingly sensitive to the concentration of legal matter in his fiction. "To me, the law as a subject is really not a presence in *No Safe Place*. And in my next book, *Steelton*, there's no trial and no defense lawyer." He may branch out even farther in the future. "Maybe one day I'll write a comic novel," he says, a raffish gleam in his eye.

In his efforts to diversify, Patterson has had to spend more time doing research. For *No Safe Place*, he sought the help of George Bush, who had written him a letter praising *Degree*. The two even became friends, Patterson says. (He laughs as he recalls his four-year-old son, Chase, running naked around the Bush's home on one trip there). "A lot of the story just became two degrees of George Bush," Patterson says. This explains a note in the acknowledgements that reads "The attitudes expressed by Kerry Kilcannon do not reflect—in fact, frequently contradict—those of the political leaders and advisers who helped enhance my understanding of Kerry's world." Those politicos include John McCain and Bob Dole (whose campaign Patterson trailed to better construct certain scenes). Bush introduced Patterson to Ron Kaufman, a campaign strategist, whom Patterson grilled to find out "how do you run a guy like Kerry," whose campaign is based on principles rather than polls. Patterson is a registered independent and describes himself as having a libertarian streak. He and his wife have supported domestic-abuse programs, and he says that while storytelling is his primary goal, he does strive to impart messages in his work. He's even considered running for office (though he says "I don't sense a really great grassroots swell").

Patterson, who calls himself a "romantic," infuses *No Safe Place* with an entirely different kind of idealism: a surprisingly sentimental love story. "I didn't think about it when I wrote it, but it occurred to me later that it's a variation on the classic theme of thwarted romance, from *Romeo and Juliet* to *The Thorn Birds*," although he believes the romance relates to the book's central theme of privacy.

Patterson's protagonists are slightly glamorous types to whom extraordinary things happen, like Tony Lord in *Silent Witness*, who is accused and then exonerated of raping and murdering his high-school girlfriend. Given Patterson's seemingly ordinary life, does he identify with, or live vicariously through, his characters? "I tend to write people who are ambitious. That's a personality type that I relate to. There is a school of fiction—*New Yorker* fiction—the premise of which is a guy gets up in the morning, brushes his teeth, decides whether to leave his apartment and by the end of the story decides not to. That is not the kind of person or the kind of fiction that engages me."

Readers don't have to wait long for the tipoff that his books are of a different ilk. *No Safe Place* begins with gory killings at an abortion clinic and moves quickly to Kerry's nightmare about his brother's assassination. "I don't clear my throat like Flaubert did in *Madame Bovary*, where he described the village brick-by-brick," Patterson says.

Like Kerry, Patterson walks a tightrope between reviewers' standards and widespread acceptance. Asked if he'd prefer his next book to be a best-selling smash and critical dud or a reviewer favorite with midlist success, Patterson looks introspective for a moment, then makes a motion to dismiss the question. "Can I know what will happen to the one after that?" When we overrule the objection, Patterson opts for commercial acceptance. "I'd have to say being read; it's the ultimate form of admiration," he says.

Taking a break from talking, we decide to drive over to a stretch of beach that Patterson and his wife own, where a key scene in *No Safe Place*—a getaway weekend between Kerry and Lara—takes place. Despite gumption and a sports-utility vehicle, massive flooding from recent storms prevents us from reaching it. Rain threatened to destroy Kerry and Lara's tryst as well, symbolic of the storm that awaits them when the national media will get wind of their affair. The coincidence is uncanny and reminds us of the tendency in Patterson's books to predict the news. "If you get things right," he says with the rhetorical flourish of a politician on the stump, "sooner or later they will happen."

STEVEN M. ZEITCHIK
July 6, 1998

204

GEORGE PLIMPTON

GEORGE PLIMPTON, THE protean journalist, editor and professional dilettante, towers over the galleys and audio cassettes amassed on his desk at the *Paris Review* and shouts amiably into the phone:

"Anne, bring me a Python. One of the longer ones."

It's not hard to imagine Plimpton—an impresario of high-spirited pranks who once claimed as an April Fool's jest that he'd been bitten by a cobra, and who tells *PW* that he's recently returned from a bird-watching expedition in the Chihuahua province of Mexico—producing a live snake. In short order, much to our disappointment, an assistant arrives unfurling a 15-foot segment of the manuscript of *Truman Capote: In Which Various Friends, Enemies, Acquaintances and Detractors Recall His Turbulent Career* (Doubleday).

Like *Edie: An American Biography* (Knopf, 1982) and *American Journey: The Times of Robert F. Kennedy* (Harcourt, 1970), both collaborative efforts of Plimpton and *Grand Street* editor Jean Stein, the Truman Capote book is what Plimpton calls an "oral biography," a tapestry of recollections and impressions assembled from interviews he conducted and then literally spliced together atop the pool table in his apartment. "It's like doing a puzzle," he says of the editing process, "trying to make one section fit to another. What I did is to paste them all together into long snakes, I call them pythons. Some of them are as long as this room. And each of these rolls, these pythons, is a chapter unto itself."

In the battleship-gray townhouse on Manhattan's East River that has served as the headquarters of the *Paris Review* since 1973, Plimpton, at 70, is surrounded by the trophies of his maverick, globetrotting career. Although he lives upstairs with his wife, Sarah, and young twin daughters (an earlier marriage produced two other children), this office is stuffed with pieces of primitive art, pictures of writers, piles of baseball hats, campaign buttons and other items that lend it the antic ambiance of an art-house fraternity.

Plimpton's life is nothing if not antic. Today, he has a cold, which imparts a world-weariness to his boyish good looks and lanky, Cat-in-the-Hat build. But neither a runny nose nor the unrelenting ring of the telephone prevents him from clearing half his day to discuss his own tumultuous writing life. After all, this editor's interviews on the craft of writing—a staple of the *Paris Review* since E.M. Forster graced the first issue in 1953—have set the standard for author interviews everywhere. A font of anecdotes and publishing lore, Plimpton proves as ready to discuss his falling out with Stein, the details of which have been well bruited about in recent gossip columns, as to reminisce about the subjects of his three biographies.

Kennedy, the dashing Democratic standard-bearer; Sedgwick, the aristocratic, self-immolating superstar; and Capote, the iconoclastic writer and cosmopolitan gadfly; each suggests a different sort of parallel life for Plimpton. With his Zelig-like gift for ubiquity, Plimpton plays a minor role in each of the books: wrestling the gun out of the hands of Kennedy's assassin, Sirhan Sirhan, mingling with the Sedgwicks at Harvard and careening around Capote's famous Black and White Ball at New York's Plaza Hotel.

As Plimpton's python lies on the floor between us, it is this particular quality that comes into sharpest focus: Plimpton's tendency to be present at spectacular events, then to withdraw to the margins, the better to provide his reader with a wide-angle report on the events he chronicles. For someone who, at every turn of his career, seems to have sought glamour, fun and access to the loftiest realms of American life, Plimpton still prefers to be seen as a kind of everyman. "I'm exactly the sort of person you are," he tells his interviewer. "As a reporter, I drift through these worlds. I think reporters tend to do this. Dip their beaks into various soups and come away."

Few reporters came of age in such prestigious surroundings. Like the Sedgwicks, whose pedigree *Edie* traces to the ruling class of 19th-century New England, Plimpton was born into an affluent family, the oldest of the four children of a well-known corporate lawyer and U.N. diplomat. "I had a very fortunate upbringing in the sense that I was surrounded by rather formidable people in the arts," he says.

Plimpton speaks with a singular accent, which he once characterized as "eastern seaboard cosmopolitan." One guesses it is the product, in part, of our most elite schools, social clubs and universities. From St. Bernard's in Manhattan, where his class of 15 included Peter Matthiessen and "Punch" Sulzberger, Plimpton traveled to Exeter and Harvard, then was drafted into the Army as "a demolition specialist" (an interest that led to Plimpton's appointment as New York fireworks commissioner in the '60s). After returning to Harvard to edit the *Lampoon* and take his B.A. in 1950, he studied at Kings College, Cambridge, but was soon summoned to Paris by Matthiessen and Harold Humes to help launch the *Paris Review.*

"I didn't think I could make it as a writer, largely because everyone around me at college seemed to write with great facility," he says. "Particularly at Cambridge, where the students have had grammar pounded into them from infancy. But I felt I could edit, I had a good eye for what was particularly well written and felt I could perhaps 'make betters,' as William Shawn used to say about writing in the *New Yorker.*"

The *Review* soon became a magnet for distinguished editors, authors and avant-gardistes of all stripes, many of whom were drawn to the saturnalian literary world, and the low cost of living in 1950s Paris. Describing a visit to New York during those first precarious days of the *Review,* Plimpton recalls a chance meeting with New Directions publisher James Laughlin. "He said 'I very much admire your publication.' I remember asking, 'Do you think I should continue with it?' And he said, 'You *must* continue with it.' It was like being touched by the hand of some great potentate. I went back to Paris mostly on that touch."

Within three years, the ever-peripatetic Plimpton had returned to New York, begun teaching at Barnard and completed a children's book, *The Rabbit's Umbrella* (Viking, 1955), all while continuing to edit the quarterly. He also wrote a series of articles for *Sports Illustrated* on Harold Vanderbilt, the 1930s America's Cup champion and inventor of contract bridge.

Emboldened by his first magazine assignment, Plimpton approached *SI* editor André Laguerre with an idea he had borrowed from former *Daily News* sportswriter Paul Gallico (today best known as the author of *The Poseidon Adventure*). "What Gallico did was to climb down out of the press box," Plimpton explains. "He thought you couldn't really criticize somebody for striking out in the bottom of the ninth inning with the bases loaded in the World Series unless you yourself had faced a major league curveball. He got into the ring with Jack Dempsey and wrote a wonderful description of what it feels like to be knocked about by a champion."

SI arranged to have Plimpton, an unremarkably talented sports fan, to pitch to a roster of major league all-stars, including Willie Mays and Ernie Banks, before a crowd of 20,000 people at a post-season exhibition game in 1960. What proved a humiliating ordeal became the basis for his first book of participatory journalism, *Out of My League* (Harper, 1961). For his next book, *Paper Lion* (Harper, 1966), Plimpton actually joined a professional football team, scrimmaging with the Detroit Lions with a pen and notepad tucked in his helmet.

He also gradually gained faith in his own skills as a reporter. "I'm very nervous about my writing because it does not come easily at all," he reflects. "When I'm praised, I tend to think they're just flattering me. As I moved along I began to learn that the one gift I have is humor." This quality is all too rare among journalists, he realized.

By the mid-1960s, participatory journalism had become Plimpton's trademark. By joining the Boston Celtics, boxing lightweight champ Archie Moore and clanging the triangle for the New York Philharmonic, Plimpton demonstrated, as Capote biographer Gerald Clarke once put it, "that in an age of constricting specialization a man can do almost anything he sets his mind to, if only for a moment."

Not coincidentally, as Plimpton was planning the first of these stunts in 1959, Truman Capote was setting out for Garden City, Kans., to cover the murder that became the subject of *In Cold Blood,* a book that shattered the conventions of true-crime reporting. Like Plimpton, Capote insisted on depicting his subject—a crime and its aftermath—from the inside, ingratiating himself into a rural community with the enchanting insouciance of Holly Golightly. Tom Wolfe would later compare the two authors in an anthology on New Journalism. Both authors, Wolfe writes, "had the moxie to talk their way inside any milieu."

If today Plimpton isn't exactly a New Journalist, he continues to bridle at the limitations of genre, preferring to explode the conventions of fiction and nonfiction with the avidity of a trained demolitions expert (his only novel, *The Curious Case of Sidd Finch,* published by Macmillan in 1987, began as an *SI* hoax about a Buddhist pitcher with a 168-mile-an-hour fastball). Plimpton has even turned to Henry Fielding for the structure of *Truman Capote,* adopting Fielding's habit of giving his chapters lengthy, discursive and often humorous titles.

In his preface, Plimpton compares this biography, with its contradictory episodes and gossip, to a cocktail party. If indeed it succeeds better in replicating the experience of table-hopping at Elaine's (another milieu familiar to Plimpton) than as an exegesis of Capote's life and work, that effect is intended.

"It's like *Rashoman*, that famous film in which you have five different interpretations of the same event," Plimpton explains. "It's one of the charms of this kind of book, these varied views, these varied glasses through which he is peered at.

"I think there are some problems with oral narrative," he continues. "One is that you don't really get an absolute fix because you have so many voices offering their opinions. There's never a point at which you synthesize all the voices and give what would be a true portrait. The image of the cocktail party is suitable because you hear inaccurate and scurrilous things about people, and the listener has to pick through all these various voices and come up with his own portrait, his own conclusion."

As Plimpton tries to envision his own next project, which could be anything from a book on birdwatching to a children's opera, the one fixed point in his professional life, besides the *Review,* is his agent, Russell & Volkening's Tim Seldes, a classmate from Exeter. "I'm supposed to be putting together a list of things I'd like to do which is very long. Tim is always trying to control me. Sometimes I go off and do these deals on my own. He's *horrified."*

Nan Talese, who edited *Truman Capote* at Doubleday, is only the latest of Plimpton's illustrious book editors, whose ranks include Cas Canfield at Harper, Jackie Onassis at Doubleday and Starling Lawrence at Norton. "I think for an editor you really want somebody who is going to feel that the book is their own," he says. "Who's going to try to get the best deals for it, make sure the right ad copy is done for it, mother you through the parties that are held for it and give you confidence. They're like guides on safari moving their clients through difficult country."

In an introduction to a *Paris Review* anthology released by Norton in 1990, Jonathan Galassi writes that "editing is nothing less than the art of the possible." That attribute may apply to all editors, but is particularly true of this snake-charming editor-author, who has not only extended the art of the possible on the printed page, but has also made it a way of life.

JONATHAN BING
November 17, 1997

DAVID REMNICK

DAVID REMNICK WROTE his 1994 Pulitzer Prize winner, *Lenin's Tomb: The Last Days of the Soviet Empire*, a kaleidoscopic epic of the fall of the Soviet Union, after a wondrous slalom through history as a *Washington Post* correspondent. Since then, he's broadened his range, but he's never left Russia behind. Indeed, his latest book from Random House is a sequel of sorts, *Resurrection: The Struggle for a New Russia*, a less sprawling yet still stirring portrait.

Though his Russian experience seems to define him, Remnick, now ensconced at the *New Yorker*, has written recently about subjects ranging from sports to politics to literature. On the day we visit his modest office overlooking 42nd Street, he's closing a *New Yorker* piece on Jack Maple, a troubleshooting New York cop in New Orleans; finishing a *New York Review of Books* essay on the Russian writer Isaac Babel; and preparing an exegesis of a different sort of babble, that of shock jock Howard Stern.

Though Remnick speaks humbly about his work, he doesn't drop his ironic edge. "I hope you forgive me," he says upon disclosing that Stern is his subject; the apology recalls his benediction "May God forgive me" in *Lenin's Tomb,* as he toasts Stalin upon interviewing an unrepentant grandson of the Father of the People.

A rangy 6′2″ in black jeans and sneakers, a reminder note inked on his hand, the curly-haired Remnick looks less the tweedy intellectual than the "standard-issue suburban jump-shooter" he was, growing up in the early 1970s in Hillsdale, N.J. His father was a dentist, his mother a homemaker; his brother, he adds, with Yiddish inflection, is "a doctuh." In high school, Remnick edited the newspaper, imbibed literature and studied Russian, the school's "one sexy topic." At Princeton, Remnick majored in comparative literature, writing his thesis on Whitman. The campus housed some eminences in Russian history and politics, but Remnick ignored them: "I was interested in the books"—Gogol, Tolstoy, Brodsky.

Like some budding writers, he studied with John McPhee, who provided "an enormous craft lesson," not just in technique but in devotion to work. Defending McPhee against those who consider him detached, Remnick wrote in the introduction to the *Second John McPhee Reader* (Noonday, 1996) that McPhee "not only is in absolute command of his craft . . . but also revels in the pleasures of a fragile world and makes sure we take note." Remnick, it seems, has also taken note.

A campus stringer for several newspapers at Princeton, Remnick parlayed those clips into two internships at the *Washington Post* and finally, into a job as a *Post* rookie, covering night police. But he rose quickly, to a sports beat and then to the writerly "Style" section, where he profiled Harold Bloom and covered the Super Bowl. "He was extraordinarily prolific," says Jeffrey Frank, a former "Style" editor now at the *New Yorker*, citing Remnick's "novelist's eye," writing speed and reporting acumen.

Remnick's interest in Russia was further whetted by a 1984 vacation trip. In 1987, he applied for a job at the *Post's* Moscow bureau. Though he lacked the foreign correspondent's usual overseas pedigree, Remnick's writing ability won him the post. He promptly began studying Russian with his fiancée (*New York Times* writer Esther Fein), got married and leaped east into history.

"Russia is extremely inviting for an American correspondent with a modicum of Russian," Remnick reflects. "What was thrilling was that everything mattered so much." He would work as late as midnight or 2 a.m., filing stories from around the country, his dispatches on the crumbling Soviet system anchored in sharp-edged human portraits.

Remnick, Fein and their baby left Moscow in August 1991, just a day before the failed coup against Mikhail Gorbachev. He rushed back for six more weeks of reporting. "History could not have asked for a more burlesque ending," he says with a laugh. While two framed book awards lie on his office floor, his wall boasts a framed *Post* front page from the coup days, when Remnick, operating on a higher plane, cranked out 3000–4000 words a day.

Though he describes himself as lucky, Remnick also knew how to further that luck. While in Washington, he'd been contacted by agent Kathy Robbins, who was scouting new talent; upon leaving for Moscow, he resolved that he'd keep notes on "this epochal transition." About a year later, Robbins got Remnick a contract for a Russia book with Linda Healey at Farrar, Straus & Giroux; after Healey left for Pantheon, Remnick moved to Jason Epstein at Random, encouraged by Epstein's ex-wife, Barbara, Remnick's editor at the *New York Review.* In *Lenin's Tomb,* more so than in his *Post* pieces, Remnick could judiciously inject his own presence, with measures of irony, empathy and even reflection on his own Russian Jewish heritage. He applied what he learned from Orwell, who was never "a hectoring moralist." Of his own book, Remnick says, "I want you to know that this story is being told not by an omniscient, perfect narrator. It is a story filtered through a human presence."

Lenin's Tomb garnered rave reviews, but the book seemingly became an exemplar of the perilous prospects of selling serious nonfiction; Random House publisher Harry Evans stated at a 1994 PEN panel that it and other notable Random books had lost major sums. But Remnick says it earned back its $200,000 advance, and Epstein predicts it will backlist quite profitably.

When he was finishing *Lenin's Tomb,* Remnick was set to become the *Post's* New York correspondent; then *Vanity Fair* editor Tina Brown—he'd written one piece for *VF* but hadn't met her—invited him to lunch at the Four Seasons. Donning his one suit, Remnick experienced what he calls Brown's Vulcan mind meld, as she sought his thoughts about the *New Yorker,* for which he'd written one article. When she was named *New Yorker* editor a few months later, Remnick was one of her first hires.

Happy with the "enormous freedom" of a magazine perch, Remnick says he owes the *Post* a significant debt. "I would not have known how to become a journalist if I'd been one of the mythical figures [legendary *New Yorker* editor William] Shawn plucked out of Harvard." He points to his office shelves: "In order to write a book like *Common Ground* or *Coming into the Country* or *The Right Stuff,* you not only have to have an artful approach to narrative and character and language; you also have to have reportorial chops."

Remnick didn't expect to write about Russia from his desk in New York: "You're not marinating in it in the same way." But he kept his ties, buying Russian newspapers from the Hotalings depot a block down 42nd Street, watching Russian news on C-SPAN and calling journalist friends in Moscow daily.

Four chapters of *Resurrection* appeared in some form in the *New Yorker.* "I think Tina is happy to have pieces about Russia; she knows it's important, but she's also happy when I write about other things," he says. "They can be just as high-minded, but a little closer to home."

So he has profiled Marion Barry, Mario Cuomo and Michael Jordan, as well as delving into the life and work of sociologist William Julius Wilson, Nobel author Kenzaburo Oe and Princeton religious professor Elaine Pagels, whose studies of the origins of Satan gave the title to *The Devil Problem and Other True Stories*, (Random House, 1996). "Collections are dying," Remnick pronounces, but thanks his publisher for allowing him "to begin publishing on things that aren't Russian."

Yet the ongoing story in Russia proved impossible to ignore, and he squeezed in three or four trips a year to Moscow. *"Lenin's Tomb* is very bulky, in some kind of Russian way almost. *Resurrection* is more focused," he says, for it addresses the changes in politics, media, business, which were centered in Moscow. While Remnick wasn't able to witness some events, such as Boris Yeltsin's 1993 confrontation with Parliament, he managed to reconstruct scenes through assiduous interviewing. Moreover, his long-established sources helped Remnick scoop the world when he reported in the *New Yorker* that Yeltsin had come close to canceling the 1996 election. And in topsy-turvy Russia, where the crusading press once published Remnick's *Post* portrait of an unregenerate Stalinist, this Yeltsin revelation was seized on by the communist press.

"Resurrection is about what changed and what persists: namely, the kind of vacuum of state structure, of ideology, of national purpose . . . and into that vacuum rushes one *goniff* [Yiddish for "thief"] after another," explains Remnick. He calls his book both "dark and optimistic," arguing that despite all the disappointment he chronicles, the world's doomsayers don't give Russia enough credit for launching a transition.

Since *Lenin's Tomb,* Remnick asserts that his main lesson was "to toughen my view of Yeltsin himself, to recognize that the guy who climbed up on that tank in 1991 is in no way the same figure who stumbled to victory in 1996 and to make one goal of this book a picture of the political, personal and moral explanation for this decay."

The self-critical author believes that his first book displays "an enormous amount of work, and patches of good work." He calls *Resurrection* "in some ways a better book, though I'm provided with a less fantastical story. It's a more disciplined book." Still, Remnick declares that "my writing is nowhere near as good as it can be." Why such restlessness? "Because I read what's on my shelves," he responds, pointing to Dreiser and Ellison, Caro and McPhee. Then again, editor Epstein, whose list is as sterling as any, calls Remnick "the most remarkable young writer I've dealt with in a long time—maybe ever."

Remnick's still adjusting to the fact that the thrill of living in a great historical moment has been supplanted by a regular life based on work and family, albeit with occasional appearances as a talking head on media shows such as *Charlie Rose*. (The family now includes two sons; Fein, after a stint reporting on publishing, now covers health care for the *Times*.) "What's the Flaubert line," Remnick asks, " 'Write as if possessed and live like a bourgeois'?"

Remnick says he'll still keep up with Russia—"It's something I care about enormously, as a human being, not just an object of observation." Still, he doesn't foresee another Russia book, unless he can find a more specific topic or narrative. Meanwhile, he's busy. His phone rings: a quick schmooze with *New Yorker* colleague Jeffrey Toobin about the latest O.J. Simpson trial.

Then he refers to the three pieces he's juggling and adds, with a self-mocking chuckle, "I'm presumably on book leave." He's planning a book on the Cassius Clay–Sonny Liston heavyweight championship fights, bouts that refracted racial and societal tensions during the turbulent 1960s. Yes, Remnick's a sports fan, but this is more than a boxing saga: "I'm interested in Ali as an inventor of rap, a figure who scared the shit out of white America.

"In some ways, this is not a good thing, but I can't help it," Remnick says of the Whitmanesque multitudes that he pursues. "If I have any virtues, it's that I'm interested in a lot of things. But one of my main *faults* is that I'm interested in a lot of things. At 38, I've not learned to remotely specialize."

NORMAN ODER
February 24, 1997

SHERI REYNOLDS

Sᴴᴇʀɪ Rᴇʏɴᴏʟᴅs ɪs sitting crosslegged in the bar of Manhattan's Intercontinental Hotel, fretting over the disappearance of the writer's callus from her right ring finger. "It's probably as smooth as it's been in my lifetime," she says, rubbing the offending digit with a fascinated grimace.

A cherub-faced, crop-haired, sturdily built woman in smock and sandals, Reynolds sports a Venus of Willendorf pendant at her neck, a grape cluster tattoo above her left trapezius and a youthful world-weariness that can transform a posh hotel bar into a personal space. Recently, however, the 30-year-old has had too much of hotels—as the concern over her writer's callus shows.

"There has been no peace in my life," she says, referring to the past four months. Peace—along with the opportunities for callus-building writing time—went out the window for Reynolds when Oprah Winfrey announced that *The Rapture of Canaan*, Reynolds's second novel, was her sixth pick for the *Oprah* book club.

Overnight, Reynolds's quiet existence as a struggling novelist and College of William and Mary creative writing instructor and English professor, living in Richmond, Va., with her roommate and close friend, the poet Amy Tooter, was gone, perhaps never to return.

"It was such a jolt," recalls Reynolds. "When I got the call, I was in the worst financial state of my life. I was living on credit cards. *The Rapture of Canaan* was being remaindered, and I didn't have the money to buy any copies. And then suddenly, boom—there were another 950,000 copies being printed. Reporters called. All my friends called. People with only the remotest connection to me called, asking me to read their manuscript." To add to the chaos, at the beginning of the summer Reynolds and Tooter relocated, with their menagerie of two dogs, two cats, two birds and two fish, to Norfolk, where Reynolds had accepted a teaching position at Old Dominion University.

The *Oprah* windfall is the kind of providential supervention that Reynolds eschews in her incantatory, viscerally honest novels. Like Dorothy Allison or Keri Hulme, Reynolds writes of women struggling with crushing personal and social burdens, who achieve a measure of peace only when they summon the courage to confront their circumstances. Transcendence, for them, is achieved through struggle and introspection, not serendipity.

In her first novel, *Bitterroot Landing* (Putnam, 1994), the heroine, Jael, is a victim of sexual abuse who finds the anonymous life she has built for herself as a small-town pastor's assistant threatened by her painful memories. Jael gradually turns to mystical rituals and a local incest survivor's group to grapple with her pain. Ninah, the teenaged protagonist in *The Rapture of Canaan* (Putnam, 1996), grows ever more restive under the harsh doctrines of the insular Pentecostal sect in which she was raised. When she becomes pregnant with her prayer partner's child, she is ostracized—and forced to define her religious faith on more personal terms. And Finch, the heroine of *A Gracious Plenty* (Harmony) has been a town pariah since a childhood accident that left a disfiguring scar on her face. A cemetery caretaker, Finch learns lessons about the living from the dead people whose graves she tends and finally finds the strength to make peace with her community.

Crown publisher Chip Gibson, who also oversees the Harmony imprint, calls Reynolds's writing "redemptive fiction," perhaps a nod to the spiritual emphasis of her books. It is also a term suggestive of the deliverance—from demons personal and social—that her heroines actively seek, something that Reynolds admits has been a goal of her own. "I am a dark person and I do dwell on some dark stuff," she says.

"There's something that happens to me when I write that's transforming, that I love, because I figure things out," Reynolds continues. "I guess all of my novels are autobiographical, not literally, but emotionally. There's some kind of parallel. Strangely enough, there was a point while I was writing *Bitterroot Landing* where I realized my character had matured more than I had. I realized that she had passed me in her ability to forgive, to not be so hasty about making judgments. And I didn't know what to do. So I just stopped writing the book. And it was real strange, because in taking Jael someplace else, I drew my own map. And I think that's why I do it."

216

Reynolds spent her childhood in rural South Carolina, in the countryside between the towns of Conway and Galivants Ferry. Her father is a former farmer who now runs a fishing equipment store and cricket farm with her brother-in-law; her mother manages a radiology clinic. She has only one sibling, a younger sister who is now a stockbroker, but describes herself as part of a "tight extended family" composed of relatives and friends in the church and surrounding agricultural community. Meals were commonly cooked outdoors, for as many as 20 or 30 at a time.

"I used a lot of that in *The Rapture of Canaan,* in terms of the sense of being part of a clan, a tribe," says Reynolds. Her settings, another deeply felt component of her books, also tend to be from her past. "In *Bitterroot Landing,* the river [where Jael suffers an emotional crisis] is completely out of my background, and it's a landscape that I love more than anything—the mossy trees, the shadows, the taste of river water," she says.

But while Reynolds formed a bond with the natural world of her childhood home that is clearly a strong source of sustenance, other aspects of her upbringing were less salutary. The strictness of her Southern Baptist/Pentecostal background left her prey to "little furies," which she says writing helped her channel: "I was always belligerent, and it was not an acceptable thing to be if you were a girl. And I couldn't disobey—it was one of the Ten Commandments. So I think I used the stories I wrote to do things that I couldn't actually do."

Today, Reynolds still uses her writing as a pulpit from which to air her differences with her family. "Sometimes I think a lot of my books have been written with my family in mind. It's like 'Hey, look at this.' And especially with religious issues," she says. The deeply sensual, pantheistic, anti-patriarchal spiritual vision that Reynolds delineates in her books (she describes her personal beliefs as "a mixture of Quakerism and Taoism, with some nature-worship thrown in") is one that would certainly shock any devout Christian. Yet her affection and respect for her Christian characters is also evident, and this moderation perhaps helps explain the warm bond Reynolds says she still maintains with her family. "I'm not taking on the biggest issues and proclaiming them from the mountaintops—just picking one up and turning it a little bit," she says.

Reynolds majored in English at Davidson College, and received a scholarship to the MFA program at Virginia Commonwealth University, where she studied with Lee Smith and Paule Marshall. In her final year at VCU, a novel-writing class with Tom De Haven produced the manuscript that became the seed of *Bitterroot Landing*. She revised it over the summer following her 1992 graduation, and that August was taken on by California-based agent Candice Fuhrman, whose name she found in *Literary Market Place* after the New York agents whom she contacted declined to read her manuscript. A contract with Putnam for a $25,000 advance followed within a year, under editor Susan Allison, after early interest from Harcourt Brace was scuttled when that company's trade division was downsized in early 1993.

"I was so happy," recalls Reynolds. "I came up to New York for the first time in my life and met all of the people at Putnam, who were so nice to me." Following the early 1995 publication of *Bitterroot Landing* (it was released as a Berkley paperback that November), Allison signed Reynolds up for two further books, the first of which was to become *The Rapture of Canaan*.

"That was a desperation book—I had only three months to write it because of a contractual deadline. I used a lot of my religious background, and my squabbles with religious Christianity," says Reynolds of the book (Winfrey would tie the book's theme in to the Heaven's Gate cult suicides when she spoke with Reynolds on her show).

Reynolds delivered the manuscript before Christmas of 1994, and a little over a year later Putnam published the novel to warm reviews, with a trade paperback edition from Berkley following a year later. Reynolds took the summer of 1996 off from her teaching job to write the second book under contract, which eventually became *A Gracious Plenty*.

"That's a book about grieving," says Reynolds, explaining that she wrote it during a period when her roommate was in mourning following the unexpected death of a close friend. "I would wake up in the morning real worried about Amy, and I would take walks in the cemetery and try to figure out how to help her."

To Reynolds's dismay; shortly after she delivered the manuscript, in September 1996, she received a letter from Putnam canceling her contract, due to the poor sales of her previous books—even though Allison had already told her how much she liked the new work. "I pretty much had my heart broken through that publisher," she says, her voice still tightening at the memory.

Such cost-cutting maneuvers have certainly become familiar to publishing industry observers in recent years, but knowing that it's a trend does little to mitigate the distress of an author whose book has been dropped. "I don't fault them: it's just that I came to understand that it's just a business, that the individual's not important. The book's important."

Seven months later, Fuhrman was struggling fruitlessly to find another publisher for *A Gracious Plenty* when Reynolds got the call from Winfrey. "I was at home reading," she remembers, "and I didn't believe it at all. First my editor at Putnam called. I hadn't spoken to her since September, and my first thought was. 'Why are you doing this to me?' And then Oprah called, but I didn't recognize her voice—I didn't think it sounded like her."

Within weeks of Oprah's announcement, *The Rapture of Canaan* was a number one Publishers Weekly bestseller. According to Putnam, prior to April the book had sold a combined 40,000 copies; currently there are over a million copies in print. *Bitterroot Landing* was also sent back to press, in a new trade paper edition.

"It felt like I'd been saved—that my career, which had been in the shitter completely, through nothing I had done, had been resurrected, also through nothing I had done," says Reynolds.

Not surprisingly, interest in Reynolds's unpublished manuscript suddenly rocketed: in May, after a hot auction (in which Putnam, ironically, was the highest bidder), Harmony bought hard/soft rights for $600,000. "Their deal made sense to me," says Reynolds, noting also that Harmony executive editor Shaye Areheart had expressed interest in the book prior to the *Oprah* bombshell. A 16-city reading tour kicks off September 22 to support an anticipated 150,000-copy printing.

Stress aside, how is Reynolds enjoying the attention? "It's a real strange thing when something that you've done because you love it becomes so commercial," says Reynolds. "And I don't know what I'm going to do about that. I do know that when this book tour's over I'm taking a break from the public part of it."

Specifically, she looks forward to spending time in her new house, where she plans to convert the attic into a study, installing the old bed, where she has written most of her novels, next to the window.

In that sanctuary, this young writer, who went from having no contract, a remaindered novel and a dim future to the sudden glare of public acclaim, hopes to recapture the private dimension that she says is so important to her craft, and that has been denied her in the hectic recent months: "I miss," she says simply, "my daydreaming time."

MALLAY CHARTERS
September 22, 1997

NORA ROBERTS

THE HOME OF Nora Roberts, hidden among the hills in the rural, western Maryland town of Keedysville, is not the Xanadu-like estate one might expect to be the abode of a best-selling romance author who by the end of this year will have written 126 novels, with over 42 million copies in print. It is in fact the same modest country ranch to which Roberts came as a 17-year-old bride over 30 years ago.

There have been some improvements, notably a BMW and a Land Rover now parked in the driveway and a fantasy closet full of designer clothes and shoes. But this is the same house in which Roberts, a 29-year-old stir-crazy housewife stuck indoors with two small sons during a snowstorm in 1979, made her first stab at writing romance fiction. And Roberts isn't going anywhere. "When I came here," she says, "I realized I was home. Sometimes you just recognize it."

Loyalty to her roots is also evident in the way Roberts manages her house of fiction. Although she broke out into hardcover bestseller-dom in 1996 with her fourth hardcover for Putnam, *Montana Sky*, Roberts, unlike some in her genre, continues to write original paperback romances. "I am a popular writer and proud of it," she says. "And I really believe in the category romances. I was there with two young kids, and the shorter format saved my sanity. I remember exactly what it felt like to want to read and not have time to read 200,000 words."

Today, Roberts has no problem with words. She's probably the fastest writer in the business, with an amazingly prolific output that pretty much makes her the Joyce Carol Oates of the romance. The occasion for this interview is the publication of her sixth hardcover for Putnam, *Homeport*, a thriller about an art historian from Maine immersed in the international world of art forgery. But Roberts was already off and running this year with the number-one mass market romance bestseller *Sea Swept*, from Jove in January, and *Secret Star*, from Silhouette in February. Also forthcoming this year are close to a dozen more books in a flurry of genres and formats.

"I just have a fast pace; it's like having green eyes," Roberts says. A petite, auburn-tressed woman with a strong-willed, practical manner, she seems to have always had boundless energy—and a free spirit. The youngest child of five, whose parents ran a lighting company in Silver Spring, Md., Roberts says her mother was ready to lock her into her room rather than let her get married as a teenager. But she was determined. After becoming a Keedysville housewife (she has since divorced and remarried), Roberts tackled leisure-time arts and crafts with extraordinary zeal. "I made jam, did the whole earth mother bit. I could have needlepointed a car."

But in an awakening that could fit within the pages of Betty Friedan's *The Feminine Mystique*, Roberts soon turned to fiction. "Subconsciously, I was looking for an outlet for creativity. When I started writing, it was like, 'This is it. Why didn't I realize it before?' "

Roberts also says that her work ethic is due to an inherent discipline that "comes from being raised Catholic—if you're not working, there's the near occasion of sin and all that." Indeed, no nun could find fault with Roberts's daily regimen: a morning swim and workout (in the small pool/gym area that used to be the basement of her home) followed by a basically nonstop 9 a.m.–5 p.m. writing stint.

Roberts entered the field at an opportune time. Although it took her three years to break into publishing, she did it with few connections or contacts. A casual acquaintance who worked as a ghostwriter in New York knew she was writing romances and tipped her off to the formation of Silhouette in 1980, an S&S imprint meant to be an American counterpart of Canadian-based Harlequin, which at that time tended to buy only British writers and had already rejected Roberts's early submissions. Roberts quickly sent some manuscripts, unsolicited, to Silhouette, "back when you could do that," and Nancy Jackson, then an acquiring editor for the house, eventually picked *The Irish Thoroughbred* from the slush pile. The manuscript, a horsebreeding tale set in Roberts's own backyard in Maryland, would become her first published romance in 1981. That, in 1984, Silhouette merged with Harlequin "has been a final irony," says Roberts. "I thought, 'Well, now they're writing the check after all.' "

For help with her first contracts, Roberts followed a friend's recommendation and called Amy Berkower, a new agent at Writers House who was looking for clients. Roberts recalls hiring Berkower "over the phone, I guess that wasn't too professional."

But it worked. Berkower remains Roberts's agent today. It was Berkower who assessed when it was time to test the waters with a trade house—Bantam, in 1987. And when that house didn't necessarily publish to Roberts's preferred pace, Berkower facilitated the move to Putnam in 1992. And although Roberts, an avid Mary Stewart fan, immediately wanted to write romantic thrillers, her agent advised her to wait. "Amy said, 'Build a foundation, just keep at the categories and put that away for a while,' " recalls Roberts. "She was right. When the time came, and I had developed a following, it was just like she said."

Berkower also managed to persuade Roberts to don the J.D. Robb pseudonym for a Berkley mass market series. Set in the year 2058 and featuring police lieutenant Eve Dallas, newly married to roguish and mysterious high-tech billionaire Roarke, the series was a Putnam response to handling the Roberts output. Although Roberts had already understood the practicality of changing a name (her birth name is actually Robertson), she was reluctant in the case of the Robb books. "I thought it would be a dilution of my readership. But Amy knows me and said, 'Look it's like having Coke and Caffeine Free Coke.' " Roberts came away convinced of the efficacy of such brand proliferation. The initials J.D. denote her two sons, Jason and Daniel, both now in their 20s, while the new surname has a distinct marketing advantage: Robb books almost always appear right next to Roberts books on bookstore shelves.

In all her writing, Roberts is known for her wry humor and the use of different narrators, two devices that were once rarities in a genre that, says Roberts, "was usually about a terrified 18-year-old young virgin and all from her point of view." Remarried 12 years ago to Bruce Wilder, a carpenter who first came into her life when he was hired to oversee her house-expansion project and now owns and operates the local Turn the Page Bookstore Cafe, Roberts says she could hardly relate to that.

"I never did 'the virgin,' " she says. "My heroine may have problems, she may be vulnerable, but she has to be strong, she has to be intelligent. She has to be independent and so does he, or I'm not interested in telling their stories."

Roberts says she enjoys the short format of category romances, which she calls "charcoal sketches," as much as she does the more fully fleshed-out plots of her hardcovers. Many of her romance series grew out of creating intertwining families and friends whose relationships and subsequent generations expanded beyond the confines of a single book. And along with other writers in the genre, Roberts keeps pushing the envelope of the romance form, writing about a hero with supernatural powers (*Night Shadows,* for Silhouette in 1991) and about witches (the ongoing Donovan Legacy series for Silhouette). Roberts credits her editors—Silhouette's Isabel Swift, who has worked with Roberts since 1983, and Putnam v-p Leslie Gelbman—for allowing her to take such leaps.

But Gelbman did initially worry that her author often relies on surfing the Internet for background research. *Montana Sky,* for example, was crafted without traveling to the state in which it is set, in part because Roberts has an aversion to flying. "I don't believe in the journalistic style," she says. "I don't have time to pop out and go there."

"I know they say, 'Write what you know,'" Roberts continues "But I write what I want to know." Her characters are as fanciful as her settings. Although *Homeport* heroine Miranda Jones has a determined air as well as "hair the color of a Tonka toy fire engine," Roberts says the resemblance stops there. "She's so much smarter than I. She's got a Ph.D. and all of that. Plus *she's* tall."

Lately, Roberts's online research has "become totally addictive," she says, and takes up several hours of her daily regimen. From her gabled top-floor windowed writing room, one of her husband's many renovation projects, Roberts now maintains various subject folders and chat rooms on America Online and other sites. One extremely vocal group of fans have their own "Nora-holics" web site and came to a signing Roberts held at her husband's bookstore (which has its own web site and does a healthy online and mail business in orders for Roberts's backlist). "It was wonderful to see how my books helped bring about relationships among these women," she says. And in a Valentine's Day promotion this year, Roberts began a tale on America Online that was completed by readers. It's a project she hopes will inspire some budding writers. "I would have loved to have had that help to get me started," she says.

But Roberts still sees red over the inadvertent "help" she gave

Janet Dailey, who last year admitted that two of her books, *Aspen Gold* and *Notorious,* and a forthcoming novel now pulled from publication, contained passages from Roberts's works. The shock that Dailey, a prolific romance writer and a longtime acquaintance of Roberts, could pirate her work even caused Roberts to stop writing for while. "It's like mind rape. To think how far along it's been going . . . it's like being stalked," she says.

As of press time, Roberts was in the pretrial discovery phase of the lawsuit she has filed against Dailey. In lieu of damages, Roberts is asking Dailey to make a donation to the Literacy Volunteers of America, a cause dear to the Romance Writers of America, an organization of which Roberts is a charter member and its first Hall of Fame inductee. Roberts is also requesting that Dailey reveal the full extent of the plagiarism so that all the tainted books can be pulled from the shelves and so that Roberts doesn't have to read through Dailey's entire body of work. "We would like to know the scope of the copying without me having to read until my eyes bleed," says Roberts. As of press time, Roberts's suit had been amended to also charge that Dailey's *Tangled Vines* plagiarizes Roberts's works. The suit estimates that Dailey has lifted from at least 13 of Roberts's novels.

While Roberts admits the media attention around the plagiarism has probably increased her name recognition ("I'm sure some people went into stores and said, 'Oh, that's her,' and picked up a book"), she says it also forced her to defend the genre against reporters who implied that all romance writing is interchangeable. "They have no business to sneer," she says. "I don't think it would have happened in any other genre. It was 'It's romance, let's take a shot. Let's talk about heaving bosoms.' Mysteries, for example, have their formulas too."

For Roberts, the romance formula leads to a "celebration of emotions," which she says readers desperately crave. She sees the experience as providing a fix of "that wonderful rush of feeling when you first fall in love." Roberts firmly believes that providing that feeling in a popular genre is an important service. "I get e-mail all the time from people who say, 'I liked this thriller, but why couldn't they have put in a love story, too?'" she says. "That's why it's always at the core of my work."

Thanks to her "magic drawer" of stockpiled romance manuscripts,

Roberts is working typically a year ahead. Although *Homeport* completes a three-book contract for Putnam, the house has already committed her to three more. And Roberts has no intention of reducing her output in order to focus on her hardcovers. "That would be only one book a year," she says. "Whatever would I do?"

JUDY QUINN
February 23, 1998

KIM STANLEY ROBINSON

N<small>O ROAD CUTS</small> through Village Homes, the Davis, Calif., housing community where Kim Stanley Robinson lives. After parking on the perimeter, it's necessary to trek in on foot, past suburban homes, wood frame houses tiled in the light pastels favored in sunny climates.

Robinson's house is Navaho White with blue trim. He meets us at the door. At 46, soft-spoken and ruggedly handsome, he betrays the occasional fidget and clockward glance of a man on a tight schedule. That's unsurprising, given Robinson's huge international readership and the fact that he's just tidying up details with James Cameron for optioning theatrical rights to his Mars trilogy—*Red Mars* (1992), *Green Mars* (1993) and *Blue Mars* (1996), all published by Bantam.

Even so, Robinson finds time to show us around the compound, from the community dance studio to the daycare center where his two-year-old, the younger of his two sons, is taking a nap, and the village garden, which is maintained by residents who've applied to a committee for a plot to tend. Robinson, who edits the community newsletter, has his own piece of turf surrounded by clover he's planted as the first step in a three-year plan to get rid of the encroaching nutgrass. Nutgrass, he says, existed back in the Pleistocene. It laughs at transients like humans and flowers. With his fingers, Robinson digs through teeming millipedes to reveal the hard root. This is clearly a man who thinks with his hands as well as his head. He has helped create everything that surrounds him here.

How natural that Robinson, a chief exponent of "eco-fiction" and architect of one of the greatest planned communities in modern fiction—embracing the entire planet of Mars—should be an active member of his own miniature society. But what of the fractious politics, the mortal struggles between ideologies that mark his stories—

even among the Utopians who make a sneak appearance in his latest novel, *Antarctica* (Forecasts, May 11), out next month from Bantam? The model for that is right here, he says with a laugh. There are endless meetings, endless debates over every detail of community life.

This tumultuous social microcosm has nevertheless provided Robinson with the perfect writer's redoubt. In his study, a picture of the Dalai Lama from an Apple Computer ad lies on an end table next to an ancient dog-eared copy of *The Worst Journey in the World,* Apsley Cherry-Garrard's classic on the ill-fated Robert Falcon Scott expedition to the South Pole in 1912. Robinson's terrace is composed of flagstones in varied, intricate and interlocking patterns. He points out two of them that look like the California coastline, north and south. A small Buddha figure sits in the far corner.

Robinson laid the stones in the summer of 1997. With his trip to Antarctica completed, and the new novel under his belt, it seemed a well-deserved interlude between projects. But arranging the stones, he found, was "an objective correlative of writing a novel": here were the same musicality and "shapeliness" that inform his fiction.

This from a writer of "hard science fiction," a genre known for its nuts-and-bolts delivery and its subjugation of such dainties as character and mood to fast action and sensational technologies? Robinson chuckles at the label. "Before the Mars series, no one called me that." His earlier novels, the California Trilogy of *The Wild Shore* (1984), *The Gold Coast* (1988) and *Pacific Edge* (1990), as well as *The Memory of Whiteness* (1985), earned him a reputation as a "humanist" SF writer in opposition to the cyberpunk writers then in ascendance. The humanist label was less a cause of chagrin, since he found the cyberpunk ethos myopic, a glorification of bad morals. But in the Mars books one finds page after page of scientific exposition.

"The novel is a very capacious form," Robinson explains. "There's no reason exposition should be less interesting than stage business."

Not that there's a poverty of drama in Robinson's work. In *Antarctica,* scientists in remote, ice-bound stations struggle to continue their work against the threat of rapacious conglomerates on the one side and ecological terrorists on the other. The novel features sabotage by ice pirates, life-or-death treks across frigid mountainous expanses, global political and economic struggles between ruthless combatants and even a love affair. Its cadences are poetic, the composition artful.

This aesthetic in itself would be enough to distinguish the book from traditional hard SF, but what rankles Robinson about the label, often applied to his work in reviews and in discussions among SF aficionados, is the politics of it. "Hard SF has traditionally been right-wing: Heinlein, Niven, Pournelle. The classic SF has been hard in attitude—like you can't let these poor ridiculous people on the starship because they aren't smart enough and it doesn't make sense. And hard SF contains a whole lot of silly fantasy elements: faster-than-light travel, talking aliens—a bunch of crap that hard SF gets away with because they've got this 'hard' attitude."

Robinson is much further to the left. While eschewing rabid polemics, he is distrustful of big corporations, and his tendencies are decidedly Green. When Carlos, a Chilean scientist in *Antarctica,* discourses on the "globally downsized postrevolutionary massively fortified stage of very late capitalism," it's very much in keeping with the critique of environmentally catastrophic practices that distinguishes all of Robinson's books, including the Mars trilogy, which pits conservationist "Reds" against the "metanats," developers on a transplanetary corporate scale.

Has Robinson ever engaged in "ecotage," a neologism he's used for ecological sabotage? The writer demurs with a grin, reluctant to invite prosecution, perhaps. But he has no problem, he says, with such acts of civil disobedience as obscuring logging road marks to slow down clear-cutting. "If you can make it a little bit more expensive than it already is without hurting anybody, then you're taking away their [the big logging companies'] profit margin, and investors might go away."

As a novelist, Robinson's main concern is artistic, not political. After growing up in Orange County, Calif., he took a B.A. and then a Ph.D. in English and American literature from UC-San Diego, writing his dissertation on Philip K. Dick. He has also been a lecturer at UC-Davis. Nevertheless, for Robinson, politics is inseparable from art and science. "The idea of art for art's sake, that you can be a great artist without being political, especially in literature, doesn't work. Great literature is always political. The meaning of life is a highly political thing."

Robinson's wife, Lisa, is an environmental chemist, and he sees in the purity of scientific inquiry a model for an ideal system of government. The problem for him as a novelist, he says, is that science does not always conform to the demands of narrative. "The way that science runs itself is slow, diffuse and undramatic; it's almost everything that stories are not supposed to be." So writing stories about science is "like trying to fit square pegs into round holes over and over and over again."

That he has succeeded in fitting those pegs into place is demonstrated by Hugos (awarded by fans for the best SF novel of the year) for both *Green Mars* and *Blue Mars,* and a Nebula (awarded by professional SF writers) for *Red Mars.* Part of the trick is Robinson's marriage of the lyrical and the scientific. In *Antarctica,* he pulls this off through the character Ta Shu, a Feng Shui artist rhapsodizing as he spins through the frozen wasteland remembering the Scott and Roald Amundsen expeditions, broadcasting live over the airwaves as he goes.

The unifying idea of the wandering Ta Shu telling the stories of the old explorers came to Robinson "like a gift." It was one of those "solutions to a technical problem that then become the most beloved thing." Or perhaps, he allows, it was his experience in the 1970s roving through the beaches of the Hawaiian islands, losing track of time, that gave rise to the idea of Ta Shu. Robinson has hiked not only in Hawaii but in the Sierras, the Antipodes, the Himalayas and Buddhist Nepal; Ram Dass, he offers, was an inspiration to him in that great transition of the '70s from drug culture to meditative practice. "The radical politics and Zen spiritualism of the '60s and early '70s certainly did shape my aesthetic and my mission as a writer," he says.

Robinson has since put his body on the line in the service of his writing. On his first trip to Antarctica in November/December 1995, underwritten by a National Science Foundation program that brings artists and writers to the Pole, Robinson visited remote outposts, talking with some of the same scientists he had consulted for the Mars project. Antarctica, it turns out, is a great laboratory for the study of Mars, because of its topographical similarities. "I had never been in a helicopter before. They call them flying refrigerators!"

In Antarctica a childlike sense of timelessness took hold of him. In that impossibly hostile landscape, one simply could not organize one's day in a civilized manner, he recalls. Some of the things he found there were "so science fictional I couldn't believe it," like the neutrino detection apparatus that uses the earth itself as a filter and the polar ice cap as a lens: a blue glow from the ice reveals the presence of subatomic particles from supernovas light years away.

"There was a lucky star over the whole experience," he says. He wrote *Antarctica* in two short bursts. Recently, Robinson was pleased to learn that his book (already published in its HarperCollins U.K. edition) was on sale at the NSF visitor's shop in Antarctica. It was a big hit among the Antarcticans. "You got it right!" one veteran of many winters told him.

Robinson's road with publishers has been smooth, informed by what he likes to call a sensible team spirit. He has only praise for agent Ralph Vicinanza, who has repped him since his previous agent, Patrick Delahunt, retired in the late 1980s. "In his last act as a good agent, Patrick found his clients another good one to recommend, which was Ralph," says Robinson.

His first novel, *The Wild Shore,* was the book that relaunched the Ace Specials, a series of trade paperbacks designed to introduce new writers. There followed a second Ace book, and several books with Tor, before Robinson migrated to Bantam for the Mars series. At Bantam he worked with such editors as Lou Aronica, Jennifer Hershey and Tom Dupree (now all at Avon). His current editor is Pat LoBrutto.

As the interview winds down, we linger by a bookcase near the kitchen where the precious original accounts of polar explorations found in old bookstores have their special place on a high shelf. This evokes memories of other old things: while in New Zealand for a recent conference, Robinson visited a museum in which artifacts of the Scott expedition were supposed to be on display. In fact, they were hidden in a box under a stairway while things were being reorganized. It took some doing to get to them, but then he was able to hold in his hands the shards of a certain Emperor penguin egg members of Scott's expedition had risked their lives to obtain. In *Antarctica,* Robinson advocates returning such artifacts to their original sites. How much more inspiring for visitors to actually come upon them *in situ.*

What are we to make of interests as diverse as the flagstone tiles arrayed on his balcony—from the cracked shell of an Emporer penguin egg to the landscape of Mars, conservation, music, Buddhism and the antipode? "That's what a novel is for me—a bunch of competing desires that I have to reconcile in each sentence, a series of problem-solving decisions. So there's a certain fine process of writing that I truly love." Robinson peers out the window at his terrace as another image strikes him. "It's like hiking in the mountains, where every footstep is a tiny little problem that you solve by where you choose to walk."

ELIOT FINTUSHEL
June 22, 1998

ROXANA ROBINSON

Roxana Robinson lives on the southern edge of the territory she has claimed for her own in fiction: New York City's Upper East Side, residential headquarters of the nation's WASP elite. Her spacious apartment between Park and Lexington Avenues is filled with antique furniture and oil paintings, one a full-length portrait of Robinson in a strapless black evening gown commissioned from an artist who later painted President George Bush. A table in the living room holds vintage snuff boxes collected by the author and her husband, investor Hamilton Robinson, as well as a silver cigarette case that belonged to his father.

Dressed in black jeans and a T-shirt topped by a printed blouse, her straight brown hair loose and her face makeup-free, the 51-year-old writer sits casually in a wing chair, her feet drawn up underneath her, nursing a cup of tea. She seems serenely at home in the advantaged world her characters inhabit in the short-story collections *A Glimpse of Scarlet* and *Asking for Love* and in her latest novel, *This Is My Daughter.* Yet it took a while, she says, to lose her self-consciousness about it as the setting for her fiction.

"WASPs have been on the top of the heap for a long time in this country, but in the '50s and '60s they started losing ground. So that any mention of WASPs is now ironic; you expect the adjective to be deprecating. It was hard for me to write about people who were affluent and privileged without a kind of conspiratorial aside to the reader that I understood that they were in some way morally deficient."

Robinson, on the contrary, treats her protagonists sympathetically and respectfully as she limns with psychological precision their complex relationships. *This Is My Daughter,* just out from Random House, chronicles the often tense interactions of Emma, an editor at an art magazine, and Peter, a lawyer, as they struggle to build a new family with the reluctant participation of Tess and Amanda, their respective daughters from previous marriages. As usual, Robinson excels in depicting the emotional fallout from divorce: Emma and Peter feel guilty, regarding the breakups as moral failures on their parts; Tess and Amanda are angry and confused; the ex-spouses, Warren and Caroline, are vindictive and not above manipulating the children to get back at their former mates.

This is familiar terrain for Robinson. The author, who has a 25-year-old daughter from a previous marriage, has touched on the divided loyalties and difficult adjustments inherent in second marriages in almost everything she's written. "I think it's a very interesting dynamic that has a very broad resonance right now," she remarks.

"The traditional love story includes two participants who are adult and who are in love. If you have children from a previous marriage, you have any number of main characters, and only the two adults are positive they want to make this work. There's this notion in America that you can always have a fresh start, but you are not starting over here: you are setting out on a whole new project with resistant partners."

The question of how to deal with these resistant partners prompts bitter arguments between Emma and Peter that frighten them both; the author makes it clear that two people who love each other might not be able to work things out. "The arguments are meant to be scary," Robinson says. "In the group I write about, arguments are repressed and postponed; these people are not used to letting off steam very easily, so when they do, it's very serious."

As in all of Robinson's fiction, her characters' financial ease and physical comfort are merely a backdrop for their internal lives. Unlike Edith Wharton or Louis Auchincloss, she does not portray people scheming to rise in society or to keep intruders out of it. Her protagonists' concerns, like their author's, are domestic. "I don't write about money and class," says Robinson. "Those things don't interest me at all. What interests me are the politics of the family. And families are families. You know, *Hamlet, Macbeth, Lear* are dramas of the family. The only reason they're perceived in a wider arena is that they're about kings, so anything that happens to them affects the whole country."

Her immediate family gave Robinson an intriguing perspective on the American elite: within it, yet not entirely of it. Both her grandfathers were lawyers, and "everybody went to Harvard," but her father, Stuyvesant Barry, declined to follow the traditional career path.

"He went to St. Bernard's, St. Paul's, Harvard and Harvard Law; he was meant to take over his father's law firm in New York," says Robinson. "Then he made a complete life change: left the law, became a schoolteacher, became a Quaker, was prepared to be a conscientious objector during the Second World War—and his father had been a colonel. My mother, Alice Scoville, was from Philadelphia, went to Shipley [a fashionable Main Line school] and Vassar, but they both took on a new sort of life. They moved down to Kentucky, where I was born, and taught at a mountain school, then went back to Pennsylvania, where he was the head of Buckingham Friends. It was an odd mix growing up, moving back and forth between my parents' and my grandparents' worlds."

Roxana Barry shared her parents' love of books, and teachers at Buckingham Friends and Shipley praised her youthful writing abilities. "Since I was ambivalent about teachers," she recalls, "it made me ambivalent about writing. I was slightly rebellious, didn't see myself as doing whatever I was told, so the fact that I was told early on that I should write put me off."

Nonetheless, she studied creative writing at Bennington with Bernard Malamud. The conjunction of a Jewish-American novelist with a scion of the WASP aristocracy may seem unlikely, but Robinson credits Malamud as a formative influence on her work. "He never suggested that I change the way I wrote," she recalls. "He gave me that sense of meticulousness that is so crucial. He was a small, methodical man, and he told us that you had to sit down and write every day—no waiting for inspiration. Of course, we all know this now, but to a 19-year-old it was a revelation. His calm, focused attentiveness to craft was what stayed with me."

The name of the contemporary writer whose books had the most profound impact on Robinson is less surprising. "Updike was the one," she comments. "If I'm a writer, it's because he taught me. I think he's the best living writer in the English language, and he's driven by compassion, which is the most interesting emotion to explore."

As Robinson discusses her work and her literary influences, the adjective she often uses to describe her characters, "conscientious," seems apt for their creator as well. She considers questions carefully and answers them thoughtfully, even phoning her interviewer later to clarify a point she felt hadn't been made lucidly enough. She saves her psychological insights for her work, sketching her personal history briefly and factually.

Robinson dropped out of Bennington after two years and got married, finishing her B.A. at the University of Michigan, where her husband was in business school, in 1969. Her major was English, but she wound up working for the next four years in the American painting department at Sotheby's in New York. "I had taken some history of art courses, and I got the job through friends. It was a wonderful education: we sold about a thousand paintings a year, and I probably looked at triple that; it gave me a range of experience I would not have gotten in school. I was writing fiction in a very secretive, ineffective way, and in fact I started publishing art history [in the mid-1970s] because I couldn't get my fiction published."

Divorced and remarried, Robinson began to break into the short-story market on both sides of the Atlantic in the 1980s. Her work appeared in *McCall's,* the *New Yorker* and the *Southern Review* in the United States. Publication in a British literary periodical, the *Fiction Magazine,* prompted a letter from an English editor asking if Robinson had a novel—"and of course I did!" *Summer Light* was issued by J.K. Dent in 1987; Viking released it in the States the following year, with a few changes made by editor Amanda Vaill (whose biography of Gerald and Sara Murphy has just appeared from Houghton Mifflin). Still in print in a University Press of New England paperback edition, *Summer Light* addresses, in a slightly tentative manner, subjects Robinson would explore more deeply in later works, including a divorced woman with a child hesitantly embracing new love and the complicated relationships among a group of intelligent, self-analytical people.

Ironically, just as Robinson felt she was settling into life as a fiction writer, she received a nonfiction offer she couldn't refuse. Edward Burlingame, a personal friend who then had his own imprint at Harper & Row, invited her to undertake a biography of Georgia O'Keeffe, who had just died. Although Robinson had recently vowed to give up art-history writing, she promptly accepted. "It was such an extraordinary opportunity," she explains. "O'Keeffe was a towering figure with a hugely powerful grasp on people's imaginations, and

236

there was very little published about her. It would be like writing a biography of Virginia Woolf if no one else had ever done it. It was just irresistible."

Immersing herself in the vast O'Keeffe archives at Yale, which included hundreds of personal letters, Robinson found that "there are a lot of ways in which biography and fiction overlap. The kind of delving into people's personalities that you do is very similar to writing fiction: you need to understand the characters as completely as possible before you write about them. But instead of creating them in my head and having to think up a plot, I could just tell the story."

Published by Harper & Row in 1989, *Georgia O'Keeffe: A Life* was nominated for a National Book Critics Circle Award and made the *New York Times* list of recommended books for the year. Burlingame also edited *A Glimpse of Scarlet,* which appeared in 1991 to excellent reviews. But when Burlingame was fired from HarperCollins following the company's acquisition by Rupert Murdoch, Robinson changed houses.

"HarperCollins was not really supportive of literary fiction, as far as I could tell," she says. "So I went to Random House." Susanna Porter handled the 1996 publication of *Asking for Love,* but "my story collections really get no editing," says the author. "I do them so exhaustively there isn't room for the shift of a comma. Susanna did suggest some cuts in *This Is My Daughter,* which I was perfectly happy about.

"The form of a novel is more forgiving and more voluminous, sort of like baggy trousers—I kept remembering that you could take a whole chapter and write about the whiteness of the whale! In a short story, nothing can be there that isn't directly germane to the last moment: not an adjective, not a sentence, nothing can be extraneous to this perfect curve that you're trying to create. In a novel that's not true; I put in lots of things just for fun. So if Susanna said, 'We don't need to know this much about such-and-such,' I said, 'Fine: take out three pages.'"

Now working on a new novel, once again about struggles within a family, Robinson hasn't written any stories since handing in *This Is My Daughter* a year ago. "I might," she says, "but maybe I'll just use all the material in my next novel instead." It's also still possible that she'll write another biography. "People ask me all the time, because biography is so popular now, but the subjects they've suggested have either not been as powerful [as O'Keeffe] or were someone everyone has heard of and read 15 books on. But it's not out of the question."

As in her fiction, Robinson doesn't make sweeping statements. She prefers to deal with the moment, and let life unfold as it will, while she observes with interest.

WENDY SMITH
June 15, 1998

JAMES SALTER

J AMES SALTER'S MEMOIR *Burning the Days* is both a literary event and the chronicle of a full, varied life.

Salter is the author of some of the most esteemed fiction of the past three decades, in particular *A Sport and a Pastime* (1967) and *Light Years* (1975), novels revered by a select and impassioned readership for luminous prose that cuts to the heart of human relationships in deceptively simple language, eschewing abstract ideas in favor of the most concrete and incisive images. Together with *Solo Faces* (1979) and the short stories collected in *Dusk* (1988), these works constitute an artistic legacy that could hardly have been imagined by the young pilot whose military experience is described with feverish immediacy in the first half of *Burning the Days*.

Born James Horowitz, the son of an engineer who developed real estate, Salter grew up on Manhattan's privileged Upper East Side between the two world wars. At the Horace Mann School, he inhaled poetry and wrote for the school's literary magazine. In 1942, at age 17, he followed in his father's footsteps and entered West Point. The memoir's riveting second chapter unsparingly describes "the forge" and young James's initial rebellion, "burning with anger against what I was required to be."

Yet this bookish misfit stayed the course at West Point and became a fighter pilot, seeing combat in the Korean War and remaining in the Air Force until the year after his first novel, *The Hunters*, appeared in 1956. (The pen name James Salter was adopted to evade regulations requiring approval of publications written by army personnel.) Those 15 years in uniform were "the voyage of my life," the author writes in *Burning the Days*. "I had come very close to achieving the self that is based on the risking of everything, going where others would not go, giving what they would not give."

That sentence will resonate for those familiar with Salter's fiction, all of which concerns to varying degrees people who find pleasure in taking large risks, sometimes in giving their all. It also displays a belief in the revelatory power of closely observed detail, a distrust for pronouncements about feelings and motivations that seems a legacy of Salter's tenure in the armed services, where what you do is more important than what you say about it.

Burning the Days (Random) has the same emotional modesty, particularly in its second half. Evocative sketches of the European and American landscapes, of his work as a screenwriter and novelist, and of people Salter knew—author Irwin Shaw, actor Robert Redford, *Grand Street* founder Ben Sonnenberg, among others—occupy much more space than the sparing descriptions of his interior life. "I'm just not given to writing a deeply analytical or confessional book," he remarks. "In many respects, I think my life is more interesting because of what I was able to observe than because of what I felt."

Interviewed at the Bridgehampton, N.Y., summer home he shares with his wife, playwright Kay Eldredge, and their 12-year-old son, Theo (they live during the school year in Colorado), Salter frequently responds to questions about why he did or wrote something either with a verbal shrug or with an anecdote that employs his dry wit to change the subject. Slim and tanned, looking closer to 52 than 72, he is a charming storyteller of the old-fashioned variety, spinning rambling yarns distinguished more by their pungency than their punchlines.

Salter's elusiveness could be frustrating, except that his asides often prove his point that "the general is uninteresting; it's the specific that's fascinating." He firmly refuses, for example, to discuss the internal forces that drove a busy junior officer to spend evenings and weekends writing fiction, but riffs compellingly on the development of his craft during those years.

"I had returned from the [Korean] war, where I'd kept a journal— I didn't know much about it; journal-keeping is a skill in itself. I don't mean a diary, where you say, 'He was ghastly to me tonight: I feel I should do this and that, and besides my mother was there'—not that kind of thing. A writer's journal usually has observations in it, scenes, words, names, things you as a writer will be able to use in the future. I had one from the war, and one day in Georgia, on an afternoon after flying, suddenly this book just came to me whole and entire. I simply jotted down very quickly maybe a page and a half with the theme, characters, and general events."

The Hunters, about combat pilots in Korea, was submitted to Kenneth Littauer, who became and remained Salter's agent until his death in 1968. (Peter Matson of Sterling Lord Literistic now represents him.) Harper & Brothers published the novel to generally good reviews, and the author resigned from the Air Force to devote himself full-time to writing.

Salter regards *The Hunters* as an apprentice work and until this year refused to permit a reprint edition. Counterpoint publisher Jack Shoemaker, who brought out *Dusk* and paperback editions of *A Sport and a Pastime, Light Years* and *Solo Faces* at North Point Press, finally convinced the writer to allow him to reissue the novel. "I really didn't want to, because it was a first book and I knew very little; I thought I would be embarrassed by it. But Counterpoint is an exceptional house and Jack's an exceptional guy; he persuaded me it was worth doing. I wasn't prepared to argue with him endlessly about it, so I said finally, 'Suppose I revised it a little bit?' He agreed, and I went through and tried to bring it up to standards."

Salter is even more dubious about Shoemaker's wish to reprint *The Arm of Flesh,* a 1961 work (also based on his flying days) that he views as deeply flawed. "That's going to take considerably more medical treatment. It's very derivative; I was powerfully impressed by Faulkner's *As I Lay Dying,* and I'm afraid the novel shows it."

The writer can be extremely critical of his work, which he holds to the exacting standards of the challenging fiction—by Gogol, Faulkner, Albert Camus, Flannery O'Connor, Marguerite Duras— that shaped his idea of what literature should be when he was a young man reading and learning on his own. (Like many autodidacts, he speaks and writes of books with a passion and discernment greater than most of his university-educated peers.) Even Salter, however, can't find anything negative to say about *A Sport and a Pastime,* the 1967 novel Reynolds Price once called "as nearly perfect as any American fiction I know." His tale of a love affair between Phillip Dean, a restless American, and Anne-Marie Costallat, an 18-year-old Frenchwoman, is notable for its matter-of-fact sexuality, its precisely lyrical evocation of provincial France (a region the author loves), and its understated tone of desire and yearning.

Characteristically, Salter replies to a question about what makes *A Sport and a Pastime* so special to him (as is evident from passages about it in *Burning the Days*) by focusing on the technical problem it presented. "Usually in books the erotic passages are an aria, and the rest is recitative. I wanted to do the reverse, in which the eroticism was the recitative and just went on all the time, since it's so much a part of life. The only difficulty I had was in making it appealing to the reader. If it had been written in the first person, it would have been confessional and nasty. If it had been written in the third person, it would have been too clinical and distanced. The idea came to me to have somebody tell this story intimately, as if telling it about another person, perhaps not knowing for certain whether all of it was true or not." The resulting narration, by an unnamed man who describes acts he could not have witnessed and teases the reader, "I cannot divulge my sources," struck precisely the note Salter sought.

In *Burning the Days,* the writer acknowledges that both Anne-Marie in *A Sport and a Pastime* and Nedra in his subsequent novel, *Light Years,* were based on actual women. The latter book, a piercingly unsentimental portrait of a seemingly perfect marriage and its eventual dissolution, raises the thorny question of the relationship between fact and fiction in Salter's work: he was divorced from his first wife, after more than two decades and four children, around the time *Light Years* was published in 1975.

Once again, the writer begins with a deliberately uninformative reply, then moves off on a more interesting tangent. "Not every character is based on a single person, but sometimes they are. So, let us use a word that we have not used yet: 'pure,' "—a joking reference to his interviewer's fruitless attempt to elicit an explanation of why that adjective turns up so often in his prose.

"You don't want to damage your characters by introducing things that are unnecessary; you may eliminate certain things to clarify," Salter explains.

"Gide has a wonderful line, 'It's unworthy of noble natures to spread round them the confusion they feel.' I think this is an obligation of the novelist: to observe and clearly set apart what is important, and to discard those confusing, extraneous, and ill-fitting things. That's what I'm about, in any case. Of course, you are absolutely entitled to use anything you see—or have heard or lived or made up—in whatever order you want. A perfect knowledge, as someone said, justifies any fiction."

Light Years brought Salter to Random House and to the late Joe Fox, who also signed up *Burning the Days* before his death. (Kate Medina did the memoir's final editing.) "Joe was the first real editor I had. Nobody said anything about the earlier books—in fact, the editor for *The Arm of Flesh* said, 'Well, I don't understand a word of this, but it's probably good'!" Harper also failed to understand *A Sport and a Pastime,* which it rejected as "repetitive and uninteresting." Only George Plimpton's faith in the book resulted in its arm's-length publication by Doubleday, which in 1967 had a contractual agreement to publish *Paris Review* Editions—but not necessarily to be enthusiastic about them.

"Joe and I became close friends as the years went on," Salter says of Fox. "I found him authoritative, but he also had that nice quality of saying, 'All right, if that's what you feel:' I think a good editor does that, unless you're obviously headed for the cliffs and have to be turned away."

Solo Faces, Salter's fifth novel, was published by Little, Brown editor-in-chief Robert Emmett Ginna in 1979. Ginna was an old friend who, during his years as a movie producer and magazine editor, had kept the well-regarded but less-than-bestselling writer solvent with screenwriting and journalism assignments.

Much of the past decade was occupied by Salter's exploration of the nonfiction skills required for *Burning the Days,* while he devoted his fictional energies to short stories. "I like stories," he says. "It's difficult to write a perfect long book, possible to write a perfect shorter one, but a perfect story, yes: there it is, it's dangling in front of you, you're snapping at it, saying, 'Maybe this will be it.' "

The idea for a new novel is germinating; Salter hopes to "sit down with it" after he finishes a fall teaching stint at Williams College. Meanwhile, the reputation of his earlier work continues to grow. It's become virtually a cliché to speak of Salter as "a writer's writer," but his fellow authors have always been his most steadfast admirers. *A Sport and a Pastime* and *Light Years* received mixed reviews when first published, and although critics eventually caught up with such Salter partisans as Peter Matthiessen, John Irving, and Kenneth Koch, his sales still suggest a readership among the happy few.

"Joe Fox always used to say, 'Forget it, you couldn't write a mass market book if you tried,' " he recalls wryly. "I'm never going to sell like Stephen King; I write a certain way, there are certain things that interest me, and if the audience for them is not vast, well, that's the way it is. I'm thrilled that other writers would want to read me; I can't think of an audience I'd rather have."

WENDY SMITH
September 1, 1997

243

WILL SELF

W<small>ILL</small> S<small>ELF</small> <small>STEPS</small> into the Groucho Club, London's exclusive watering hole for people in the arts, hops on a barstool, orders two bagels with lox platters, a beer and a Bloody Mary with a double shot of vodka. At 6'5", everything about him seems extreme—an impression that he clearly enjoys projecting.

As a journalist (he was a regular columnist for the London *Observer* until he was "fired in a rather high-profile incident" in May), Self estimates that he published a quarter of a million words last year alone. *Great Apes* (Grove/Atlantic) is his fifth book in seven years.

In a conversation that spans a manic run through Soho, a ride on the Underground and a tour through the Natural History Museum with his two children, the writer—and his thoughts on the writing life—remain constantly captivating, if difficult to pin down. Fluctuating between the brash, self-contradictory manner of the enfant terrible often portrayed in the British press, and the somewhat surprising persona of the serious writer and family man, Self at times seems to suffer from the same fate that afflicts the simian art critic in *Great Apes* who can no longer "tell himself whether or not he was being ironic."

Self's fiction, too, is riddled with contradictions, combining explicit violence and a vicious sense of humor that often borders on the misanthropic, with characters who are surprisingly accessible, even sympathetic. A rough division can be made between what he has referred to as his "nasty books," *Cock & Bull* and *My Idea of Fun*—in which a woman grows a penis and becomes a rapist and a man fornicates with the neck of a decapitated tramp—and his collections of short stories that are more like intellectual puzzles, with narratives that turn in on themselves and texts within texts.

Great Apes has elements of both. Like many of Self's stories, the novel is built around a central conceit—chimps have swapped places with humans in the evolutionary hierarchy. The idea of a London overrun by monkeys—climbing everywhere, stuck in traffic and mating at art openings—is made more plausible by the predicament of Self's protagonist, Simon Dykes (an artist who first appeared in his short story collection, *Grey Area*). Dykes begins the book as a human, and wakes up in the alternate ape-world convinced he is still a man. As the novel progresses, the habits and language of the chimps grow familiar, and as the doctors gradually convince him that he is deluded, the reader is convinced as well. "There are two ways of getting someone to suspend disbelief," Self explains. "One is just to present a fantastic conceit—like Kafka—and the other is to very gradually try and convince somebody of something utterly preposterous."

Self traces his enthusiasm for art and literature to his adolescence in London, as the child of an American mother who worked in the production side of publishing and a father who was an academic. It was a strained relationship that ended in divorce, and Self mentions in passing that in his own "very troubled teens," he was "diagnosed as a borderline schizophrenic and put on very heavy drugs." This experience explains in part the distrust of psychiatry that is a common theme in his fiction. "I always wrote," he says. There were "failed, pretentious novels in my late teens and early 20s"; then, a few years after he graduated from Oxford with a degree in philosophy in 1982, Self found himself running a trade-magazine publishing company.

"It sounds grand, but I had only five or six people working for me, and I used to have to do everything. I would go out and take photos, I'd do the reporting, the desk-top stuff, lay the whole thing out and print it. It sounds odd, but that's when I really learned to write to order. It disciplined me. Then I started writing seriously and I wrote my first book."

At the suggestion of his ex-girlfriend, an editor at Bloomsbury, he submitted an un-agented manuscript of his first collection of short stories, *The Quantity Theory of Insanity*. Bloomsbury bought it for £1,700 and published it as a paperback original in 1991. The book was soon lauded by Doris Lessing, Martin Amis and a *Granta* panel comprised of Salman Rushdie, Bill Buford and A.S. Byatt that designated Self one of the best young writers in Britain.

"It was a terrible baptism of caresses for a writer, because I didn't receive one negative review at all," says Self. "Of course, that tees up the next generation of critics to really savage you and also gives you a completely unrealistic idea of what it's like to publish books."

Quantity Theory was not published in the U.S. until 1995. Self met his American publisher, Grove/Atlantic's Morgan Entrekin, in 1992. From the beginning, Self recalls, it was an "astonishingly serendipitous" partnership. Self was visiting the States with a friend, who knew Entrekin's foreign rights director, Juliet Nicholson, who had just finished reading *Cock & Bull*. When Self's friend called her up to invite himself to the Hamptons, he "said I've got this friend Will Self with me, and she said 'What? I've just put down his book. It's a complete rave. We want it, we want it.' " And so Self went to meet Entrekin.

"At the time I'd written about half of *My Idea of Fun* and I pitched it to him like a character out of *The Player*. Entrekin acquired both *Cock & Bull* and the not-yet-written *My Idea of Fun*, deciding to postpone the publication of *Quantity Theory* until Self was better known in America. "It was the classic canard about being unable to flog short stories," Self recalls.

Entrekin is the only editor who has ever done extensive editing of Self's work, helping him revise *My Idea of Fun* (which appeared Stateside in 1993) at an early draft. His Bloomsbury editor, Liz Calder, is "terribly sort of dégagée," he says. "She's brilliant. She has an absolute nose for books. She's made her career on being able to spot Atwood, spot Rushdie. She'll get a manuscript and she'll say, well, I thought you might do X, and Y, and they'll be two tiny little points. And you'll think, bloody hell, I just submitted a 130,000 word manuscript, and then you'll actually think about it, and you'll think, yeah, those are good points, and that's it."

Self now counts Entrekin as a close friend. "There are terrible rumors about me and Morgan—that we check into a brothel in New Orleans for a month every year, where 40 whores cover us in cocaine." He laughs. "It's an astonishingly staid world, books. If you've got any kind of dash at all you become like Scarface."

Staid is not a word one associates with Self. He started using drugs at 12, and fought addiction throughout his teens and early 20s. He spent the years after university traveling around Australia and India and then went into rehab in 1986, and as he tells it, kicked the habit. Self admits freely to being a drug user now but is adamant that, for more than a decade, he has never found himself addicted.

In general, the media's obsession with Self's drug use has merely enhanced the stereotype of the high-flying anarchist the writer has so strenuously sought to cultivate. But this May, weeks before *Great*

Apes came out in England, his well-publicized audacity suddenly backfired, as another reporter leaked a rumor that Self had been taking heroin on John Major's press plane before the election; he was forced first into avoiding the charge and then into publicly admitting it. The incident ended with his being fired from his job at the *Observer*, which he had held for a couple of years, and having his face on the cover of every tabloid in town.

Self radiates a flippancy about how he is perceived by others, so it is somewhat surprising to hear him say that he hasn't been able to sleep since the whole debacle occurred. "It's been pretty bad. Enormous public humiliation, your face smeared over every paper, paparazzi at my door. We had to virtually go on the run and live out of my car for a week."

What worries Self most is that the attention will take away from serious consideration of his novel. Otherwise, he says, "I can sort of take it—I have had such heavy personal criticism for so many years now—I'm not saying that I've become inured to it, but yes, I have become inured to it. . . . Before the election, I was having a lot of difficulty accepting that I was famous. I was finding it very hard to deal with. And now I've sort of given up."

It seems ironic that the fuss about him using heroin would erupt now, when his life seems comparatively stable. Recently remarried, he has moved into a new house in Stockwell in South London with his second wife, Deborah Orr, who edits the *Guardian's* weekend magazine, and they are expecting a baby this fall. He still gives the impression of getting out and about more than most, but he also seems to have gotten into the rhythm of being a productive writer.

He credits Orr with helping him a great deal with *Apes*. "She puts a 90-page newspaper out every week, so she really knows how to deal with text. I've shown her far more than I've ever shown anybody before. I feel odd saying it, but I do regard it as a bit more of a cooperative exercise, without her turning into Mrs. Nabokov and having to accompany me to all my lectures."

Asked what he's working on now, he reels off a number of projects that include writing for American magazines ("The British press doesn't deserve me," he says), and a film adaptation of *The Picture of Dorian Gray* set in contemporary London. "Then there's a new novel and various other things. It just goes on and on and on. When I started seriously on my career, I was like, When are you going to be able to relax? How many books will you have written? And gradually it's begun to dawn on me that this is not going to happen. I'm feeling much more relaxed about it now because I know it's never going to stop . . . unless I dry up."

Self clearly sees writing as an integral part of the way he makes sense of his life, fueling an insatiable interest in anthropology, psychology and semiotics. But pressed to discuss his deeper motivations for writing, the same contradictions in his persona emerge. At one moment he seems passionately engaged, and at the next he presents himself as a dried-up cynic, driven to bloodlessly observing human behavior out of an overdose of ennui.

"If you're very committed to writing, it is the way you interpret the world," he says. "I suppose what writers try to score for, the writer's heroin, really, is that moment when you read a work of fiction and you think to yourself, I completely identify with that sentiment or idea or that experience and I've never heard it articulated to me in exactly that way. It's essentially a new coinage of sympathy. And if you can do that once or twice a book, you're doing really well. If you can do it once or twice a page, you're Tolstoy."

It seems typical of Self that he starts backtracking here, as if he doesn't want to get caught sounding too earnest about anything. "I basically write to amuse myself, and for money. I do it for money because I'm unemployable in any other context, and I do it to amuse myself because I get really bored the whole time."

Self bristles when it's pointed out that money and boredom can't possibly be his primary motivations, and he leans forward to emphasize his point. "I'm telling you the absolute fucking gospel truth. You can't sit down as a satirist and think, 'oh, these people are behaving dreadfully badly. I must write this satire about apes to show humans that they've all got to be much nicer to each other. I'm very upset about it and I'm going to lock myself up in this room. . . . ' It doesn't work like that. You just get very bored, and start writing books."

ANNA HENCHMAN
September 8, 1997

STUDS TERKEL

WHEN STUDS TERKEL meets a journalist in late May, it's the day after he has been inducted into the American Academy of Arts and Letters, bringing a certain street credibility to an eminent but starchy institution. While he enjoyed re-encountering authors and artists he'd interviewed over the decades, Terkel claims his initial impulse was in the spirit of Gore Vidal's crack: "I already belong to the Diner's Club."

However, at 85, with blockbuster oral histories like *Working* and *The Good War* to his credit, Terkel still wonders whether he's the real thing, a writer: "After all, I've been accused of just being a recorder." So, despite his qualms, Terkel joined: "I figure, what the hell, I've proved something." *My American Century,* his latest book from the New Press (a "quasi-anthology of my eight oral journals"), also seems more a validation than a valedictory. With introductions and excerpts from each book (plus his introduction to the 50th anniversary of *The Grapes of Wrath,* which had been requested by John Steinbeck's widow), this volume displays Terkel's pen and voice as much as the stories he elicits. In his foreword, Robert Coles lauds Terkel as "our foremost documentarian, our leading student of American variousness as it gets embodied in human particularity."

Terkel meets *PW* at the New Press's office in a warehouse-like building in the grungy district near New York's Port Authority bus terminal. It seems more suited to Terkel than the offices of the plush Random House empire, where he was long published by André Schiffrin, now director of the New Press. The elfin Terkel dresses in a uniform of sorts: herringbone tweed jacket, blue sweater, tieless red-and-white checked shirt, a rubber band wrapped around his right wrist. His socks are red. Wisps of longish white hair crown a strong-featured face that got him cast as a gangster in his early days as an actor.

When *PW* asks Terkel to talk about his new book, he doesn't quite comply. "We'll come to the book," he declares, indicating his preference for a "sort of jazz conversation, improvised." Even so, Terkel—a self-described "hambone actor" with "a touch of logorrhea"—has memorized many of the riffs. He has a prodigious memory and the energy to animate anecdotes and characters; then again, Terkel aficionados might recognize some stories as direct lifts from his oral memoir, *Talking to Myself,* or Tony Parker's oral biography, *Studs Terkel: A Life in Words.*

His epitaph, Terkel once wrote, should be "Curiosity never killed this cat." Asked to elaborate, he reflects on the working-class men's hotel his mother ran in Chicago, a place where young Louis Terkel watched the men drink and argue—and saw those pastimes distorted by the Great Depression. "How could I deny the Wells Grand and its influence on me—far, far more than the University of Chicago Law School?" He studied law during the Depression, "dreaming of Clarence Darrow, but I got Contracts and Real Property."

His regular streetcar ride to Chicago's South Side nonetheless took him past storefronts playing "race records" that fueled his love of music and gave him his entrée into Chicago's black culture. Growing up with an emotionally volatile mother fostered his sensitivity; living with brothers—one studious, the other genial—also helped ripen his eclecticism. And yes, Chicago's broad-shouldered mix of ethnicity and industry furthered Terkel's American grain. He puts it another way: "Chicago is a city that grew out of improvisation."

His career developed similarly. "My dream was to have a civil service job, go to movies, see ballgames and plays, and read." But his clerk's work in the treasury department led to a labor theater group and ultimately a disc jockey job and a measure of fame. From 1950 to 1952, Terkel hosted the local TV talk show, *Studs' Place,* but his support for left-wing causes and his refusal to sign a McCarthy-era loyalty oath cut short that career. Locally blacklisted and struggling for gigs, Terkel returned to WFMT radio in 1952 and developed a long-running public affairs program that mixed literature, music and—increasingly—interviews.

To Terkel, a good interview requires curiosity and preparation. "If it's [with] the author of a book, I read [the book] and sometimes I put music to it" as an introduction. Nicknamed "Studs" for his identification with novelist James T. Farrell's dissolute, macho Studs Lonigan, Terkel still sports old-time slang like "dough" and "scram." Indeed, his books show not only an affection for the ordinary person but also a certain delight in types like the eloquent gangster. He avoids lofti-ness in interviews; at times, he wrote in the introduction to *Division Street: America*, "I was impelled to use self-deprecatory profanity to clear the air." Nonetheless, he peppers his patter with offhand erudi-tion, references to Chekhov, Whitman and Walker Percy.

In Chicago, Terkel palled around with Nelson Algren and debated God on the air with Mahalia Jackson. Traveling for WFMT, he turned his recorder toward luminaries like Bertrand Russell and South African Nobelist Albert Luthuli. He took his microphone on a train to the 1963 March on Washington, but, for the most part, didn't interview ordinary folk until he launched into books. In the early 1960s, transcripts of some Terkel interviews from South Africa, pub-lished in the WFMT magazine, found their way to Schiffrin, then at Pantheon. Schiffrin had just published Jan Myrdal's *Report from a Chinese Village* and wanted a book on an "American village." Thus emerged *Division Street* (1967), in which Terkel asked Chicagoans about their changing city.

Since then, Schiffrin has served as Terkel's editor, muse and goad. "Three months later, it's André again. I'm an innocent Adam. Here he comes, the serpent with the apple, and says, the kids don't know about the Great Depression." Thus came *Hard Times* (1970) and then *Working* (1974), an international bestseller with its panoramic view of people struggling with labor and identity. Some books, like the memoir, were more Terkel's idea, but Schiffrin's had a hand in them all. Traversing America's past and its soul, they include *The Good War; Race; American Dreams: Lost and Found; The Great Di-vide;* and, most recently, *Coming of Age*, about energetic oldsters.

"Without André, I'd have a wholly different life," Terkel reflects. "I realize now, my life is an accretion of accidents." And when Schiffrin founded the New Press in 1992, after his forced resignation from Pantheon, Terkel brought *Race* with him, bringing the fledgling house its first bestseller, a dose of credibility and some revenue to plow back into the not-for-profit enterprise. "People say, that's so great, you were loyal to André," Terkel recalls. "I say, no, what's so unusual about loyalty? He's the guy who created me, for Chrissakes."

To find subjects for his books, Terkel once wrote, he uses "hunch, circumstance, and a rough idea"—a chance meeting with a cabbie, a friend's recommendation, a woman featured in the local news. With such people, an interview is a conversation: "sitting, talking, having a cup of coffee" before taping.

"Is everybody I interview a so-called ordinary person?" Terkel asks rhetorically. "They're ordinary, but they speak for others." And sometimes they don't know what they think till he elicits it. One woman, upon hearing her voice on tape, told him: "I never knew I felt that way." Marvels Terkel: "What a moment, not only for her, but for me."

To orchestrate such conversations for his books, he takes 60 pages of a transcript and distills it into some eight pages. "Of course I transpose the sequences," he says, "but the words are the words of the person." For his books, Terkel habitually took about three months off from WFMT, placed some classic shows on repeat and edited at home in his bathrobe, "mining for gold." Perhaps his favorite interviewee in *My American Century* is C.P. Ellis, the ex-Klansman from *American Dreams* who, to Terkel, symbolizes the human capacity for redemption. He's also glad he included Jerome Zerbe, the condescending society photographer, from *Hard Times*. From *Working*, Terkel chose the dignified fireman Tom Patrick ("I can look back and say, I put out a fire"), but he regrets he didn't keep the spirited parking attendant "Lovin' Al," with whom he smoked 15-cent cigars. Terkel originally wanted this new book to contain just his own writing; Schiffrin suggested that Terkel add interview excerpts, so *My American Century* "would be a kind of history of the 20th century."

Terkel, who reads lefty publications and damns those who protest the "liberal media," doesn't deny his politics, but he resists critics who condemn him wholesale on ideological grounds. "Of course I have a point of view, it's in my introduction," Terkel acknowledges. "But I want my people to be free."

Not every Terkel project has worked out. A book on power was short-circuited when moguls he interviewed lacked candor, and Terkel proved too venerable for a book on youth. Terkel regrets he hasn't trained a corps of oral historians—"My life's been ad hoc"— though Sydney Lewis, a former assistant, produced the oral history *Teenagers*, for the New Press, using Terkel's techniques, he says. But the frequent classroom adoption of books like *Working* has inspired many students to start taping.

In January, following his annual New Year's show, Terkel will give up the WFMT gig and prepare for the millennium. "In the 21st century, what will the kids know about this country? It'll be the traditional stuff about the big shots, the presidents." But he has a unique library, some 8000 hours of tapes, most from his show, the rest from the books. Working at the Chicago Historical Society, he envisions creating programs for schools or communities. (Schiffrin, however, would like some books.) "Is the civil rights movement just Martin Luther King, or is it the train I was on?"

Terkel, who doesn't drive, has long resisted technology. In fact, his fumbles with the tape recorder are almost a strategy to show ordinary folk his own vulnerability. But the quintuple bypass he endured last year put his Luddite leanings in perspective. "Technology saved me. So here I am, the ungrateful wretch." He remembers more: the surgeon was—in Terkelian high praise—"a skilled craftsman."

When Terkel's first books appeared 30 years ago, themes like race and the Vietnam War were vivid, immediate. Now, allows Terkel, "it's a strange moment. Something's happening to the American dream. The haves and the have-nots gap is greater, but the business section says we're on the way up. So we have a switch. And labor's having a hard time."

But Terkel recalls a reason to be optimistic. Waiting for the bus in Chicago, he recalls, he got a ride from a union rep, a longtime fan of his. The man told him that labor has a new constituency—women and immigrants—"and they're good." To recall the moment, he looks for the man's business card, shuffling through a stack as if playing speed solitaire. Along the way, he finds a 1923 card advertising a Socialist and Labor candidate for Chicago's Board of Aldermen. It warms him. "So I have these adventures."

Terkel and his wife, Ida, a former social worker, live in "a have-section in a have-not area—I wouldn't dream of living in a suburb." And he's been rewarded. His title for *Division Street* was metaphorical, not literal, though Chicago has a street of that name. But sometimes life imitates books. Now, over the Chicago River at Division Street, a bridge bears the name of Studs Terkel.

"People say I'm retired," he says, apropos of "Vox Humana," his new project to distill stories from his archive, to continue in what he calls "the arena of unofficial truth." "On the contrary, there's a new challenge. I've always had these accidental changes, but this one I'm thinking about. I want to spend a year listening to these voices, me and"—he can't resist the quip—"Joan of Arc."

NORMAN ODER
July 28, 1997

JOANNA TROLLOPE

A JOURNALIST INVITED TO visit Joanna Trollope in her greystone, peak-roofed home in Coln St. Aldwyns, Gloucestershire immediately sees the vitality and matter-of-fact charm that define her sharply nuanced and witty portraits of English middle-class life. Although Trollope doesn't usually allow reporters into her home, she has broken her rule for *PW*, greeting us as she would a long-awaited weekend guest.

Tall, blonde, riding-crop-thin and dressed English country casual, Trollope ushers us into a capacious study where two upholstered, high-backed chairs sit perpendicular to a welcoming fireplace. She's already launched—as so many middle- and upper-class Britons are regularly compelled to do—into some form of an apology.

"I hope you understand my reluctance to invite you here," she says as she and her playwright husband Ian Curteis see to our trenchcoat and scarf, "but it has to do with English journalists. They know everything there is to know about me and so they only come here to look at the decor and go away and say something nasty. I thought that if I'd decided I could no longer have them, I had to extend that to all journalists. It's to do with class, of course. They want to know whether I have everything, and then they criticize it."

Sitting at that fireplace only minutes away from Curteis's cheerful arrival with tea and strips of carrot cake, one wonders what there is to find wrong with this perfectly agreeable room—idyllic for any writer, actually, in its just-this-side-of-cluttered mix of furniture and bric-a-brac. Trollope, who's all angles in her chair, explains this is Curteis's room. Pointing more or less directly above her, in a voice that's both chipper and no-nonsense as well as paced at something of a gallop, perhaps to match the horse-country setting, she says, "I work in a small room up there."

Trollope's sixth novel on these shores, *A Spanish Lover*, (Random House) is already three books old in England, a publishing pattern—

"bizarre" is Trollope's word—partially dictated by the successful American television airings last year and the year before that of her earlier novels, *The Choir* and *The Rector's Wife*, both of which were published here by Random House in 1995. "It isn't hard to remember them," she says of her Rural Domestic narratives. "Of course, I remember the storyline—this is not Proust," she comments. "Readers are always writing me about all my books. I have to say I have the nicest readers in the world."

A Spanish Lover concerns the changing fortunes of 39-year-old twin sisters Lizzie and Frances. The first has married and started a successful business with her husband Robert; the second runs a travel agency but has declined to marry. "You may remember in *The Men and the Girls*—the novel before *A Spanish Lover*—there were little boy twins," Trollope says. "I'm interested in this business of twins, of twinship, particularly when it's women. Sisters don't leave sisterhood alone. There are competitivenesses. There is the twitch upon the thread. They feel each other's pulse."

Pulse rates in *A Spanish Lover* quicken and slow as the 1980s run out on Robert and Lizzie, forcing them to downscale, just as Frances meets a married Spaniard called Luis with whom she falls in love and by whom she contrives to have a baby he has made clear he doesn't want. This scheme is also an outgrowth of another of Trollope's writerly impulses. "I like looking at clichés to see if they hold good or not. What's more cliché than the myth of the holiday romance? What's more cliché than the woman from the North being emotionally unlocked by the man from the South?"

As with all of what Trollope calls her "JTs" (to distinguish her contemporary novels from historicals she began to write in the late '70s under the name Caroline Harvey) the ending of *A Spanish Lover* is calculatedly unresolved. Although Luis accepts his new son, it's at the cost of his love for Francis. The plangent minor chord coda is typical of Trollope's works—reminiscent, for instance, of the fade-out in *The Men and the Girls*, where Kate, having left her husband James, a man much older than she, returns to offer a reconciliation just a few days too late. Trollope insists on ambivalent endings that don't "patronize the readers. If I tidied up the endings, they'd fall flat. As a reader I don't like having *my* mind read." She simply wants to present her contemporary figures as objectively as possible in all their familial dilemmas. "I'm not going to judge them," she says. "It all comes from a Philip Toynbee quote I have on the wall upstairs—

255

'The definition of moral progress is the realization that other human beings are fully as human as oneself.' "

A speech in *The Men and the Girls* goes some way towards summarizing her fictive interests. In it, James, the older husband, says, "When things change, you simply have to learn to adapt to them, don't you? And I suppose, if you're lucky, you might learn to like the change, or at least get perfectly used to it." Trollope explains: "Life is a series of changes. That's the human condition. If you stop changing, that's when a certain fossilization begins. You pull in your horns. It's a recipe for a diminishing life. There's a Sylvia Townsend Warner letter about life being a series of losses of homes. The first home is the womb, isn't it."

Trollope's fiction is also imbued with disappointment. It afflicts the dramatis personae of just about every one of the JTs, which to date include, in order of their composing, *The Choir, A Village Affair, A Passionate Man, The Rector's Wife, The Men and the Girls, A Spanish Lover, The Best of Friends, Next of Kin* and *Faith,* a short paperback original that's part of the Bloomsbury Quid series. About her dedication to parsing the fine points of setback, she says, "I have known considerable disappointment, and I think disappointment is tremendously underestimated. It's thought of as a minor incident in a life, but it isn't minor. It's a very necessary part of life. The darkness of life is crucial. It has to be harnessed. One of the good things about getting older is that one fears [disappointment] less."

Born in Gloucestershire in 1943, Trollope had a father who was a Royal Engineer and who, it being wartime, "begat me and disappeared" for the duration of WW II. She spent much of her childhood with her brother and sister in Surrey with her mother's parents. Her grandfather was a country parson whose type, Trollope says, is "now as dead as the dinosaur." Her grandmother, as Trollope sees it, "had no outlet for her fantastic talents"—and therefore partly inspired the spirited protagonist of *The Rector's Wife.* Her mother kept an anthology—a loose-leaf booklet—of her favorite writing, and Trollope's time was spent being read aloud to and reading on her own. "I'm sure it was that upbringing that hooked me on words. People who know the wonder of words know it early, don't they?"

Although she was raised a Trollope, she merrily confesses that her often-misreported relationship to Anthony, the man to whom she refers as "the real Trollope" "is very disappointing. I'm of the same family but not his branch. We're from the trade side that left Lincolnshire early in the 19th century to come to London. The grand family is always terrified I'm going to claim closer kinship. I'm really some remote kind of cousin. But I have to say I do admire him astoundingly. What I like most about him is his benevolence. He really likes humanity. I think great writers do."

With so many influences acting on her, Trollope nonetheless took her time admitting to herself and the rest of the world that she was a writer. Her first novel remains unpublished and "is upstairs under lock and key so the children don't find it." (Trollope has two daughters from a previous marriage and two step-sons). More than a decade after graduating from Oxford, having put in time as a civil servant and a teacher, she published her first Caroline Harvey novel in 1978.

"We haven't tried Miss Harvey on America," Trollope says about volumes called *Legacy of Love, Second Legacy, Parson Harding's Daughter* and *Steps of the Sun*. Trollope imagines Caroline Harvey as quite distinct from herself. "I see her as given to Anita Brookner cardigans and perhaps with a cat. But it's all silly. It's me." Nevertheless, there is a wide disparity between the two kinds of novels to which she's devoted her time. For Trollope, Caroline Harvey is "less satisfying to write. It's not as rich and as deep. I suppose I know I'm dealing with a certain kind of reality, but it isn't the deepest kind."

Nevertheless, it wasn't a simple matter for the CHs to become JTs. "I felt like a vehicle up a cul-de-sac without a reverse gear," Trollope says. "It was Ian who gave me the idea during one of our endless discussions over dinner. His exact words were, 'It's time you went to Sainsbury' [the large British supermarket chain]. I was terrified. I thought, 'You'd hidden behind pre-Freudian psychology for so long.' Ian got me out of that, too. He said, 'Why not choose a social problem you don't know anything about?' I'd sat next to a dean at a lunch some months before and he'd said something about possibly having to close down the choir. This little nugget went down into this useful creative compost." And became *The Choir*, the first JT and a comprehensive fictional study of a town caught up in the religious and political ramifications of putting an end to its boys' choir. And that put Trollope on the literary map. Today, she says with a certain amount of pleasure, there may not be "a day when there isn't a letter from a reader in the post—some of them addressed only 'Joanna Trollope, Gloucestershire, England.' "

Trollope continues to write as both Caroline Harvey and herself.

In fact, the next CH—*The Brass Dolphin*—is due out in England soon and for the first time will have an up-in-the-air ending. "Anymore the suggestion of a happy ending fidgets me," she declares.

Of her writing habits, Trollope will only say that she matches, quite by coincidence, Anthony Trollope's 1000 words-per-hour rate when she's on a roll, which she usually is early in the day, and she always writes the first chapters and then the ending before filling in the middle. "I work office hours," she reports, "but the creative bit is in the morning. It's a long morning. I write in long-hand very fast. But I have to say that the administration of a writer's life takes much more time than it ought."

Once Trollope has written a book—on the right-hand side of the foolscap so she can tweak on the left-hand side—she gives the manuscript to a friend who puts it on disk. That's when she can get objective and become "ruthless." She says, "I require editing. I don't think there's a manuscript in the world that doesn't need editing. The trouble begins when you get too prima donna-ish." She's edited in England by Bloomsbury head Liz Calder and in America by Random House's Suzanne Porter, although Porter generally only changes the occasional Briticism. Trollope also switched agents when Lizzie Grossman at Sterling Lord Literistic moved to Oregon, and Pat Kavanaugh at Peters Fraser & Dunlop, the English agency, thought a British author being handled from Portland didn't make a great deal of sense. Kavanaugh's suggestion for a replacement was Joy Harris of Lantz Harris Literary Agency, and Trollope couldn't be happier—"I think she's wonderful." *The Best of Friends* is promised to Random House but *Next of Kin* isn't and Trollope is uncertain if RH will remain her American publisher. "I don't want to make too much of this, but I'm considering *A Spanish Lover* a make-or-break book."

The fire in Curteis's study is still blazing. A late English afternoon has set in. Trollope still talks a country-mile-a-minute. "To be a great writer, or even good," she says, patently meaning to have it understood that she places herself in the latter category, "you have to have a real sympathy, a tolerance, for the human condition. It isn't much slaying dragons. It's bearing things."

DAVID FINKLE
February 3, 1997

GARRY WILLS

Garry Wills strides into his Evanston, Ill., home only to pause suddenly on the threshold of his elegantly appointed living room. The meticulously kept house seems an incongruous backdrop for the tall, rugged, broad-featured writer, clothed in outdoors garb and outsized footwear—from which, he has just realized, snow is melting onto the gleaming floor. With a wry expression, Wills delicately retreats to the doorway to remove his boots. This adjustment made, he turns to the task at hand: conversing about the hard work of living the life of the mind.

We have ventured here this frigid winter morning to discuss Wills's latest book, *John Wayne's America: The Politics of Celebrity,* (Simon & Schuster). As we sit and talk in his living room, the author comes into better focus. Up close, it becomes apparent that Wills's pullover and chinos are made from fine-textured fabric; his trademark glasses, boxy and black, appear to be fashionably designed. Like the man himself, Wills's oeuvre is at once larger-than-life and highly polished.

Wills has now published 15 books, ranging from his groundbreaking analyses of Nixon and the Kennedys to studies in Greek tragedy and Shakespeare and his recent bestsellers *Certain Trumpets: The Call of Leaders* (1995) and *Lincoln at Gettysburg* (winner of both a Pulitzer and an NBCC award in 1992). In all of these works, Wills clearly and insightfully examines the power dynamics of public performances and the intertwining of theater and politics. But in the years since Wills published the 1979 account of his evolution away from the political right, *Confessions of a Conservative,* his own powerful rhetorical performance has seldom been publicly examined. How does Wills himself continually perform so effectively?

Part of the answer lies in Wills's determination to wrestle with many of the same grand themes in book after book, gradually refining a formidable political sensibility. *John Wayne's America* might seem to mark a departure for an author known above all for shrewd portraits of political leaders, past and present. Yet its title echoes its companion-piece in the Wills canon: 1987's *Ronald Reagan's America*. "In Reagan's case," Wills points out, "you have the politician as showman; in Wayne's case, the showman as politician." Both case studies illuminate America's romance with its own image, as reflected to it by Hollywood.

Where his own work is concerned, Wills eschews showmanship. He stays out of the spotlight, away from the coasts. He and his wife, Nathalie, came to Evanston, outside of Chicago, in 1980, when Wills took a post at Northwestern University. Two of their three children now have jobs in the book world: John, a Michigan Ph.D., works for Borders in Ann Arbor; Lydia is a New York literary agent who counts Elizabeth Wurtzel among her prominent clients; a third child, Garry, is in the midst of a round-the-world bicycle journey.

Since the beginning of his career, Wills says, he has been advised by colleagues that " 'you have to move to New York, that's the only place where you can keep up the kind of ties in the publishing world that you need to get ahead.' That never appealed to me," he avers, shaking his head. "Later, a lot of people said I should move to Washington, because I was writing more on politics—but I didn't and I'm glad. I think that kind of networking consumes too much of people's lives. I don't know when they get their work done. Here I'm just remote enough that I can get to places when I want to, but I'm not surrounded by the industry. Even my daughter," Wills adds, smiling, "has to surface occasionally, get her head above water, come home and get back to normal."

Wills, whose clear, matter-of-fact statements are punctuated by frequent sotto voce amendments and qualifications, describes writing habits that are a picture of diligence. "I write in the morning, almost every morning. I usually go to libraries in the afternoon and do research, except when I'm teaching, but now I teach only one course a year, so that's not a part of my regular routine. I write by hand, and have a typist type it up." Occasional trips abroad vary the established procedure, but only, it seems, to a degree. "Usually I go away in February to get away from the cold, and to get outdoors—I write and walk and read outdoors, when the weather allows. My wife's family is from Italy. We get there once or twice a year, and that's just pure enjoyment, although I do usually get an article out of it."

Wills came to Northwestern as a full professor, but "the crushes to find time to write" drove him to give up tenure for his current adjunct position. He teaches a course every year, usually in American cultural history, though he maintains his interest in the Classics, a field which he feels to have been invigorated by recent academic movements.

"I'm a multiculturalist," Wills avows: "I'm a Classicist, but I think that the best thing that has happened to Classics is multiculturalism, women's studies, slave studies."

If certain moments, like this one, find Wills speaking in a professorial mode, he easily moves into a more informal manner when he talks about his life experience. Wills was born in 1934, a child of the Depression. His family traveled about the midwest as his father sought work. In his late teens, Wills entered a Jesuit seminary. He was still a seminarian when, in 1957, William F. Buckley discovered a submission from Wills in the slush-pile at the *National Review* and brought him on board as a regular contributor. Wills subsequently earned his Ph.D. in Classics from Yale, writing for *NR* all the while.

Wills credits one of his mentors at *NR* in particular, book review editor Frank Meyer, for schooling him about the book world. Wills recalls that Meyer, who died in 1972, "was very curious and intellectually restless. He had this phone network of people he would call late at night. I was a night person in those days, and what I learned about books and other people often had to do with him." Meyer's young acolytes at *NR* also included Arlene Croce, John Leonard and Joan Didion.

As to Wills's subsequent choices of venues for his journalism, he says there's been "no grand plan, I go where I'm invited." By the late 1960s, Wills was writing regularly for *Esquire*, where Harold Hayes was his editor. At *Esquire* Wills covered the death of Jack Ruby, the assassination of Martin Luther King Jr. and other major events of the day. The fast pace of change in those years led him to begin a syndicated column, which he has continued to write regularly ever since.

Wills identifies 1970's *Nixon Agonistes* as marking his emergence into the major leagues of book publishing. The Nixon project originated with an article on Nixon's 1968 campaign, commissioned by Hayes for *Esquire*. Dorothy de Santillana, an editor at Houghton

Mifflin, called Wills, he says, "the minute she read it," offering a book contract. "She got me my first really considerable advance. Without having to spend my own money, I followed Nixon for the rest of the campaign," Wills recalls. While *Nixon Agonistes* inaugurated what became a long sequence of books on presidents and power. Wills calls it "the book that I would least have expected to write." *Esquire* called him, Wills notes, only after Murray Kempton had to bow out of the assignment; hence, he claims, "it was just by accident that I wrote it."

Wills recalls how he became fascinated by Nixon's theatrics, by "the whole interplay between private and public man, which is what caught Dorothy de Santillana's eye in the article." He describes a moment from the piece, when "I'm in the airplane with Nixon, for my interview that I'd been leading up to in the article—earlier on I've seen him in glimpses, and this is the first time I'm really close, right across the aisle—and he switches off the lights so that I can't see him. She [de Santillana] liked that approach."

If there is a single hallmark of Wills's writing, it is this capacity to wear lightly his own accomplishments. In Wills's books, broad depictions of historical figures stand out, but they subtly mesh with the detailed accounts of situations and motivations that provide their background.

Wills found de Santillana, who at the time was nearing retirement, "absolutely wonderful; there's a whole club of people who did one book with her, and loved her. David Halberstam is one; in fact, he dedicated *The Best and the Brightest* to her. The house was kind of stingy with advances, so it was hard for the editors to keep their authors."

The books since have been many, but Wills's editors have been few. After the success of *Nixon Agonistes*, Wills went to Ken McCormick at Doubleday, who was "the editor I had the longest, and most unfailingly wonderful relationship with," says Wills. After McCormick's retirement, Peter Davies lured Wills to Little, Brown where *The Kennedy Imprisonment* became a bestseller.

Yet for his next book Wills moved to Alice Mayhew at Simon & Schuster, who remains his editor today. "I'd known Alice for years because she was involved with the whole *Commonweal* Catholic writers group. We came up with a three-book contract, and I've actually written four books with her, and now a fifth." Wills's only recent non-S&S book is *Witches and Jesuits,* his recent essay on *Macbeth.* Originally a series of lectures given at Oxford, it was published by Oxford University Press in 1995.

Mayhew's input has had an important role in shaping at least one of Wills's recent triumphs: *Certain Trumpets,* his collective profile of various effective leaders. "Alice was trying to come up with names of other sorts of people to write about—you do get into a niche of people who just write about presidents—and as she was going through these various leaders, we started sifting the criteria for choosing leaders. Oddly, the choice of the people came first, and not the theory."

Ted Chichak of the Scott Meredith agency was Wills's agent into the 1980s—*Under God,* Wills's study of religion in the 1988 campaign, is dedicated to him. When Meredith died, Chichak moved on, and so did Wills, first to Janklow & Nesbit, and then, last fall, to Andrew Wiley. Wills connects his latest move to the unfolding of his daughter Lydia's career. "I think a lot of my feelings for the agency had to do with the fact that she was there, and when she moved [to Artist's Agency] I was not as tied to them."

His current project is a book about the political situation after the Cold War, though he is hesitant to talk about a work in progress, demurring that he is "still formulating my ideas." Of course, ideas about Cold War politics inform both *John Wayne's America* and *Reagan's America.* The development of such "parallel studies" is not a new strategy for Wills. "I've done that in the past; you do it automatically, because you're working on things at the same time. For instance, my *Cincinnatus* [George Washington] and *Kennedy Imprisonment* books were meant to be two studies in power, one on a person wielding power, the other on power wielding the person."

Wills recently gave the Storrs lectures at Yale Law School on Shakespeare's *Julius Caesar.* He is happy to talk about how he has "always been interested in performance." But asked to reflect on the rhetorical dimension of his own writing, Wills grows laconic. "Oh," he accedes, "I suppose you certainly are managing your effects."

Wills is similarly reluctant to dilate on his role as a leading public intellectual. Yet he argues vigorously that writers remain crucial actors in the public sphere. "Writers were very important in the women's movement, for instance, more important I think than politicians."

At the end of the session, Wills tours his guest through his cozy upstairs study, a sun-filled corner room. Above Wills's desk is a special-edition copy of the Gettysburg Address, mounted in a frame on the wall: a gift to Wills from the Library of Congress. The gift, and its current location, seem appropriate. Although himself quite a private person, Wills can truly be said to work under Lincoln's sign, circulating commentaries on the events of his era, which are, like Lincoln's, timely, deeply thoughtful and finely crafted.

SAMUEL BAKER
March 24, 1997

TOM WOLFE

IT TOOK A decade to write. It is the panoramic saga of a hot-house Atlanta society on the verge of being burned to the ground. Its headstrong protagonist is an enduring symbol of American enterprise. It received rave reviews but was such a popular sensation that it demolished the barrier that traditionally separates literary from commercial fiction. The book is of course *Gone with the Wind,* but if you were to mistake the above description for that of Tom Wolfe's latest novel from FSG, *A Man in Full,* you wouldn't be far off the mark.

Lest you think that this eminent social satirist, known for his savage critiques of American pomp and pretension and for his ferocious, era-capping pronouncements, is ill-served by a comparison to the author of the most beloved potboiler of all time, rest assured; it's a comparison that he encourages. "I love being in the same paragraph as Margaret Mitchell," he says over breakfast at the Ritz in Atlanta. "In literary circles, you're not supposed to say that. But you could argue, and I would if anyone would listen, that *Gone with the Wind* is the greatest American novel ever written." Just two days after the National Book Foundation denied him a second NBA, it's not surprising to find this genteel contrarian slyly thumbing his nose at literary elitism. But rarely has Wolfe made his ambitions to write for the widest possible audience so unabashedly clear.

Thus far, readers have been happy to oblige him. No novel this year has been saddled with the high expectations that awaited Wolfe's first book since *Bonfire of the Vanities,* and no novel this year has made such a splash in the publishing pool. The ravenous news media that, in *The Right Stuff,* Wolfe famously decried as a "consummate hypocritical Victorian Gent," have seized the author by his high-peaked lapels and refuse to let go. He has landed on the cover of *Time* magazine (one of a handful of authors this decade to do so), been profiled by newspapers from coast to coast and has been featured in seven separate articles in the *New York Times* alone, all of which has helped him set sales records at bookstore appearances during the most competitive book-selling season of the year.

When we last heard from Wolfe, the publishing industry was a different place. When *Bonfire* appeared in 1987, well before the advent of the one-day laydown, it came with a first printing of 200,000 copies, an ambitious sales projection in its day, and one that depended on the hand-selling efforts of a vibrant independent bookseller network. *A Man in Full* steps into a different world, sporting a first printing of 1.2 million, with its eye trained on a wide range of retail accounts, from independents to K-Mart to Amazon to the massive chain-owned superstores. The one-day laydown, meant to maximize a book's chances of immediately capturing the top slot of the bestseller list—a feat usually only achieved by the likes of a Grisham, Clancy or King—proved successful, and at press time, that's where the book remains. "It's surprising," says Irwyn Applebaum, who will publish the book in trade paperback at Bantam sometime next year, "that Tom Wolfe, who many consider a literary author, would be able, two out of two times, to attract such keen interest."

But is Wolfe a literary author? In the modern entertainment market, serious fiction has always been overshadowed by commercial fiction, film and TV. As *Time* Magazine book critic Paul Grey puts it, "The notion that literature occupies a higher cultural niche has gone by the boards." But can Wolfe's novel, an ambitious, multilayered feat of story-telling that hit the marketplace like a commercial heavyweight, safely be defined as either literary or commercial? Would this doorstopper of a novel, published by a mid-size house known more for Nobel laureates than bestsellers, command the interest of so large a readership if it weren't also such a pop phenomenon?

These questions were foremost in our mind as we set out to follow Wolfe from reading to reading during the breakneck swing through Atlanta that promised to be the most highly charged stretch of his book tour. Ever since the headline of a *Wall Street Journal* article screamed "Fiddle-dee-dee! Wolfe Burns Atlanta," the capital city of the New South was spoiling for a showdown with the cosmopolitan author who seemed poised to bring more attention to Atlanta than any event since the centenary summer Olympics.

The specter of Atlanta in flames certainly haunts the novel, whose myriad plotlines depict the decline and fall of local real estate titan

Charlie Croker, proprietor of a quail plantation called Turpmtine; the political brushfire touched off by the accusation that a black Georgia Tech football star has raped the daughter of a white business tycoon; a mayoral race tinged by the vexed politics of a city unable to put to rest the racial conflagrations of the past; and the bizarre odyssey of a worker laid off from one of Croker's frozen food warehouses who finds himself on a collision course with his CEO.

When asked if he intended to write an inflammatory tract, Wolfe almost admits as much by voicing an opposite fear: "I was worried that people were expecting a firebomb or a blowtorch and that it was a warm bath." In his words, "The book is neither pro-Atlanta nor anti-Atlanta. It *is* Atlanta." But the controversial thrust of the book has paid off amply, helping to generate the storm of publicity that greeted him immediately upon his arrival here.

From the moment he touched down at Hartsfield International Airport, Wolfe was surrounded by a battalion of TV cameras and reporters from news organizations across the country. The most ubiquitous were those representing the *Atlanta Journal-Constitution* gossip column "Peach Buzz," which ran a weeklong segment called The Wolfe Watch, illustrated at the top with a Mr. Peanut-like caricature of the author, to track his travels about town and contretemps with reviewers and local politicians. Eyebrows rose when former mayor Sam Massel rescinded an offer to have Wolfe speak at a meeting of leading businessmen, and when the current mayor, Bill Campbell, who is black, boycotted all of Wolfe's appearances. Which of the self-made Atlanta real estate moguls is Croker supposed to be? (Wolfe calls him a composite.) Is the fictional mayor's effort to "pass" as a darker-skinned man based on a very real controversy surrounding Atlanta's last mayoral campaign?

According to FSG marketing v-p Laurie Brown, the fast-breaking, true-to-life elements of the book fundamentally shaped the marketing campaign, from the decision to publish after the November elections, a strategy that paid huge dividends when the novel hit a news vacuum in its first week of publication ("You can always lose a *Time* cover to an Israeli peace agreement," says Brown in jest), to the house's decision not to release advance galleys. Indeed, the news angle is what influenced *Time* to put Wolfe on the cover a week before pub date, despite the fact that authors don't generally sell well on newsstands. Sales of the Tom Wolfe issue "weren't great," according to *Time* managing editor Walter Isaacson, but featuring Wolfe on the cover was important to Isaacson because "it helps push a form of fiction that is engaged in the world."

Talk about engaged! In Atlanta, Wolfe had so many commitments that he barely paused to eat or sleep. Although the novel painstakingly chronicles Atlanta's diverse and polarized social strata, Wolfe zeroed in on consumers more likely to afford his $28.95 hardcover. For three days, he crisscrossed the city's wealthier enclaves, from a black-tie benefit for the Margaret Mitchell House at the Atlanta History Center to private lectures and readings at the Four Seasons and at the Piedmont Riding Club in Buckhead, the city's most affluent district. At the Borders store there, a carnivalesque atmosphere prevailed, as roughly 1100 customers, waiting in line for hours, found diversion from an "electric kool-aid" stand (minus the LSD), a large screen TV running a videotape of *The Right Stuff* and a bookseller in an astronaut suit. At the Hartsfield Airport Waterstones, Wolfe signed 200 copies of the novel in just over 30 minutes.

Some may find it surprising that Atlantans opened their arms to welcome an author who has aired so much of their city's dirty laundry. More surprising perhaps is how Wolfe, who has made a hobby of skewering sacred cows and bloated egos, continues to find subjects who will let their guard down in front of him. But finessing his way into strange and often exclusive milieux has long been his trademark. Asked how he does it, Wolfe explains, "Usually, I just start with one person. In effect what I try to do when I go somewhere is say, 'I'm going to be your chronicler. If you're interested, tell me a story.' And this is my one contribution to psychology, what I call Informational Compulsion. Most people have a story to tell and they're delighted when somebody arrives and wants to listen to it." As he says this, one sees how quickly Wolfe could disarm almost any adversary with his easygoing, soft-spoken demeanor and impeccable Southern manners. "There's a lot more everyday casual courtesy in the South than in other places," he observes. "There is such a thing as Southern hypocrisy. But it's always couched in courteous terms and that makes life a lot smoother."

Wolfe says that he made dozens of visits to Atlanta to research the novel, and traveled to quail plantations in the company of his friends Mack and Mary Rose Taylor, who are among the book's dedicatees (Mack is a leading Atlanta real estate developer and, coincidentally, the father of publishing PR guru Camille McDuffy). At the Atlanta

History Center, when one wag in the audience stood up and asked whether, on one of these trips, Wolfe shot a bird, he puckishly replied, "I'm not sure which kind you mean. They were too smart to let me shoot a gun." What Wolfe shot instead was a lurid snapshot of conspicuous consumption, South Georgia-style. Turpmtine is eerily suggestive of the ante-bellum South—"29,000 acres of fields, woods, and swamp, plus the Big House, the Jook House, the overseer's house" and a landing strip for Croker's Gulfstream Five, all maintained by an extensive African-American staff dressed in yellow overalls.

As difficult as it may be to envision Wolfe in his cream suits, spats and speckled socks, prowling for quail in the moist Georgia sedge, it's clear that his wardrobe is, in effect, a form of camouflage deflecting attention from the inner man to his exterior. "Early in the game," Wolfe says, "when I was writing articles about all sorts of new social phenomena, I realized I was not going to blend in no matter what I wore. When I was covering Ken Kesey and the Merry Pranksters, they were always astounded that I would show up in a jacket and necktie." The product of a small Richmond boy's school where a strict dress code was enforced, Wolfe was still a reporter at the *New York Herald Tribune* in the 1960s when he upped the sartorial ante considerably, adapting the style of an insouciant planter that he maintains to this day.

His wardrobe has also helped make him a pop icon, instantly recognizable from across the room or on the page of a magazine. "Tom is a star in a way that writers usually are not," says his editor, Jonathan Galassi. As FSG's Brown puts it, Wolfe "lives a life outside of the spotlight, but when he's ready to step back into the spotlight, it's ready for him."

In this millennial year, the desire for books that define our times has grown intense, and Wolfe doesn't shrink from the task. Making an appearance at the National Press Club in Washington, which was televised on C-Span, Wolfe declared that the "money fever" of the 1980s has been replaced by the "moral fever" of the 1990s. Such proclamations have become as much a hallmark of Wolfe's as his clothing. On stage or on TV, Wolfe can be a magnetic showman, a deadpan raconteur with stark features and dark, expressive eyes.

Lynn Nesbit, who has represented Wolfe since his first book, *The Kandy-Kolored Tangerine-Flake Streamline Baby*, was issued by FSG in 1965, insists that the author's star power has little to do with his present success. "Maybe he has a persona but I don't think that should be emphasized." It's the quality of this book and that alone that has made it so popular, she says. That may be, but FSG has certainly capitalized on Wolfe's celebrity status by setting his name on the dust jacket in type that's roughly 10 times larger than the title of the book.

The cult of personality surrounding Wolfe's work also helped keep the hype engine revved during his long years of silence. Until recently, few people knew what his new novel would be about. Though never catalogued before this year, FSG hoped it would be ready earlier. It was to be called *The Mayflies*, then *Red Dog*, then *Cracker Heaven*. But as word spread that Wolfe had undergone quintuple bypass surgery and was suffering from depression, its imminent release seemed unlikely. As it turned out, the delay had more to do with Wolfe's uncertain plans for the book than anything else. "We all know that Tom is his most severe critic as well as his most exacting editor," says Nesbit. "It's not that he wasn't writing. He was cutting, revising, taking certain things out." In retrospect, Wolfe says he "wasted colossal amounts of time trying to put this book in New York." Six years into it, he sent Galassi an 830-page manuscript and met him for lunch shortly thereafter. "I found myself telling stories about Atlanta," Wolfe recalls. "And I said, 'I should have written about Atlanta.' Without skipping a beat, Jonathan said, 'That would be a good idea.'

That was his very subtle way of saying this book wasn't panning out."

It was a gamble for FSG to indefinitely absorb the cost of a long-unfinished book contract with an advance reported to be roughly $6 million. But their forbearance was crucial, says Wolfe. "I was so glad, when this played out the way that it did, that I was with Farrar, Straus. They never put any kind of pressure on me. I don't think that a lot of the publishers that were interested in me after *Bonfire of the Vanities* would have had the faith or the patience to wait for this thing."

Wolfe finished the novel in August (he works on a manual typewriter and the complete, triple-space manuscript came in at 2100 pages). In order to meet the November release date, says Galassi, FSG had to "turn on a dime." One of the unorthodox production measures they devised was to divide the book into two sets of proofs. The two halves of the manuscript were read in shifts (which "drove the copyeditors crazy!" says Galassi). Even *Time*'s Paul Grey says that he received the manuscript in two installments, one in July and one in August. Notorious for making enormous changes at the last minute, Wolfe was tightening the book until the very end.

The publicity campaign was to prove just as unorthodox. Though sources at FSG insist that no title on the fall list was sacrificed to the *Man in Full* juggernaut, FSG's Brown says, "There's no question this book was discussed every day for months, and fretted over, as we tried to get the right number of books shipped."

From the start, the marketing campaign was designed to strike at an elusive segment of the market: male readers of literary fiction. The sheer heft of the book, combined with an ultra-sleek book design, in which a hulking businessman gazes Rasputin-like through a dust jacket window, telegraphs that the author of *The Right Stuff* remains resolutely interested in the question of what defines the late 20th-century male.

The book has been carefully positioned in places where business travelers, and men in particular, are likely to see it. The marketing budget, said to be $500,000 (an unprecedented sum for FSG), will be used during the frantic book-buying weeks ahead for full-color ads in newspapers, on the sides of buses in midtown Manhattan and in lightboxes at airports in Atlanta, New York, Washington and Boston.

It's hard to say how much the stellar sales of *A Man in Full* should be attributed not to the engaging narrative that Wolfe has written, but to the fact that it was published and marketed so well. Nor is it easy to predict how the circumstances surrounding this publishing event will align themselves around future novels that ambitiously take as their subject the whole breadth of contemporary American life. But it's worth remembering that what eventually undoes Wolfe's protagonist, Charlie Croker, is the hubris that leads him to think that he controls the real estate market rather than the other way around. "A real-estate developer is a one-man band and the band is called Me, Myself and I," says Wolfe. "They have the gambling instinct and always want to roll the dice." In the case of *A Man in Full,* an ad-hoc coalition of publishers, booksellers and arbiters of popular taste rolled the dice simultaneously. And they've rolled a winner.

JONATHAN BING
December 7, 1998

CONTRIBUTORS

JOHN F. BAKER was editor-in-chief of *Publishers Weekly* for 12 years. Now he is editorial director.

SAMUEL BAKER, a Chicago-based freelance writer, is a frequent contributor to *Publishers Weekly*.

JOHN BLADES is a former book editor with the *Chicago Tribune* and author of the novel *Small Game*.

MALLAY CHARTERS is a journalist and postbaccalaureate pre-medical student.

TRACY COCHRAN is co-author of *Transformations: Awakening To the Sacred In Ourselves*.

MICHAEL COFFEY is managing editor of *Publishers Weekly*. His second book of poems, *87 North*, was published by Coffee House Press.

MATTHEW DEBORD is a contributing editor at the on-line magazine *FEED*. He lives in Brooklyn.

DAVID FINKLE writes frequently about books and the arts.

ELIOT FINTUSHEL is a Santa Rosa, California-based mask and mime showman and science fiction writer.

ELIZABETH GAFFNEY is editor-at-large of the *Paris Review* and the translator of *The Pollen Room*, a novel by Zoe Jenny.

ANNA HENCHMAN is a doctoral candidate in English at Harvard and a freelance writer.

IVAN KREILKAMP is a freelance writer living in Chicago.

RENÉE KRIST's writing has appeared in the *Village Voice, Spin,* the *San Francisco Bay Guardian* and other magazines.

COLIN LACEY is a freelance writer living in County Kerry, Ireland.

SUZANNE MANTEL is a contributing editor at *Publishers Weekly* and arts editor of the weekly paper, *New Times Los Angeles.*

NORMAN ODER is an editor at *Library Journal.*

JUDY QUINN is book news editor at *Publishers Weekly.*

CALVIN REID is news editor at *Publishers Weekly.*

SUSAN SALTER REYNOLDS is an assistant editor at the *Los Angeles Times Book Review* and a book critic for the Life & Style section of the *Los Angeles Times.*

JEAN RICHARDSON is the London correspondent for *Publishers Weekly.*

MICHAEL SCHARF is a contributing editor at *Publishers Weekly.*

JENNIFER SCHUESSLER is a freelance writer living in Brooklyn.

WENDY SMITH, the author of *Real Life Drama: The Group Theatre and America, 1931–1940,* is a frequent contributor to *Publishers Weekly* and to book review sections in many periodicals.

LORIN STEIN, a former contributing editor at *Publishers Weekly,* works at Farrar Straus & Giroux.

SYBIL STEINBERG is senior editor in the Forecasts department of *Publishers Weekly.*

JEFF ZALESKI is editor at large in the Forecasts department of *Publishers Weekly.*

STEVEN ZEITCHIK is editor of *PW Daily* at *Publishers Weekly.*

BIBLIOGRAPHY

(Books currently in print by interviewed authors)

BERYL BAINBRIDGE

An Awfully Big Adventure, Carroll & Graf, paper, 1995
The Birthday Boys, Carroll & Graf, 1994; Carroll & Graf, paper, 1995
The Bottle Factory, Carroll & Graf, paper, 1994
The Dressmaker, Carroll & Graf, paper, 1996
English Journey, Carroll & Graf, paper, 1997
Every Man for Himself, Carroll & Graf, 1996; Carroll & Graf, paper, 1997
Forever England, Carroll & Graf, 1999
Master Georgie, Carroll & Graf, 1998
A Quiet Life, Carroll & Graf, paper, 1999
Something Happened Yesterday, Carroll & Graf, 1998
Young Adolf, Carroll & Graf, paper, 1998

ANDREA BARRETT

The Forms of Water, Pocket Books, paper, 1994
Lucid Stars, Dell, paper, 1997
The Middle Kingdom, Washington Square Press, paper, 1992
Secret Harmonies, Delacorte, 1989; Washington Square Press, paper, 1991
Ship Fever, Norton, 1996; Norton, paper, 1996
The Voyage of the Narwhal, Norton, 1998

FREDERICK BARTHELME

Bob the Gambler, Houghton, Mifflin, 1997; Mariner, paper, 1998
The Brothers, Penguin, paper, 1994
Chroma, Grove Atlantic, paper, 1996
Double Down, Houghton Mifflin, 1999

Moon Deluxe, Grove Atlantic, paper, 1995
Natural Selection, Viking, 1990
Painted Desert, Penguin, paper, 1999
Second Marriage, Grove Atlantic, paper, 1995
Two Against One, Grove Atlantic, paper, 1996

JOHN BAYLEY

Elegy for Iris, St. Martin's, 1998
Leo Tolstoy, Univ. of Mississippi, paper, 1996
The Red Hat, St. Martin's, 1998

BILL BRYSON

I'm a Stranger Here Myself, Broadway Books, 1999
Made in America, Avon, paper, 1996
The Mother Tongue, Avon, paper, 1991
Neither Here Nor There, Avon, paper, 1993
Notes from a Small Island, Morrow, 1996; Avon, paper, 1997
A Walk in the Woods, Broadway Books, 1998; Broadway Books,
        paper, 1999

CALEB CARR

The Alienist, Random House, 1994; Bantam, paper, 1995
Angel of Darkness, Random House, 1997; Ballantine, paper, 1998
The Devil Soldier, Random House, 1995

MICHAEL CUNNINGHAM

Flesh and Blood, Farrar, Straus & Giroux, 1995; Scribner, paper,
        1996
A Home at the End of the World, Farrar, Straus & Giroux, 1990;
        Farrar, Straus & Giroux, paper, 1998
The Hours, Farrar, Straus & Giroux, 1998

EDWIDGE DANTICAT

Breath, Eyes, Memory, Soho Press, 1994; Vintage, paper, 1998
The Farming of Bones, Soho Press, 1998; VHPS, paper, 1999
Krik? Krak!, Soho Press, 1995; Vintage, paper, 1996

MIKE DAVIS

Burning Our Illusions Tonight, Holt, 1999
City of Quartz, Verso, 1990; Vintage, paper, 1992
Ecology of Fear, Holt, 1998; Vintage, paper, 1999

DON DELILLO

Americana, Penguin, paper, 1989
The Day Room, Penguin, paper, 1989
End Zone, Penguin, paper, 1986
Great Jones Street, Vintage, paper, 1994
Libra, Penguin, paper, 1991
Mao II, Penguin, paper, 1992
The Names, Vintage, paper, 1992
Players, Vintage, paper, 1989
Ratner's Star, Vintage, paper, 1989
Running Dog, Vintage, paper, 1989
Underworld, Scribner, 1997; Scribner, paper, 1998
White Noise, Penguin, paper, 1991

DOROTHY DUNNETT

Caprice and Rondo, Knopf, 1998; Vintage, paper, 1999
Checkmate, Vintage, paper, 1998
The Disorderly Knights, Vintage, paper, 1997
The Game of Kings, Vintage, paper, 1997
King Hereafter, Vintage, paper, 1998
Niccolo Rising, Vintage, paper, 1999
Pawn in Frankincense, Vintage, paper, 1997
Queen's Play, Vintage, paper, 1997
Race of Scorpions, Vintage, paper, 1999
The Ringed Castle, Vintage, paper, 1997
Scales of Gold, Knopf, 1999
The Spring of the Ram, Vintage, paper, 1999
To Lie with Lions, Vintage, paper, 1999
Unicorn Hunt, Vintage, paper, 1999

FANNIE FLAGG

Daisy Fay and the Miracle Man, Warner, paper, 1992
Fannie Flagg's Original Whistle Stop Café Cookbook, Fawcett,
    paper, 1995
Fried Green Tomatoes at the Whistle Stop Café, Random House,
    1987; Fawcett, paper, 1997
Welcome to the World, Baby Girl!, Random House, 1998

MARIA FLOOK

My Sister Life, Pantheon, 1998
Open Water, Ecco Press, paper, 1997
Reckless Wedding, Carnegie-Mellon Univ., paper, 1996
Sea Room, Wesleyan Univ. Press, paper, 1990
You Have the Wrong Man, Pantheon, 1996

ALLEGRA GOODMAN

The Family Markowitz, Farrar, Straus & Giroux, 1996; Washington
    Square Press, paper, 1997
Kaaterskill Falls, Doubleday, 1998; Dell, paper, 1999

MARY GORDON

The Company of Women, Ballantine, paper, 1986
Final Payments, Ballantine, paper, 1986
Men and Angels, Ballantine, paper, 1986
The Other Side, Penguin, paper, 1990
The Rest of Life: Three Novellas, Penguin, paper, 1994
The Shadow Man, Random House, 1996; Vintage, paper, 1997
Spending, Scribner, 1998; Scribner, paper, 1999

SUE GRAFTON

A Is for Alibi, Holt, 1995; Bantam, paper, 1987
B Is for Burglar, Holt, 1995; Bantam, paper, 1986
C Is for Corpse, Holt, 1995; Bantam, paper, 1987
D Is for Deadbent, Holt, 1995; Bantam, paper, 1988
E Is for Evidence, Holt, 1995; Bantam, paper, 1989

F Is for Fugitive, Holt, 1995; Bantam, paper, 1990
G Is for Gumshoe, Holt, 1995; Fawcett, paper, 1991
H Is for Homicide, Holt, 1995; Fawcett, paper, 1992
I Is for Innocent, Holt, 1995; Fawcett, paper, 1993
J Is for Judgment, Holt, 1995; Fawcett, paper, 1994
K Is for Killer, Holt, 1995; Fawcett, paper, 1995
L Is for Lawless, Holt, 1996; Fawcett, paper, 1997
M Is for Malice, Holt, 1997; Fawcett, paper, 1998
N Is for Noose, Holt, 1998; Fawcett, paper, 1999
O Is for Outlaw, Holt, 1999

DONALD HALL

The Bone Ring, Story Line, paper, 1987
Death to the Death of Poetry, Univ. of Michigan, paper, 1994
Fathers Playing Catch with Sons, North Point Press, paper, 1984
Goatfoot, Milktongue, Twinbird, Univ. of Michigan, paper, 1978
The Happy Man, Random House, paper, 1986
Life Work, Beacon Press, 1993, Beacon Press, paper, 1994
The Man Who Lived Alone, Godine, 1998
The Museum of Clear Ideas, Houghton, Mifflin, paper, 1994
Old and New Poems, Ticknor & Fields, paper, 1990
Old Home Day, Browndeer Press, 1996
The Old Life, Houghton, Mifflin, 1996; Houghton, Mifflin, paper,
    1997
The One Day, Ticknor & Fields, paper, 1988
Poetry and Ambition, Univ. of Michigan, 1988
Seasons at Eagle Pond, Ticknor & Fields, 1987
String Too Short to Be Saved, Godine, paper, 1976
Their Ancient Glittering Eyes, Ticknor & Fields, paper, 1993
The Weather for Poetry, Univ. of Michigan, paper, 1982
Without, Houghton, Mifflin, 1999

JANE HAMILTON

The Book Of Ruth, Houghton, Mifflin, 1996; Anchor Books, paper,
    1990
A Map of the World, Doubleday, 1995; Anchor Books, paper, 1992
The Short History of a Prince, Random House, 1998

ROBERT HUGHES

American Visions, Knopf, 1997; Vintage, paper, 1998
Barcelona, Knopf, 1992; Vintage, paper, 1993
The Culture of Complaint, Oxford, 1993; Warner Books, paper,
    1994
The Fatal Shore, Vintage, paper, 1988
Nothing, If Not Critical, Penguin, paper, 1992
The Shock of the New, Knopf, paper, 1991

GARY INDIANA

Gone Tomorrow, High Risk Books, paper, 1995
Let It Bleed, High Risk Books, paper, 1997
Rent Boy, High Risk Books, paper, 1994
Resentment, Doubleday, 1997; Bantam, paper, 1998
Three-Month Fever, Cliff Street Books, 1999

RONA JAFFE

An American Love Story, Delacorte, 1990
The Cousins, Mira Books, paper, 1996
Five Women, D.I. Fine, 1997; Mira Books, paper, 1998

JAN KARON

At Home in Mitford, Viking, 1998; Penguin, paper, 1996
A Light in the Window, Viking, 1998; Penguin, paper, 1997
The Mitford Years, Viking, 1997; Penguin, paper, 1999
New Song, Viking, 1999
Out to Canaan, Viking, 1997; Penguin, paper, 1998
These High, Green Hills, Viking, 1995; Penguin, paper, 1997

ALFRED KAZIN

An American Procession, Harvard, paper, 1996
God and the American Writer, Knopf, 1997; Vintage, paper, 1998
The Inmost Leaf, Harvest Books, 1979
A Lifetime Burning in Every Moment, HarperPerennial, paper,
    1997

New York Jew, Syracuse Univ., paper, 1996
On Native Grounds, Harvest Books, paper, 1995
Starting Out in the Thirties, Cornell Univ., paper, 1989
A Walker in the City, Harvest Books, paper, 1969
Writing Was Everything, Harvard, 1995

FAYE KELLERMAN

Day of Atonement, Fawcett, paper, 1992
False Prophet, Fawcett, paper, 1993
Grievous Sin, Fawcett, paper, 1994
Justice, Avon, paper, 1996
Milk and Honey, Fawcett, paper, 1991
Moon Music, Morrow, 1998; Avon, paper, 1999
Prayers for the Dead, Morrow, 1996; Avon, paper, 1997
The Quality of Mercy, Fawcett, paper, 1990
The Ritual Bath, Fawcett, paper, 1987
Sacred and Profane, Ballantine, paper, 1998
Sanctuary, Avon, Paper, 1995
Serpent's Tooth, Morrow, 1997; Avon, paper, 1998

STARLING LAWRENCE

Legacies, Farrar, Straus & Giroux, 1996
Montenegro, Farrar, Straus & Giroux, 1997; Berkley, paper, 1998

BRAD LEITHAUSER

Cats of the Temple, Knopf, 1986
The Friends of Freeland, Knopf, 1997; Vintage, paper, 1998
Penchants and Places, Knopf, 1995
Seaward, Knopf, 1993
Very, Knopf, 1998

JOHN LEONARD

The Last Innocent White Man in America, New Press, 1993; New
        Press, paper, 1997
Naming in Paradise, Oxford, 1990
When the Kissing Had to Stop, New Press, 1999

JONATHAN LETHEM

Amnesia Moon, Harcourt Brace, 1995; St. Martin's, paper, 1997
As She Climbed Across the Table, Doubleday, 1997; Vintage, paper,
    1998
Girl in Landscape, Doubleday, 1998; Vintage, paper, 1999
Gun, with Occasional Music, Harcourt Brace, 1994; Tor Books,
    paper, 1995
Motherless Brooklyn, Doubleday, 1999
The Wall of the Sky, the Wall of the Eye, Harcourt Brace, 1996; Tor
    Books, paper, 1997

PATRICK McCABE

Breakfast on Pluto, HarperCollins, 1998
The Butcher Boy, Fromm International, 1993; Dell, paper, 1994
Carn, Dell, paper, 1997
The Dead School, Dell, paper, 1996

JAY McINERNEY

Bright Lights, Big City, Vintage, paper, 1984
Brightness Falls, Vintage, paper, 1993
The Last of the Savages, Knopf, 1996; Vintage, paper, 1997
Model Behavior, Knopf, 1998; Vintage, paper, 1999
Ransom, Vintage, paper, 1985
The Story of My Life, Vintage, paper, 1989

JAMES M. McPHERSON

The Abolitionist Legacy, Princeton Univ., paper, 1976
Abraham Lincoln and the Second American Revolution, Oxford,
    1991; Oxford, paper, 1992
Battle Chronicles of the Civil War, 6 vols., Macmillan, 1990–1991
The Battle Cry of Freedom, Oxford, 1988; Ballantine, paper, 1989
Civil War and Reconstruction, St. Martin's, paper, 1999
Drawn with the Sword, Oxford, 1996; Oxford, paper, 1997
For Cause and Comrades, Oxford, 1997; Oxford, paper, 1998
Gettysburg, Rutledge Hill, 1998
In Blood Thicker than Water, Vintage, paper, 1999

Marching Toward Freedom, Facts on File, paper, 1994
The Negro's Civil War, Ballantine, paper, 1991
Ordeal by Fire, 2 vols., McGraw-Hill, paper, 1993
Struggle for Equality, Princeton Univ., paper, 1964
What They Fought for, 1861–1865, Louisiana State Univ., 1994;
    Anchor Books, paper, 1995

THOMAS MALLON

Aurora 7, Norton, paper, 1992
A Book of One's Own, Hungry Mind, paper, 1995
Dewey Defeats Truman, Pantheon, 1997; St. Martin's, paper, 1997
Henry and Clara, Picador USA, paper, 1995
Stolen Words, Ticknor & Fields, 1989

DANIEL MENAKER

The Old Left, Knopf, 1987
The Treatment, Knopf, 1998; Washington Square Press, paper, 1999

RICK MOODY

The Black Veil, Little, Brown, 1999
Garden State, Pushcart Press, 1992; Little Brown, paper, 1997
The Ice Storm, Warner Books, paper, 1995
Purple America, Little Brown, 1997; Little, Brown, paper, 1998
The Ring of Brightest Angels Around Heaven, Little, Brown, 1995;
    Warner Books, paper, 1996

BRIAN MOORE

Black Robe, Plume, paper, 1997
Cold Heaven, Plume, paper, 1997
Lies of Silence, Doubleday, 1990; Avon, paper, 1991
The Lonely Passion of Judith Hearne, Little, Brown, paper, 1988
The Magician's Wife, Dutton, 1998; Penguin, paper, 1999
No Other Life, Doubleday, 1993; Plume, paper, 1997
The Statement, Dutton, 1996; Plume, paper, 1997

LORRIE MOORE

Anagrams, Warner Books, paper, 1997
Birds of America, Random House, 1998
Like Life, Knopf, 1990; Plume, paper, 1991
Who Will Run the Frog Hospital?, Knopf, 1994; Warner Books, paper, 1995

STEWART O'NAN

The Names of the Dead, Doubleday, 1996; Penguin, paper, 1997
A Prayer for the Dying, Holt, 1999
Snow Angels, Doubleday, 1994; Penguin, paper, 1995
The Speed Queen, Doubleday, 1997; Ballantine, paper, 1998
A World Away, Holt, 1998; Owl Books, paper, 1999

RICHARD NORTH PATTERSON

Dark Lady, Knopf, 1999
Degree of Guilt, Ballantine, paper, 1997
Escape the Night, Ballantine, paper, 1997
Eyes of a Child, Knopf, 1995; Ballantine, paper, 1996
The Final Judgment, Knopf, 1996; Ballantine, paper, 1997
The Lasko Tangent, Ballantine, paper, 1997
No Safe Place, Knopf, 1998; Ballantine, paper, 1999
The Outside Man, Ballantine, paper, 1997
Private Screening, Ballantine, paper, 1997
Silent Witness, Knopf, 1997; Ballantine, paper, 1997

GEORGE PLIMPTON

The Best of Plimpton, Atlantic Monthly, paper, 1991
The Bogey Man, Lyons Press, paper, 1993
Fireworks, Doubleday, 1984
Mad Ducks and Bears, Lyons Press, paper, 1993
The Open Net, Lyons Press, paper, 1993
Out of My League, Lyons Press, paper, 1993
Paper Lion, Lyons Press, paper, 1993
Shadow Box, Lyons Press, paper, 1993
Truman Capote, Doubleday, 1997; Anchor Books, paper, 1998
The X Factor, Norton, 1995; Norton, paper, 1996

DAVID REMNICK

The Devil Problem, Random House, 1996; Vintage, paper, 1997
King of the World, Random House, 1998
Lenin's Tomb, Vintage, paper, 1994
Resurrection, Random House, 1997; Vintage, paper, 1998

SHERI REYNOLDS

Bitterroot Landing, Berkley, paper, 1995
A Gracious Plenty, Crown, 1997; Crown, paper, 1999
The Rapture of Canaan, Berkley, paper, 1996

NORA ROBERTS

All the Possibilities, Harlequin, paper, 1992
The Art of Deception, Silhouette, paper, 1993
Blithe Images, Silhouette, paper, 1993
Born in Fire, Jove, paper, 1994
Born in Ice, Jove, paper, 1995
Born in Shame, Jove, paper, 1996
Boundary Lines, Silhouette, paper, 1994
Brazen Virtue, Bantam, paper, 1998
The Calhoun Women, Harlequin, paper, 1996
Captivated, Silhouette, paper, 1992
Captive Star, Harlequin, paper, 1997
Carnal Innocence, Bantam, 1999; Bantam, paper, 1992
Command Performance, Silhouette, paper, 1993
Convincing Alex, Silhouette, paper, 1994
Dance of Dreams, Harlequin, paper, 1994
Dance to the Piper, Mira Books, paper, 1994
Daring to Dream, Jove, paper, 1996
Divine Evil, Bantam, paper, 1992
Finding the Dream, Jove, paper, 1997
For Now, Forever, Harlequin, paper, 1992
For the Love of Lilah, Harlequin, paper, 1991
From the Heart, Jove, paper, 1996
Genuine Lies, Bantam, paper, 1991
Hidden Riches, Jove, paper, 1995
Hidden Star, Silhouette, paper, 1997
Holding the Dream, Jove, paper, 1997

Home for Christmas, Harlequin, paper, 1986
Homeport, Putnam, 1998; Jove, paper, 1999
Honest Illusions, Jove, paper, 1993
Hot Ice, Bantam, paper, 1987
Irish Rose, Harlequin, paper, 1992
The Last Honest Man, Mira Books, paper, 1995
The Last Honest Woman, Harlequin, paper, 1990
Local Hero, Silhouette, paper, 1994
Loving Jack, Silhouette, paper, 1994
The MacGregor Brides, Harlequin, paper, 1997
The MacGregor Grooms, Silhouette, paper, 1998
The MacGregors, Harlequin, paper, 1998
Megan's Mate, Silhouette, paper, 1996
Montana Sky, Jove, paper, 1997
Night Moves, Harlequin, paper, 1992
Nightshade, Silhouette, paper, 1993
Once More with Feeling, Harlequin, paper, 1995
Once Upon a Castle, Jove, paper, 1998
One Man's Art, Harlequin, paper, 1992
Playing the Odds, Harlequin, paper, 1992
Prime Evil, Bantam, paper, 1995
Private Scandals, Jove, paper, 1994
Public Secrets, Bantam, 1997; Bantam, paper, 1998
Rebellion, Harlequin, paper, 1999
The Reef, Putnam, 1998
Reflections, Harlequin, paper, 1992
The Return of Rafe Mackade, Silhouette, paper, 1995
Rising Tides, Jove, paper, 1998
Sacred Sins, Bantam, paper, 1987
Sanctuary, Putnam, 1997; Jove, paper, 1998
Sea Swept, Jove, paper, 1998
Secret Star, Silhouette, paper, 1998
Skin Deep, Mira Books, paper, 1995
Sweet Revenge, Bantam, paper, 1989
Tempting Fate, Silhouette, paper, 1992
True Betrayals, Jove, paper, 1996
Unfinished Business, Harlequin, paper, 1992
Untamed, Silhouette, paper, 1992
Waiting for Nick, Silhouette, paper, 1997

The Winning Hand, Harlequin, paper, 1998
Without a Trace, Mira Books, paper, 1996

KIM STANLEY ROBINSON

Antarctica, Bantam, 1998; Bantam, paper, 1999
Blue Mars, Bantam, paper, 1997
The Gold Coast, Tor Books, paper, 1988
Green Mars, Bantam, paper, 1995
Icehenge, Tor Books, paper, 1998
Pacific Edge, Tor Books, paper, 1995
The Planet on the Table, Tor Books, paper, 1987
Red Mars, Bantam, paper, 1993
A Short, Sharp Shock, Bantam, paper, 1996

ROXANA ROBINSON

Asking for Love, Random House, 1996
Georgia O'Keefe, HarperCollins, paper, 1989
Short Stories, Penguin, paper, 1999
Summer Light, Hardscrabble Books, paper, 1995
This Is My Daughter, Random House, 1998

JAMES SALTER

Burning the Days, Random House, 1997; Vintage, paper, 1998
Dusk and Other Stories, North Point Press, paper, 1989
The Hunters, Vintage, paper, 1999
Light Years, Vintage, paper, 1995
Solo Faces, North Point Press, paper, 1988
A Sport and a Pastime, Vintage, paper, 1995

WILL SELF

Cock and Bull, Vintage, paper, 1994
Great Apes, Grove, 1997; Atlantic Monthly, paper, 1998
Grey Area, Grove, 1996; Atlantic Monthly, paper, 1997
My Idea of Fun, Vintage, paper, 1995
The Quantity Theory of Insanity, Vintage, paper, 1996
Tough, Tough Toys for Tough, Tough Boys, Grove, 1999

STUDS TERKEL

American Dreams, Ballantine, paper, 1985
Coming of Age, New Press, 1995; St. Martin's, paper, 1996
Division Street: America, New Press, paper, 1993
The Good War, Ballantine, paper, 1985
The Great Divide, Avon, paper, 1989
Hard Times, Pantheon, paper, 1986
My American Century, New Press, 1997; New Press, paper, 1998
Race, Anchor Books, paper, 1993
Talking to Myself, New Press, paper, 1995
Working, Ballantine, paper, 1985

JOANNA TROLLOPE

The Best Friends, Viking, 1998; Berkley, paper, 1999
The Brass Dolphin, Viking, 1999
The Choir, Random House, 1995; Berkley, paper, 1997
The Men and the Girls, Bantam, paper, 1994
Next of Kin, Bantam, paper, 1997
Other People's Children, Viking, 1999
A Passionate Man, Bantam, paper, 1994
The Rector's Wife, Berkley, paper, 1996
A Spanish Lover, Random House, 1997; Berkley, paper, 1998
A Village Affair, Bantam, paper, 1994

GARRY WILLS

Certain Trumpets, Touchstone, paper, 1995
Inventing America, Vintage, paper, 1979
John Wayne's America, Simon & Schuster, 1997; Touchstone, paper,
    1998
Lead Time, Doubleday, 1983
Lincoln at Gettysburg, Touchstone, paper, 1993
Under God, Touchstone, paper, 1990
Witches and Jesuits, Oxford, 1995; Oxford, paper, 1996

TOM WOLFE

The Bonfire of the Vanities, Farrar, Straus & Giroux, 1987; Bantam,
    paper, 1988

The Electric Kool-Aid Acid Test, Bantam, 1983

In Our Time, Farrar, Straus & Giroux, 1980

The Kandy Kolored Tangerine-Flake Streamline Baby, Farrar, Straus & Giroux, 1987

A Man in Full, Farrar, Straus & Giroux, 1998

Mauve Gloves and Madmen, Farrar, Straus & Giroux, paper, 1988

The Painted Word, Farrar, Straus & Giroux, 1975; Bantam, paper, 1982

The Pump House Gang, Farrar, Straus & Giroux, paper, 1987

The Purple Decades, Farrar, Straus & Giroux, 1982

Radical Chic and Mau-Mauing the Flak Catchers, Farrar, Straus & Giroux, paper, 1987

The Right Stuff, Farrar, Straus & Giroux, 1979; Bantam, paper, 1983